C0-ARR-924

developmental
language programming
for the retarded

developmental

language programming

for the retarded

Rolland J. Van Hattum
Professor, Communication Disorders
State University of New York, College at Buffalo

Shaw University Library

Allyn and Bacon, Inc.
Boston, London, Sydney

371.9
V254

Copyright © 1979 by Allyn and Bacon, Inc., 470 Atlantic Avenue, Boston, Massachusetts 02210. All rights reserved. No part of the material protected by this copyright notice may be reproduced or utilized in any form or by any means, electronic or mechanical, including photocopying, recording, or by any information storage and retrieval system, without written permission from the copyright owner.

Library of Congress Cataloging in Publication Data

Van Hattum, Rolland James, 1924–
    Developmental language programming for the retarded.

    References: p. 245
    Includes index.
    1. Mentally handicapped children—Education—Language arts. 2. Mentally handicapped children—Language. 3. Communicative disorders in children. I. Title.
LC4616.V36   371.9'28   78-10720
ISBN 0-205-06452-3

Printed in the United States of America.

AAE-6027

To Rhonda Marie Cassavitis
Because her brother cared so much for her.

107981

CONTENTS

preface

This book provides practical information and suggestions for teachers, speech clinicians, and parents in planning and implementing language programming for the mentally retarded or anyone exhibiting delayed language. The goal is to provide basic practical language information; suggestions for informal diagnosis to aid in program placement and format as well as a core of material to serve as a basis for planning a language program. The information pertaining to language in the early chapters is intended to serve only as background for the information on which the programming suggestions are based.

Chapter 1 discusses the importance of language and its relation to mental retardation. Chapter 2 proceeds to a basic overview of language intended primarily for teachers of the retarded. Types of grammars, the organization of language and communication, and the development of language and speech are included.

Chapter 3 includes discussion of the relative roles of the speech-language pathologist and teacher of the retarded as well as other school personnel and persons in the home. Aspects of program organization are discussed and a brief overview of pertinent factors pertaining to mental retardation presented as well as considerations in program planning. Finally, the use of program models, language diagnosis, and planning conferences is mentioned.

In Chapter 4, the importance of parent participation is reviewed. Since parents are the first teachers of their children, involvement of parents in planning and program presentation is stressed. Suggestions for relating to parents and providing them with support and encouragement are presented as well as advice for programming which they can provide.

Under diagnosis, in Chapter 5, an overview of the early development is included as a means of providing diagnosis for programming purposes. Cooperative diagnosis is emphasized and methods of record keeping outlined. Particular mention is made of the need to differentiate various types of "nonverbal" children. The use of behavioral language development landmarks is meant to emphasize the thesis of this book that the child's language behavior should be studied independent of traditional labels. The important factor is those language behaviors the child does or does not have.

The presentations of syntax and classroom programs in Chapters 6 and 7 are intended to assist the teacher and SLP by providing a framework on which to build the total habilitative program. It is recognized that no program materials could be presented which would be applicable for the needs of all children. The speech-language pathologist possesses the skills to provide remedial programming and although those materials included are appropriate for use by the specialist, this is not the primary intent. The sequencing of programming should be to improve attending and listening skills and to develop basic vocabulary and the grammatical system based on the specific needs of children before including all children who can benefit in classroom programming. Limitations for some children are recognized. In other words, children should proceed along the developmental sequence until they reach the limits of their abilities.

The first of the units on habilitative suggestions deals with the development of attending behaviors and a basic grammatical system, the second with a classroom program aimed at improving receiving, thinking, and expressing skills. The third, in Chapter 8, presents exercises in the three areas to supplement programming or to provide for the specific needs of individual children.

Finally, Chapter 9 consists of a list of commercial products. This is followed by a glossary of terms. This glossary is intended to assist the teacher and speech-language pathologist to better understand terminology associated with speech, language, mental retardation, and psychology. The commercial materials offer further possibilities for supplementing the materials presented.

ACKNOWLEDGEMENTS

A large number of persons contributed in various ways to the final product presented here, none more so than Dr. Norman J. Niesen, who participated in the initial planning of the text. I am indebted to him for his contributions and assistance. Dr. Douglas Wiseman helped focus my attention on language and the retarded in ways which were meaningful to me and provided me with information which served to direct me toward the programming which is presented here.

Several professionals provided their expert assistance. These persons included Lois Conway, Mary Loj, Sandra Landy and Cynthia Anthony. Dr. Maxine Mays was particularly helpful in editing and rewriting material found in the outcomes charts and language activities in Chapter 7.

A number of typists provided their skills in various stages of the preparation of the preliminary and final manuscripts. They were: Joyce Van Hattum, Gesua Van Hattum, Susan Van Hattum, Judith Janus, Lynn Vassallo, Delores Gibbs, Carol Rizzo, Christina Pena and Doris Trudeau.

A portion of this book reflects the efforts of experienced Teachers of the Retarded and Speech-Language Pathologists who participated in institutes sponsored jointly by the Exceptional Children Education Division of the State University of New York, College at Buffalo and the United States Office of Education Bureau for the Education of the Handicapped in 1967 and 1968.

These persons were:

Linda Bilderback	Anna Mae Jones	Richard Reece
Adele Cheskin	Susanne Kubanek	Nancy Rieman
Patricia Cohen	Virginia Lashinsky	James Schaaf
Brian Colpoys	Lola Lee	Elizabeth Schuman
Carolyn Crosby	Betty Lenz	Russell Siraquse
Jean Danahy	Marie Marillo	Sister M. Vincent
Margaret Davis	Colleen Marks	Frederick Soplet
Sandra Durfee	Marsha McCarthy	Helen Spicer
Paul Fedkiw	Molly McNamara	Anna May Thornton
Dominic Futia	Sarajane McNess	Joella Turner
Mary Donnelly Hardy	Marie Mordeno	Mary Jane Verbier
Camille Heeb	William Nelson	Patricia Weinreich
Anita Hormann	Dianne Oaklander	Jeanette Wiede
Teresa Ianacone	Geraldine O'Brien	Margaret Winkler
Janet Jacobs	Delores Phalen	Gloria Wolkenstein
Florence Johnson	Lynn Pitasky	

Finally, the author wishes to extend appreciation to Dr. Horace Mann, formerly Director, Exceptional Children Education Division, and Dr. Keith Curry, formerly Chairman, Department of Mental Retardation, State University College at Buffalo, for their interest and encouragement.

Mentally retarded children can live better lives if their communication skills are improved. The schools presently hold the greatest promise for providing the needed assistance. I hope that this book will encourage more planning and assistance for retarded children. If it does, my efforts will have been amply rewarded.

Rolland J. Van Hattum

developmental
language programming
for the retarded

chapter one
introduction:
language and
retardation

Communication is of vital importance to each of us. The extent to which we develop an efficient and effective communication system has a significant effect on the quality of our lives. This is as true for persons of lowered intellectual functioning, the mentally retarded, as it is for all people, probably even more so. Major contributors to the development of the communication systems of the mentally retarded are the family, the teacher, and the speech-language pathologist (SLP). The SLP also has the responsibility for aiding in the remediation of communication disorders that may be present. This book is intended to provide practical information and suggestions for teachers of the retarded and SLPs in planning and implementing language programming for children labeled mentally retarded. A basic philosophy of the text is that language should be judged independently of the labels associated with the retarded. However, since specialists are familiar with so-called I.Q. categories, the reader should be aware that the material is particularly useful with the mildly (educable) and moderately (trainable) retarded, of some but more limited use for the severely retarded, and of limited use for the profoundly retarded.

The information presented regarding language and retardation is not intended to completely explain either. Rather, it is intended to provide practical background and suggestions in planning and implementing language programming. The goal is the provision of basic practical language information, suggestions for informal diagnosis to aid in program placement and program format, and a core of material to serve as a basis for planning language programs. Although the focus is on the retarded child, the material has application for all children who can benefit from language programming.

Although all of us who possess the ability to communicate adequately are somewhat aware of its importance to us, we seldom reflect on this to any great extent; rather, we accept this important ability as part of our being. If we have occasion to observe persons who display difficulty with communication, we are sympathetic if we are a casual observer and distressed if we are in some way associated with the individual. In such cases we are apt to say, "If only he could talk better," often blaming any and all the individual's problems on his communication deficit.

The phrase "if only he could talk better" should have significance for all of us. It is highly probable that each of us could improve educationally, socially, and occupationally if only we could talk better; as good speech-language is important for such success. However, for those persons who possess significant deficits in speech-language there is a critical need for the provision of concentrated services to eliminate those deficits. The children labeled mentally retarded are among those requiring such help.

The pages that follow have as their goal the provision of information and programming suggestions for enhancing communication abilities among mentally retarded children so they can learn to communicate more efficiently and effectively. This requires improved language skills, the basis for effective communication. Language is obviously a very complex subject. The complexity is even more obvious to those who have studied the words of the experts in the many fields impinging on the area of language. Hopefully, it is not necessary to master all the complexities of language in order to develop programming that will be beneficial for mentally retarded children. For if it were, there would not be a sufficient number of experts to provide for all those in need. By developing a respect for the importance of language, by achieving a basic understanding of language and how it is used in human behavior, and by visualizing these factors through schemata or models for easier understanding, motivation to provide much needed programming will be fostered and practical understanding can be obtained to aid in practical diagnosis and remediation of those language deficits that may interfere with the communication skills of mentally retarded children and prevent them from functioning at more effective levels. Acquiring basic skills in understanding language should be only a beginning. Speech-language pathologists and teachers of the retarded should make continuing efforts to increase their knowledge and skills in the vital area of language.

LANGUAGE

Obviously, language has been with us for centuries, but only recently have we begun to understand the depth and breadth of its effects. In fact, the recent increase in interest in language might lead one to suspect that language had only recently been invented. Such is obviously not the case. Anthropologists have been interested in language for years as a means of understanding various cultures. Grammarians have been interested in studying the structure of language. Psychologists have been interested in the function of language as it is related to, influences, and is influenced by intellectual and behavioral aspects of human existence. Speech-language pathologists and audiologists, initially interested in language deficits caused by brain damage and by hearing impairment, now have expanded their efforts to include other areas of language deficit. Educators in both regular and special classes have been interested in the role of language in learning and as a part of the subject area of "language arts." Language has occupied the interest of a wide and diversified group of scholars for centuries. Even Joseph Stalin (1951, p. 11) expressed considerable interest in language and wrote, "Language is directly concerned with man's productive activity, as well as with his other activity in all his spheres of work without exception." Many nonprofessionals have revealed interest in language, particularly those who have recognized its impact on personal, social, emotional, intellectual, and occupational activities.

The divergent paths that various specialities have taken owing to their particular areas of interest have led to a growing body of literature too vast for almost any individual to completely explore and almost too diverse to be integrated into a meaningful body of knowledge. Thus, each specialty tends to isolate those aspects of the literature pertinent to its special interests, defines its terms, and proceeds from this base.

DEFINITIONS

Persons writing in the language area often begin with definitions of terms. The need for definitions of terms is a fitting demonstration of the complexity of language and the divergent views of its nature. An exception will not be made here.

Language is an acquired system of structured but arbitrary vocal, graphic, and gestural signs and symbols that provide meaning by cataloging and representing people, places, things, and feelings and other abstract concepts. *Speech* is the audible motor production of sounds and sound patterns, including voice quality and rhythm, used to produce oral language. *Communication* is the process whereby information, images, thoughts, feelings, ideas, and concepts are transmitted between or among individuals, primarily through the use of various forms of language.

In this text, emphasis will be on oral-verbal language. The reader can assume this in interpreting the term "language," unless otherwise stated.

IMPORTANCE OF LANGUAGE

Although some recent studies of chimpanzees (Premack, 1976) have suggested some relatively basic language skills in primates, the ability to acquire and use complex language is unique to humans; it sets us apart from all other living things. The gift of language enables us to more fully enjoy, control, use, and relate to all things in our environment. Humans have developed complex language systems whether their culture be primitive or sophisticated. During our entire recorded history we have used language as our prime method of communication. To contemplate the importance of language to us is an interesting, even awesome, experience. In fact, after the individual's physical health, it is likely that language is the next most important aspect of the individual's existence. When the persons mentioned earlier say, "If only he could talk better," they are probably stating a greater truism than they realize. The use of language in communication is readily recognized, but more in terms of conversing with others than delivering messages in order to relay ideas, thoughts, and feelings. We display what we are like in personality and character, what we believe. We may, however, reveal what we want people to think we are like and what we want people to think we believe. One serious reservation of language is that we cannot always depend on its appearance. Language can be used to distort as well as to accurately represent. Both extremes are used in the attempt to influence us in such activities as advertising, propaganda, and politics. The mentally retarded have little protection against abuses of language.

As we reveal ourselves through language, so do others, and we use this in making judgments about others. We use language recreationally in a manner described by such terms as "shooting the bull," "rapping," "yakking," "passing time," and other similar terms. We also use language as filler, continuing a conversation with nonessential material until meaningful message transfer occurs. Rather than being discrete categories, performed one at a time, our communication tends to be interwoven with the many types of language we employ.

The internal uses of language are at least equally important and varied. We mediate our thoughts through language and interpret our environment by translating our sensory experiences into language symbols. We evaluate our world and our relationship to it through the language symbols we use. This is strongly related to that aspect of behavior labeled "adjustment." We "think" through language. We organize incoming information, store it for future use, and then plan our utilization of this information in problem solving through language. We guide our physical activity, commune with ourselves, fantasize and dream and amuse ourselves with idle thoughts and humor using language activity.

Language and Thought

Of particular importance to our interest in mental retardation is the relationship between language and thought. Whorf (1956) states that all higher levels of thinking are dependent on language. He adds that the revolutionary changes that have occurred in the world of science have been due to new ways of thinking about facts, not merely the discovery of new facts; or even more accurately, these changes have been due to a new way of talking about facts. Although he believes that thought and language have different genetic roots, Vygotsky (1962) supports the importance of language in thought. He states that the development of thought is determined by language and the child's intellectual growth is contingent on his mastering the social means of thought or language.

Luria (1963) states that language is not only a means of communication but an instrument for thinking. He feels that even physical activity is governed in part by the use of language in thought. Frost (1967) notes that language is so closely related to thinking that many psychologists consider them to be identical. Joseph Stalin (1951, p. 36) summarized it: "It is said that thoughts arise in the minds of men prior to their being expressed in speech, that they arise without language material—but this is absolutely wrong. Whatever the thoughts that may arise in the mind of men, they can arise and exist only on the basis of the language material. . . . Pure thoughts, free of language material . . . do not exist."

Language, Intelligence, and Learning

The role of language in intelligence and learning has not been clearly established. However, if language is basic to thought, it plays a strong role in both areas. Frost (1967, p. 19) states, "It is not clear whether the child gains language power as a result of high intelligence or gains high intelligence as a result of language power—conditions of either are essential for the growth of both." We note that, in general, persons judged to be intelligent tend to have good language facility and those persons judged to be less intelligent have poorer language facility. Intelligence tests are heavily weighted with language materials, suggesting that experts in the area of intelligence recognize a strong relationship between language and intelligence. It is not surprising that a child's success in school correlates highly with her scores on the major intelligence tests.

We are not surprised when language-competent persons are found to be good learners. In fact, we expect them to be.

Language and Adjustment

Another critical area of language usage is not often considered in this regard. Our ability to use language accurately and positively plays a role in our adjustment. Perhaps it is more accurate to say that the manner in which we use our language system determines our adjustment. Whorf (1956) was particularly interested in the role language played in adjustment, or, more accurately, how an individual's language shaped his or her view of the environment. He felt that words influenced behavior. In his linguistic relativity principle, he states that markedly different grammars point their users toward different types of observations and different evaluations of externally similar acts of observations that result in different views of the world.

Miller (1963) notes that the more language a child has, the better will be his relationships with family, relatives, and playmates. We know that as communication ability develops, temper tantrums decrease almost directly proportionally. Frost (1967) indicates that personality problems nearly always accompany language disabilities. He adds that social growth is closely interwoven with language power. Jordan (1967) states that behavioral status and language status are interrelated, and Luria (1963) advises that if one wishes to become a controlled individual she should talk to herself, since we have verbal control over our behavior. Almost every psychotherapeutic method that attempts to improve the adjustment of individuals uses alteration of the language system as its basic tool. Actually, Norman Vincent Peale's book entitled *The Power of Positive Thinking* (1975) should have been *The Power of Positive Language*.

Each individual perceives reality differently. In effect, reality becomes of secondary importance to our perception of reality, and in large measure, our perception is based on the language symbols we use to interpret it. Thus, our view of reality is shaped by our language. Adjusted persons are those who possess and utilize accurate and positively oriented language systems.

Language, intelligence, learning, and adjustment are interrelated in unique and critical ways. Thus, mentally retarded individuals may suffer wide-ranging and significant effects from their language limitations. Improving language function would result not only in significant benefit to their functioning in school but in their entire lives.

LANGUAGE AND MENTAL RETARDATION

Because of the recognition of the importance of language to all of us, the development of effective language and speech through the education process has long been described as a major concern of school programs. However, only recently has widespread interest been shown for the incorporation of language development activities in special education programs provided for the mentally retarded, and only recently have many of these children been scheduled for assistance by SLPs. In most instances, much more of each service is needed.

The condition of mental retardation and generalized poor language and speech performance has long been associated. Binet and Simon (1914) identified verbal communication difficulties as a prime factor in defining and classifying mental retardation. A mass of studies followed this early observation that clearly established that the retarded often exhibited speech and language performance that was defective in a number of specific ways. These findings were used frequently to support writing and thinking which tended to view the condition of mental retardation as the cause of poor language performance and became the basis for a widespread pessimistic attitude toward providing specialized speech and language help to the mentally retarded enrolled in special education programs. The net result was that the mentally retarded were often denied participation in remedial speech and language programs because it was reasoned that they would not profit sufficiently for the time, effort, and money expended.

INCREASED INTEREST IN LANGUAGE

In the mid 1950s there were several occurrences that proved to be of critical importance to both the communication disorders and mental retardation professions. First, the appearance of Chomsky's *Syntactic Structures* (1957) stimulated new interest in the study of language. The literature abounds with articles taking positions in defense of or opposition to Chomsky's beliefs. Second, an increasing number of children were identified whose major problems appeared to be in the language areas. Attempts by SLPs to use traditional testing were not productive. The labels "aphasia" or "childhood aphasia" were not appropriate for many of these children.

Often the communication difficulty was much less noticeable in social settings than in academic settings. In spite of the lack of medical evidence, various labels began to be applied to these children such as "brain-damaged" or "minimal brain dysfunction." Speech-language pathologists were asked to assist or to provide for suggestions as to how the teacher could assist these children, even those without specific speech symptoms but with problems described as "language problems that were interfering with learning." Not all of these problems were in the auditory or vocal areas. In fact, many of the problems were in areas not traditionally considered the province of the SLP. The speech and hearing profession responded slowly to the need for formal standardized testing and remedial procedures. The field of mental retardation did not. Kirk and his associates recognized the need for a test that could isolate specific deficits and developed the Illinois Test of Psycholinguistic Abilities (1961) based on Osgood's model (1957A, 1957B). Though criticized by some, the test provided opportunity for new terminology, new dialogue, and new research. It helped to focus attention on language and the benefits are still in evidence. Perhaps a major contribution of the test has been to make language deficits seem like a manageable item due to more easily understandable terminology. Such labels as "auditory-verbal channel deficit" were more manageable to SLPs who previously had displayed little activity in language deficits. On the other hand, some persons might complain that this led to oversimplification of a difficult process. Both views are probably partially correct.

Many of these children just referred to tested below normal intellectual limits and were placed in classrooms for the mentally retarded. These classrooms contained children whose delays in learning were of diagnosed organic etiology and those whose learning delays appeared related to familial factors. These latter children have been referred to as the "original mentally retarded." Classrooms for the mentally retarded also became a rapidly expanding educational placement for those children whose environments had not prepared them for academic settings and for whom many school personnel held little optimism. Regular education's failures became special education's responsibilities. Finally, it is likely that children were placed in these classes when the academic difficulty was caused by the blocks that emotional problems may impose on learning. While "acting out" children tend to be labeled emotionally disturbed, mildly or moderately withdrawn children sometimes mistakenly may be labeled mentally retarded. As special education programs increased and the number of classrooms for the retarded grew, the heterogeneity of the population increased. This was a national happening and only recently has the process slowed.

If one were to visit special classes for the mentally retarded from New York to California, certain variations in I.Q. limits and terminology would probably be noted. However, many similarities would exist. A group of children would be assembled who had been found through intelligence tests, achievement tests, and school performance to function at significantly lower academic levels than other children of similar chronological age. Quantitatively, these children would present similar test scores. Qualitatively, the children would likely present a wide range and variety in factors such as etiology, academic performance, social skills, patterns of adjustment, and communication skills. The program these children would be receiving would likely be devoted to self-care and socialization skills if the class were for moderately retarded (trainable) children and to developing minimal academic skills, improving social skills, and developing some degree of occupational adequacy if the class were for mildly retarded (educable) children. Educational programming would focus on quantitative differences in academic achievement, but little provision for the qualitative differences likely would be observed.

ALTERED DEFINITION OF MENTAL RETARDATION

Yet, there are qualitative differences. In presenting the changing view of retardation in 1954, the Nomenclature Committee of the American Association on Mental Deficiency (Sloan, 1954) states that mental retardation is a symptom complex that may result not from defects of the central nervous system alone but from defects in the psychological and sociological spheres. Dever (1969) points out that it is common to find children whose performance scores are normal or nearly normal and whose verbal score is so low that the full scale falls in the retarded range. These "half-normal" children are nevertheless considered retarded, labeled retarded, and educated retarded. Capobianco and Dunn (1968) note a lack of agreement in terminology in mental retardation. They state that there is some agreement between educators and psychologists that mental retardation should be used as a broad generic term that includes a wide range of psychological and physical syndromes that have as a common denominator subnormal intellectual development.

Several authorities suggest viewing the retarded from other than etiological standpoints. Quoting Wepman (1967, p. 11): "It is of greater importance, it seems to me, to study the behavior of the retarded rather than to search for the ever elusive cause until we can demonstrate that etiology plays a significant role in the learning capacity or learning potential of the child."

TYPES OF PERSONS VIEWED AS RETARDED

More recent views are departures from the earlier definitions that viewed retardation as a static condition caused by unavoidable genetic factors and emphasized etiology more than educational needs. The current definitions suggest that classrooms for the retarded contain considerable heterogeneity, since it is likely that there are four general types of causes of learning problems found in classes for the mentally retarded: (1) learning deficits caused by genetic limitation of intellectual skills, (2) learning deficits caused by damage to a central nervous system that otherwise might have been capable of higher intellectual function to some degree, (3) learning deficits in children who possess potential for normal intellectual function but whose environments have limited their ability to utilize their inherent intellectual skills, and (4) learning deficits in children who possess potential for normal intellectual functions but whose personal adjustment makes it impossible for them to utilize intellectual skills.

In regard to those children labeled mentally retarded as a result of forces associated with an environment inappropriate for learning the language used in the schools, adequate language is built upon many varied experiences, but the environment of some retarded children often is markedly deficient in providing these. The environment may offer little encouragement to the child for talking since it may be a physical rather than a verbal world that may be emotionally cold rather than warm and encouraging. Adequate school language models may not be available for the retarded child to imitate, nor interested adults who will listen to and talk with the child. Moreover, the environment may be devoid of stimulation, and this substantially contributes to the depressed language ability.

In particular, many children from minority groups are penalized in school because of their nondominant language usage. Among black children such labels as "culturally deprived" and "culturally disadvantaged" inaccurately overlook the richness of the culture from which these children come. They may be disadvantaged in attempting to function in a dominant culture that is different from theirs but, hopefully, these terms will disappear from usage by informed individuals. It is true that these children are culturally *different,* including some of their social behaviors, value systems, and, importantly, their language systems. Understanding and acceptance of these differences by persons in their educational environments is critical to improving educational success for these children, often mistakenly classified as mentally retarded. It cannot be denied that some of these children are mentally retarded by any standard. However, many of them primarily lack necessary competence in the language system of the dominant culture. They are educationally retarded. What to do about it is highly controversial, even among black educational leaders. Unfortunately, many issues have been emotionalized to further cloud even the clear statement of the problem and, consequently, make more difficult the determination of possible solutions.

Baskervill (1975) states it well when he says, "It must be understood that children need certain basic skills which will hopefully enhance them academically and economically in their adult lives. It seems that it boils down to the fact that competency in the communication skills is most essential in developing other skills that are considered important for scholastic and economic success." He further points out that it is the fact that some of these children may be speaking non-standard forms of English, which makes it difficult for them to achieve adequately, particularly in developing reading skills. He concludes that "it must be recognized that the tools for learning in school are delivered in a standard English package." Another factor for consideration is that whereas the entire lexicon of American English exceeds 500,000 words, the lexicon of black language is approximately 500 words. Thus, if children are restricted only to black language usage, they may be denied the wisdom of the ages contained in the literature of the culture.

Baskervill (1975) also notes that the teacher's understanding of the language system of the black child is an important factor in assisting the child. He includes the information contained in Figure 1.1 to assist teachers in noting, understanding, and accepting the communication behaviors of these children in their classrooms. Part A notes differences in syntax, the manner in which words are combined, and Part B the differences in phonology, the sound system. Recognition of the demarcation between difference and disorder may help to reduce the penalties black children may experience educationally.

In summary, the aspect of human behavior that suffers as a result of genetic inferiority, brain damage, environmental differences, or poor adjustment would appear to be language. As one attempts to converse with the so-called withdrawn child, as one observes the efforts of the child with suspected brain damage to perform simple organizational tasks, as one sees the child called "familial retarded" mired in verbal reasoning behavior, or as one overhears a conversation between two children from different cultural backgrounds, the impact of language on the child's total being becomes clear.

The differences that cause various children to be labeled mentally retarded might not be as important if the pessimism that accompanies the label were not so great. The former view that mental retardation is a static condition, incapable of change, has contributed to the lack of development of remedial measures. Greater optimism and better lives for the retarded are possible if we develop an attitude of "*how* can we improve language function of the retarded leading to improved total function?" rather than "can we?" The label of mental retardation is a particularly unfortunate one when it is used to excuse us from showing better progress in the education of children so labeled. To alter an overused phrase, mental retardation often is a self-fulfilling label.

A. EXAMPLE OF RULE VARIANCE FOR SYNTAX

Subject-verb disagreement
1. The *chairs is* in the hall.
2. They *was* going to the movie.

Zero copula verb
1. *He going* to the store.
2. *What that* thing?

Hypercorrection
1. The *peoples* will be there at noon.
2. *I walks* to school every day.
3. The *mens* are in the car.

Deleted plural
1. It cost four *dollar* to go.
2. He saw three *movie* last week.

Deleted possessive
1. My *mother* book is on the table.
2. We went to *Tom* house to play.

Invariant "be"
1. He *be* living in New York.
2. My mother *be* working hard all day.

Double negatives
1. I *ain't* got *no* money.
2. You *don't* get *no* more.

Pronomial apposition
1. *John he* rides his bike to school.
2. My *sister, she* went to the store.

B. THREE EXAMPLES OF VARIANCE
FROM STANDARD ENGLISH PHONEMES

1. Omissions of reductions of: /d/, /t/, / /, and /n/.
2. Substitutions: f/   , d/   , and v/   .
3. Morphemic deletions of: /l/, /r/, /s/, /z/, / /, and /t/.

FIGURE 1.1   Examples of black language variance. (Baskervill, 1975)

From the standpoint of improved educational function, it would appear that it is more important to isolate, understand, and improve the language deficit than to make assumptions based on medical terminology or assumed etiology; thus, this presentation is based on discussion of language deficit. The heterogeneity of this total population is not overlooked. In fact, heterogeneity by language deficit is probably greater than by etiology.

chapter two
exploring some aspects
of language

Although the teacher of the retarded cannot be expected to be an expert in language, an overview of certain aspects of language can serve to provide an appreciation for the complexity of language, reduce some of the confusion regarding the basis of variations in views expressed by various authors, make the teacher more conversant with the terminology used in the literature, and assist the teacher in understanding the basis for some of the programming material. The complexity of language creates a difficult and confusing situation for those primarily interested in providing habilitative measures. Further, as Miller (1963) pointed out, an added problem is that one must use language to discuss language. The material presented in this chapter is intended to provide background for programming. It includes information that should be considered in program development to ensure that the many facets of language are included in program planning and that materials are presented in a developmental order. Utilization of the order of communication development in "normal" children is the most defensible method of program presentation. For more complete information on language, the reader is referred to *Language Development, Structure and Function* (Dale, 1972) and for information on language problems to *Language Disorders of Children, The Bases and Diagnoses* (Berry, 1969) and the chapter "Language Remediation in Children" (McConnell, Love, and Clark, in Dickson, 1974).

ORGANIZATION OF LANGUAGE AND COMMUNICATION

A brief overview can serve to illustrate the components of the language system we use in communication. Although this text focuses on the oral-verbal aspects of language, consideration of the components will aid in better understanding an individual's total communication functioning. Figure 2.1 presents an overview of the organization of language. Communication is divided into two major parts: verbal and nonverbal. Verbal suggests the use of words, and nonverbal suggests communication accomplished other than through the use of words. Actually the dichotomy is primarily illustrative. Verbal and nonverbal communication often occur simultaneously and in some instances it is difficult to determine how to label a particular aspect. For example, finger spelling used by the severely hearing-impaired employs the alphabet and is verbal but not oral. However, it does not involve writing and reading. Thus, the material presented should be viewed only as a representation of the organization of language.

13

Verbal					
Receiving	*Thinking*	*Expressing*	*Reading*	*Thinking*	*Writing*
Oral			*Nonoral*		
Phonology Morphology Syntax Prosody Semantics Pragmatics			Alphabet Words, syllables, letters Syntax Punctuation Semantics Pragmatics		
Nonverbal					
Interpreting	*Thinking*	*Acting*	*Interpreting*	*Thinking*	*Producing*
Behavioral			*Synbols*		
Costuming Cosmetics Oculesics Proxemics Chronemics Haptics Objectics Kinesics Facial expression Body gestures			Signs Codes Signals Symbols		

FIGURE 2.1   Organization of language.

Verbal Behavior

Verbal behavior is divided into oral and nonoral. Oral-verbal signifies that words are used in a speaking-listening mode whereas nonoral-verbal suggests that words are primarily used in a reading-writing mode.

ORAL-VERBAL LANGUAGE

Receiving, Thinking, and Expressing

Receiving is the process in which incoming stimuli are received and, if the hearing mechanism is intact, the sensory stimuli impinges on the individual's central nervous system. Merely "hearing" the incoming stimuli is not sufficient. The individual must interpret it based on previously acquired information. Some stimuli require a response that has already been "programmed." In other words, the individual has some automatic responses to some frequently occurring stimuli. However, most incoming stimuli require the individual to call upon previously learned information and skills for interpretation. The use of this processing is referred to by many labels and has been labeled "thinking" in this presentation. Thinking has been described as including such activities as comparing, contrasting, matching, sorting, evaluating, remembering, storing, solving, combining, inducing, deducing, reducing, and many other activities that occur in our brain in ways we are still attempting to understand. It has also been simply described as the intermediary activity that occurs between receiving and expressing or between expressing and receiving. This is also the function in which the individual uses many of these same types of activities to prepare a response. After the individual has decided on a response she must create the language to be used to produce the desired response. When one considers that this entire procedure must occur in fractions of a second, it is surprising that more persons do not have communication deficits.

Under receiving, thinking, and expressing, the oral-verbal functions are divided into phonology, morphology, syntax, prosody, semantics, and pragmatics. To communicate with others in one's community, the individual must use the system of language consistent with that used by the other members of the community. The language used by the community is determined by its members and is initially arbitrary. For example, any word can be used to represent an object. However, once a community has determined which word will represent the object, the arbitrariness is eliminated. From that point on each individual must learn the language of the community and use it, or his ability to participate will be reduced, if not eliminated.

Phonology

Phonology is the sound system used. However, it is more than a "sound alphabet." We do not form words by sequencing sounds as though they were blocks placed in a row. Rather, sounds are combined and blended in manners that go beyond the scope of this presentation. In English we use a number of vowels and consonants that are differentiated by several distinctive features. The major features that differentiate one sound from another are method of resonation (nasal or oral), manner of articulation (plosives, fricatives, glides or semi-vowels, and retroflex), place of articulation (bilabials, labio-dental, dental, alveolar, palato-alveolar, palatal, velar, and glottal), and voicing (voiced or unvoiced).

The terms phonemics and phonetics are often used synonymously in describing the sound system. However, phonemics refers to the families that are similar enough to be recognized as distinctive from other sounds. Phonetics implies a much more rigid examination of each sound, attending to very minor differences among even sounds in the same phoneme family. In transcribing sounds, the International Phonetic Alphabet (IPA) is used. Of the many symbols in the IPA about thirty-eight or thirty-nine are used in the English language, depending on the geographic area where the speaker learned to talk or was influenced in his speaking. In the IPA, each sound has only one symbol and each symbol represents only one sound. Another similar and frequently used term in education, *phonics,* refers to the sound values of each of the twenty-six alphabet letters.

When we wish to analyze or inventory an individual's sound repertoire, we administer a phonetic analysis. This term has become adopted even though, considering the previous discussion, it is really not accurate. Actually, the individual is given a phonemic analysis because only gross evaluations are made of the individual's ability to produce the sounds. Usually, the child is presented with a card with a picture depicting the sound at the beginning, in the middle, and at the end of words. The child says a stimulus word aloud and the examiner judges whether the sound is produced accurately, is left out (omitted), is substituted for (substitution), or is produced somewhat incorrectly (distortion). An entry is made on a record sheet that serves as an analysis of the child's articulation ability. It is suggested that the teacher of the retarded observe the SLP administer phonetic analyses to gain better understanding of this procedure and herself administer one analysis under the guidance of the SLP. The teacher of the retarded should not use the results of this analysis in making a diagnosis, only for a screening evaluation.

Morphology

Morphology includes the words (lexicon) of the language and also units that are not ordinarily thought of as word units. These include the (-s) that pluralizes a word, the (-ed) that denotes past tense, the (-er) and (-est) that provide comparative information, the (-ing) that produces a gerund or participle, and so on. Both types of units, words and "part words" are called morphs. Morphs such as "jump," "big," and "cry" are referred to as "free" forms since they can stand alone, and the others, such as -er and -est, as "bound" forms since they cannot stand alone.

The words of a language are often additionally classified as nouns, pronouns, verbs, adjectives, adverbs, auxiliary verbs, prepositions, conjunctions, and articles. When we examine the frequency of occurrence of these various "parts of speech," as they have been traditionally referred to, a clearer picture of the nature of language emerges. The fabric of the language consists of carrier words and connecting words that are repeated frequently. Meaning is added through many nouns and verbs and their modifiers. In other words, the auxiliary verbs, prepositions, conjunctions, pronouns, and articles provide the vehicle for language and the nouns, verbs, adjectives, and adverbs provide the meaning. French et al. (1930) analyzed words occurring in telephone conversations they audited. They counted the total number of word occurrences (tokens) and the total number of *different* words (types). In other words, the first time a word occurred it was counted as both a token and a type. In succeeding occurrences it was counted again as a token but was not counted again as a type. In the phrase "the girl and the boy" there are five tokens, but since "the" occurs twice there are only four types. When the information was tabulated, they found the information presented in Figure 2.2.

This supports the previous description of language in that there were 34,090 occurrences of nouns, verbs, adjectives, and adverbs with a large number (2,119) of different words used. On the other hand, there were 45,300 auxiliary verbs, pronouns, prepositions, conjunctions, and articles but only 121 different words.

Syntax

When words are combined to produce meaning, syntax results. Syntax describes the manner in which words are connected, including rules pertaining to word order, agreement of subject and verb, and other aspects of sentence construction. Some persons know a few words of a foreign language. However, until one is able to combine these words in proper syntactic form, one cannot be considered a speaker of the language. The same is true of American English. The individual must be aware of and use the rules of syntax before she can be said to have adequate command of the language. Grammar includes syntactical relations but also includes the classes of words and their inflections.

Prosody

Prosody, prosodic features, paralanguage, or suprasegmental all refer to the contributions to meaning added by stress, phrasing, voice quality, rhythm, pitch,

Parts of speech	Tokens	Types
Nouns	11,666	1,029
Adjectives, adverbs	9,880	634
Verbs	12,550	456
Auxiliary verbs	9,450	37
Prepositions, conjunctions	12,400	36
Pronouns	17,900	45
Articles	5,550	3
Total	79,390	2,240

FIGURE 2.2   Analysis of tokens and types occurring in telephone conversations. (Based on French, Carter, and Koenig, 1930)

loudness, and rate. A sentence such as, "You expect me to go" can be changed considerably simply by varying the stress from word to word: "*You* expect me to go," "You *expect* me to go," "You expect *me* to go," and "You expect me to *go*" all contain the same words but vary in meaning because of variance in prosody.

Semantics

Semantics refers to the meaning of words and the relationship between the word and what the word represents. The word "tree" is a highly arbitrary combination of sounds we have chosen to represent a woody, growing thing. We could as easily have called it a "baum" as the German language does. As mentioned previously, a person must use words accurately to participate in the community and to affect adjustment and/or to avoid conflict or misunderstanding. Behavioral disciplines often use alteration of the person's semantic system to improve adjustment. In this sense, *semantics* as a behavioral discipline attempts to aid the individual in a better understanding and use of the language.

Pragmatics

Pragmatics refers to the relationships between the individual and his or her language. Whereas semantics deals with the relationship between the word and that which it represents, pragmatics focuses on the *user* of the words and how the user influences and is influenced by his or her use of language. An individual can be better understood by studying the words he or she uses. Our vocabulary reflects our interests, priorities, and emotional status. A common method of studying a culture is through study of its language system, particularly the vocabulary. This, too, reflects the cultural content, value system, and other aspects that reveal much about the culture.

Writing, Thinking, and Reading

Since the focus in this text is on oral-verbal communication, only cursory attention will be given to the nonoral-verbal modes of communication. They are, nonetheless, important aspects of the individual's total ability to communicate adequately. Although the exact nature of the relationships between spoken language and read language are not known, we do know that we first learn to hear, then to speak, then to read, and then to print and write. The written word provides a more precise and accurate aspect of communication, but it is the oral mode that we use more frequently and, for most of us, has the greatest impact on our lives.

In writing and reading, the alphabet consists of 26 characters, or graphemes, in American English. Although several of the symbols are the same, the written code and spoken code use some different symbols. Thus, one sound may have more than one symbol and one symbol may represent more than one sound. This often causes problems for the beginning reader.

The morphology in the nonoral mode is very similar, if not identical, to the oral mode. Syntax also is similar. In both instances, the written and read language tends to be more precise. It is easier to correct written material than spoken. Persons who have had the experience of transcribing speeches are often hard pressed to sort out the inaccuracies, false starts, and other errors we all make in spontaneous speech production.

Punctuation provides a further precision lacking in spoken language. However, the shadings imposed by prosody are missing in this dimension. Semantics and pragmatics are applicable in this area as well as in oral language. It is strange that the educational system has neglected the oral-verbal language so badly when it is so basic to the reading process. To learn to read language, the child must be able to understand language.

Nonverbal Language

In addition to the verbal aspects of language, there are other important nonverbal aspects of communication that are frequently overlooked. These can be divided into behavioral activity and graphic activity, referred to here as "synbols."

Behavioral Activity

Understanding behavioral activity can assist us to better understand and accept persons from other national, religious, and racial backgrounds. Each of these factors often influences and is influenced by the manner in which an individual functions and, consequently, the manner in which an individual is viewed by others. Those behaviors that we find strange may well be very normal behavior in a different cultural setting. An important factor is that they are determined by different beliefs and different environments. The teacher and SLP who accept the fact that differences are part of a multi-cultured world will be better able to relate to children whose behavior is in variance with their own experiential backgrounds and value systems. Even persons with similar backgrounds may well develop life styles which are different but neither better nor worse, and many of these differences may be revealed in behavioral activity.

Organismics pertains to the individual's physical presentation, such as eye color, shape, and positioning; body size, shape, and configuration; hair color, texture, length, and styling; skin color and texture; facial appearance including nose, mouth, ears, chin, facial hair; and the remaining parts. Costuming refers to the individual's choice of wearing apparel including the style, colors, uniqueness, costliness, and what we judge to be the appropriateness. Cosmetics refers to externally imposed materials that the individual applies to herself such as hair coloring, hair oils, powders, rouges, and the like. Oculesics refers to the manner in which the individual uses his eyes in communication. We make judgments about persons who are "shifty eyed" or who do not look us in the eyes or who stare. We consider some uses of the eyes "seductive" and others "frightening." The lack of eye contact by some black children may be misunderstood, for example. It is often a cultural factor and should be considered acceptable behavior.

Proxemics notes the individual's use of space in communication. The distance two speakers stand from one another is not a matter of chance but is culturally determined. We sometimes grow uneasy when someone violates the distance expectancy by standing too close to us. Yet, many Europeans and Latin Americans use a closer communicating distance than we do. We may feel rejected when someone stands too far away when we are attempting to communicate. Yet, the English generally prefer a greater communication distance than do Americans. Chronemics describes the effect of time on communication. Some persons respond immediately to a question or to a statement needing a response whereas others pause briefly. Some persons allow lapses in conversation whereas others will go to great lengths to avoid any time-space in conversation. On a larger scale, we usually plan our theater arrival with the understanding that the performance will begin 5 or 10 minutes late. This is our cultural understanding of time. We value "promptness" on the job; yet many American Indians have little concern regarding exact time schedules. Ceremonial activities may begin several minutes or several hours late to the consternation of persons who are not aware of this cultural difference. In many American Indian cultures time is not an important factor and things are done when people "are ready." Our concern for time is a part of our culture that most of us consider important. Those who do not may appear to be in conflict with the culture.

Haptics refers to the role of touch in communication. A pat, a slap, or a hand on an arm or shoulder may all communicate significant messages. Objectics describes the manner in which objects affect communication. An individual's car or house, for example, suggests a great deal about that person. Kinesics pertains to the role that body movement plays in the communicative process. Some persons use their bodies very expressively and even those who reveal little body activity tell us something, accurately or inaccurately, about themselves.

Facial expression and the use of gestures all reveal considerable meaning to the observer. Sometimes they enhance communication, and sometimes they are the means of communication.

Synbols

The term *synbols* is a neologism used to include signs, signals, codes, and symbols that represent meaning without using our alphabet. Hieroglyphics, cuneiform, and cave signings are earlier sign systems whereas American Indian sign language and signing used by the hearing-impaired are more recent methods. The systems of symbols used to mark highways (railroad crossings, curves) and to advertise (trademarks, billboards) and those used in safety (poison) are all examples of nonverbal symbols. Codes include mathematical symbols and formulas, Braille, sporting events box scores, and playing card markings. Signals include traffic lights, a starter's gun, and emergency flares. The intent here is not to present a classification system but only to illustrate the scope of nonverbal communication.

We communicate in a wide number of ways. We devote a great deal of our time and energy to communication. This is a fitting demonstration of our great desire to interact with other human beings, which appears to be a natural part of our being. It is no wonder that the individual who is lacking in any aspect of communicative ability is penalized by society in many ways. It also serves to point out again the importance of assisting each mentally retarded individual to achieve the best form of communication of which he or she is capable.

VIEWS OF LANGUAGE

In the study of language, confusion is often created by the philosophical differences regarding the nature of language. A basic understanding of the nature of these differences should aid in interpreting the proponents' views. Four identifiable types of grammar studies have been identified by Thomas (1963). These are traditional grammar, historical grammar, descriptive-structural grammar, and transformational-generative grammar.

Traditional Grammar

Traditional grammar had its foundations in the eighteenth century and was based on efforts to formulate definitive rules of syntax and usage. The advocates' rules assumed an ideal language. They tended to ignore historical change and to view change as harmful to good usage. Rules were based not only on Latin but also on the intuitive knowledge of experts on the "correctness" of language.

Historical Grammar

Historical grammarians attempted to explain aspects of the intricacies and irregularities of the English language. They turned to history for explanations rather than to their views regarding the correctness of grammar. This school of thought based its beliefs on language families and traced the change of word forms. These scholars explained irregular verbs, variation of pronunciation and spelling of a word, and various other idiosyncrasies of language.

Descriptive-Structural Explanations

One of two major groups today, the descriptive-structural advocates include a diverse group of scholars and are roughly akin to the behaviorists. The origin of structural linguistics is credited to Bloomfield (1933), who separated the form or structure of language from the meaning of language, dividing language study into syntax and semantics. Experts in this group describe the structure of language as it exists. They do not evaluate language but record it and describe usage. To accomplish this, they have presented the ideas of syntactic levels such as phonemes, morphemes, and the phrase structure level. This structural or descriptive group emphasizes methodology and language content. The behaviorists, sometimes referred to as the empiricists, generally relate their theoretical constructs of language to learning principles while their methodology includes the description of language based on operant conditioning and associational principles. They have provided data regarding the development of phonology and morphology, size of vocabulary, sentence length, and other information presented in charts of language development. Skinner (1957) explains the development on the basis of stimulus, response, and reinforcement principles of learning. The process of imitation is an important part of the theoretical concepts of these persons. Thus, the child is viewed as beginning with little more than a central nervous system governing a speech and hearing mechanism. This mechanism first gathers stimuli from the environment and later, through the process of imitation, responds with associations that are at first random and meaningless. Later, through a process of reinforcement, these associations become the intentional and meaningful means of communication by the individual. Most SLPs have been exposed to this viewpoint since it has been the most prominent in standard texts. More recently, the beliefs of this group have been subjected to considerable scrutiny by psycholinguists. This has resulted in refinement of theoretical concepts such as by Osgood (1967), who added computer terminology to the production of grammar. Osgood states that the mind, in the production of language, functions in a manner similar to a computer. From the base possibilities beginning at the form pool, there is a progression of sorts labeled grammatical, associational, affective, and denotative.

Transformational-Generative Grammar

The second major current group has been labeled as the transformational or generative grammarians, but other labels such as rationalists have been applied. This group points to a complexity of language and argues for explanations that include an innate language capacity. Chomsky (1957) argues that the behaviorists offer little of significance in their explanations and that the principles of conditioning, no matter what the extent of higher orders or complexity that may be added, cannot account for language learning. Experts in this group feel that imitation plays a negligible role in language development since it cannot adequately account for the entry of new features into a child's grammar. Thus, the basic tenets of the structuralists are rejected. This group suggests that there are language universals common to all languages so that the child's initial task is to select out the language of the culture in which she finds herself. Support for this is taken from the evidence that language acquisition occurs in the extremely brief period of approximately 24 months. Smith and Miller (1966) point out that grammatical speech does not begin before 1½ years and the basic system is complete by 3½ years.

McNeil (1966) adds that early language is not an abbreviated and distorted form of adult language but the product of a unique first grammar. He views a young child as a fluent speaker of an exotic language. He also argues that the speech of the child cannot be explained on the basis of imitation of adult speech. He notes that children produce sentences that cannot be accounted for as reductions of adult sentences ("He goed") and feels that the transformations appear rather late and that the child appears to build up his transformational competence by successive approximations, passing through several steps that are not yet English but are, nonetheless, transformational.

Chomsky's three parts of grammar, illustrated in Figure 2.3, are described as phrase structure, transformational structure, and morphophonemics. Part 1 of this grammar is a noun phrase that includes a determiner, a noun, plus a morpheme that signifies plurality. A verb phrase is similar. Part 2 includes rules for combining phrases or explanations of grammatical relationships. Part 3 incorporates additional development of structural grammar and historical grammar. In the operation of this grammar the rules of Part 1 produce the elemental phrase or kernel sentences of language. Part 2 includes obligatory transformations such as agreement between subject and verb and optional transformations such as the optional inclusion of adjectives or negatives. If the appropriate word form rules of Part 3 are then applied, a grammatical English sentence will result. If only obligatory transformations are applied, a kernel sentence will result. All sentences in English are either kernel sentences or are generated from kernel sentences by optional but invariable transformations.

Chomsky distinguishes between competence and performance in language. He defines competence as basic language ability and performance as language use. Understandably, the study of language is based primarily on the performance of children. Yet more recent studies of performance have yielded more objective results than had been previously available. Chomsky also differentiates between "deep structure," the semantic or meaning level that the communicator wishes to convey, and "surface structure," the phonetic interpretation that represents the communicator's utterance.

Although transformational experts have divergent viewpoints, they generally agree that children are born with some sort of competence to acquire the language of their culture. The child acquires holophrases (single-word sentences), then two-word combinations. The child then begins to develop competence in the use of

Part One—A Noun Phrase
  A determiner, a noun, a morpheme signifying plurality:
    "The girl" or "The girls"
  A verb phrase:
    "eating the cake"
  Kernel sentence: "The girl is eating the cake"
                 (noun phrase) + (verb phrase)
  A kernel sentence is simple, active, declarative with no complex noun or verb
  phrases (no adjectives, adverbs, conjunctions, prepositions, etc.)
Part Two—Obligatory Transformations (rules for combining phrases such as agree-
  ment between subject and verb)
    "The girl*s are*"
  Optional transformations (inclusion of adjectives or negatives):
    "*The tall* girl"
    "The girl is not"
  Sentence tense (active, passive, etc.):
    "The girl *has eaten*"
    "The cake has been eaten"
Part Three—Rules Concerned with Phonemes
    "man" plus the plural morpheme equals "men"
    "thief" equals "thieves," etc.
  Kernel sentences develop ("generate") sentences by optional but invariable
  transformations:
    "The tall girl is eating the cake"
    "Is the girl eating the cake?"
    "The girl isn't eating the cake"
    "What is the girl eating?"
    "The cake is being eaten by the girl"

FIGURE 2.3   Chomsky's three parts of grammar.

kernel sentences and then transformations, and then progresses to sentences of
increasing complexity.

For SLPs and teachers, it is not necessary to accept one philosophy. In fact,
they are in the advantageous position of being able to borrow from the best features of both.

DEVELOPMENT OF LANGUAGE

Since the dominant belief at present views the language performance of the child
labeled retarded as developing in the "normal" sequence except either more slowly
or as arrested at some stage of the developmental process, an understanding of
language development is another important aspect of diagnosis.

An explanation of the development of communication can only reflect the views of the author. With this in mind, communication developments consists of inherent abilities aided by hearing, observing, and imitating. The readiness to produce language is dependent on a system capable of producing the sounds of the language; developing the words of the language through combining the sounds to produce them; developing knowledge of what the words represent; being able to combine the words in the ordering the particular language uses to provide meaning; and using stress, loudness, rhythm, and many other nuances of expression appropriately. In addition to learning these aspects, the process consists of imitating basic structures (words, phrases, sentences) while developing the inflectional forms through learning structural rules. Thus, to this author, language is not solely a process of imitation or of learning rules, inflections, and transformations but a combination of the two.

The child does not appear to progress in a neat stage-by-stage manner, mastering one language skill before proceeding to the next. Rather, the child appears to expressively produce the skills he or she has mastered while receptively learning new skills. One might hypothesize that some children may attempt to master one skill completely before progressing to the next skill. Perhaps some children labeled mentally retarded develop communication in this less efficient fashion.

Communication develops in a series of three major steps. In the "average child" the first step occupies approximately the first 18 months and consists primarily of observing and developing cognition in regard to environmental events, maturing of the neuromuscular system responsible for communication, and linking of the individual's own capacity to verbalize with those external verbal activities that are heard. In other words, the child must develop the awareness that she is capable of performing those verbal acts that she hears and sees about her. The quotes surrounding "average child" are significant. Although landmarks are presented, there is wide variation in individual development.

The infant's breathing, crying, feeding, cooing, and babbling, although having other uses, are preparing the infant for aspects of speech and language behavior. The first month is characterized by nonpurposeful crying behavior. During the second month the child begins to cry in response to the environment, specifically because of discomfort, hunger, pain. During the third to fourth months the child may also initiate social crying, crying to gain attention. This entire period is also spent in developing awareness of the sights and sounds of the environment. Reflexive babbling begins and the sound repertoire begins to include some recognizable English sounds.

At about the sixth month the child repeats sounds randomly or babbles. The child may repeat her own speech sounds or those with which she is stimulated if the receptive or hearing mechanism is intact. Thus imitation begins. The entire process of hearing and seeing continues. The child builds a significant number of verbal and visual images prior to any observable use of this material.

The child first observes objects and develops the awareness that things have verbal symbols. This occurs largely through the processes of visual and auditory stimulation. First words, near the end of the first year, are largely manipulative and do not involve the process of semantic realization. In other words, the infant is only aware that making certain sound combinations produces manipulation of the environment. This is crucial to the further acquisition of communication. Thus, up until the end of the first year, the child observes, accepts auditory signals, and rehearses activities necessary for the acquisition of communication. For the most part, this learning is not intentional on the part of the infant but is a natural process in the acquisition of neuromuscular skills used in respiration and feeding. By the age of 1 year the child produces some relatively simple sound combinations such as "mama" and "dada."

At approximately 15 months the child develops semantic realization. The infant becomes aware that verbal symbols represent specific objects. After this occurs there is a relatively rapid proliferation of vocabulary (semantic proliferation). At this time the child recognizes that verbal symbols represent actions as well as objects. The child begins to use single words to represent his feelings and desires. This results in holophrases, or one-word sentences. The word "ball" may mean, "I see the ball," "I like the ball," "I want the ball," "It's my ball," "The ball is pretty," or whatever other message the child has in mind regarding the ball. The child tends to hear the strings of sounds but tends to select out those key object and action words that comprise his first vocabulary and becomes his first syntax. Whereas the adult listens for content, the infant listens for words.

The child uses this simple process in expression while noting and implanting more complex structures through the auditory processes. In the development of modifiers and prepositions, the child develops the cognitive knowledge through his observations, notes his descriptive deficiencies, attaches the adult method of verbalizing these aspects of language, and ultimately uses them in verbal expression. Thus, much time is spent developing a higher level of verbal functioning while the child is using a lower level of functioning.

As soon as the child develops a language concept, there is a rapid proliferation of that concept. Usually the child will attempt a new concept and await verification of the appropriateness and correctness through reinforcement from the environment. If the child receives no reinforcement, she may abandon the concept, continue to utilize it and habituate it, or alter the concept in light of new information obtained from observation or from alteration by her environment (correction). Where the child habituates a concept, she may do so with an erroneous one and later have difficulty abandoning the error. For example, the child may say, "Me go too." If this remains unchallenged, she may view this as appropriate and may utilize this in future expression. If it becomes habituated, it may prove difficult to eradicate. The more frequently used verbal symbols such as this may be more difficult to eradicate than those used less frequently, since the habituation is stronger. At the end of this first 18-month period, the child should possess the ability to understand a large number of words even in some fairly complicated syntax and should be able to produce a basic vocabulary, particularly nouns and verbs. The second stage, from the nineteenth to forty-eighth months, is spent in enlarging expressive vocabulary spectacularly and in developing the basic linguistic system.

At approximately 20 months, the child has expanded his vocabulary significantly and begins to produce two adjacent words. Initially the two words are only adjacent to one another. For example, "mama bye-bye" means "that's my mama" and "mama is going bye-bye." It does not mean "mama is going away." The child enlarges these presyntactic utterances until, at about 24 months, the process of syntactic realization occurs. At this time the child develops the recognition that verbal symbols, when strung together, reveal the actions of objects and are more efficient in that they carry more meaning than simple word adjacency. At the end of this period the child can understand most of the 3,000 most commonly used words in almost any context.

The third stage includes the maturation of speech skills at about the 7½-year level and the continuing ability to use more complex linguistic structures. The child utilizes simple sentences and increasingly more advanced transformations while building an inner repertoire of more advanced structures. After the child has developed the ability to produce compound and complex sentences, she possesses the ingredients to produce the infinite variety of transformations in language. Then follows the lifelong process of enlarging both receiving and expressing vocabularies. The expressing vocabulary is never as extensive as the receptive vocabulary, implied in the often-used statement, "Impression precedes expression." The extent to which the child's verbal communication develops is based on the inherent capacities of her central nervous system, the models available to her, the experiences she has that aid in the development of additional labels, the desire or motivation she has to increase her ability for self-expression, and her commitment to the integrity of expression. The first 4 years are critical.

SPEECH DEVELOPMENT

In addition to language development, speech also follows maturational patterns.

Voice

The production of voice is maturational until 7 or 8 years of age. However, changes occur throughout the individual's lifetime. There is voice quality associated with infancy, early and later childhood, adolescence, preteen and teen, young adult, middle age, and the elderly. There is a wide range of acceptability within each age range. Diagnosis of voice differences is the responsiblity of the SLP and the medical specialist.

Vowels	Van Riper (1964) 50%	Templin (1957) 75%	Poole (1934) 90%	Wilson (1966) (3)
p	3	3	3.5	4 to 5
b	3	3	3.5	4 to 5
m	3	3	3.5	4-5
t	3	6	4.5	4-7
d	3	4	4.5	4-5
n	3	3	4.5	4
k	5	4	4.5	4-7
g	5	4	4.5	6-7
ng	(1)	3	4.5	6
y	(1)	3.5	4.5	6
w	3	3	3.5	4
h	3	3	3.5	4
f	5	3	5.5	5-6
v	5	6	6.5 (2)	7-9
l	6	6	6.5	7-8
r	6	4	7.5	9
sh	6	4.5	6.5	(1)
zh	(1)	7	6.5	(1)
th (unvoiced)	(1)	7	7.5 (2)	9
th (voiced)	(1)	6	6.5	9
s	6	4.5	7.5 (2)	(1)
z	6	7	7.5	(1)
ch	6	4.5	(1)	(1)
j	(1)	7	(1)	6.7
blends				

FIGURE 2.4   The development of speech sounds: (1), not reported; (2), sound appears at an earlier age, disappears, and returns as indicated; (3), Wilson reports on age levels of educable retarded children by position in words. Ranges are shown.

Fluency

Fluent speech may not be obtained by some children until 7 or 8 years of age. Boys tend to develop fluent speech later than girls. A wide range of fluency exists at all levels and only when signs of speech struggle are noted need there be concern. Professional diagnosis by the SLP should be sought at that time.

Articulation

The development of the speech sounds is orderly, cumulative, and generally predictable. Figure 2.4 notes age levels of expectancy. It should be noted that these norms tend to be based on middle-class children without physical handicaps, that boys tend to be slower in the development of articulatory proficiency than girls, and that, with the exception of the Wilson data, the norms appear to be more closely related to mental age than chronological age.

This information reveals variability among the reports of experts. However, the percentage notes the criterion utilized and makes the age levels more comparable. In other words, Van Riper (1964) reports the average ages (50 percent), Templin (1957) reports age levels when 75 percent of children he studied produced the sounds, and Poole (1934) reports the ages at which 90 percent of the children had mastered the sounds. The studies are based on children within the normal range of intelligence. Wilson's study (1966) was based on a study of mentally retarded children. He included age levels for various positions in words. The ranges are presented here by sounds only. Although age levels for vowels are not reported, most authorities believe that the vowels should be accurately produced by 3 years of age. The consonants are presented as alphabet representations of the sounds rather than phoneme symbols.

This overview of language serves as an introduction to the diagnosis of language behavior and developmental and remedial programming for mentally retarded children. Language is a fascinating aspect of human behavior. Specialists are encouraged to continue its study.

CHAPTER THREE
THE SPECIALIST AND
PROGRAM PLANNING

INVOLVEMENT OF SPECIALISTS

In the past, the primary interest of the SLP has been generally restricted to only certain aspects of communication. When the SLP diagnosed a disorder in these aspects of communication, remedial measures were instituted to correct, or at least reduce, them. The "certain aspects" referred to have been almost exclusively speech: articulation, voice, and rhythm. A cursory examination of any of the major texts prior to the 1970s will support this contention. The classifications of symbolic disorders, aphasia, and language are often present but receive a minimal number of pages. It is really only aphasia that has received any significant amount of attention. In fact, until the early 1960s, the works of psycholinguists, anthropologists, and grammarians had been largely ignored by many SLPs as they functioned in training programs or in clinical activity.

Speech-Language Pathologist

For the SLP, a basic understanding of language, language development, and mental retardation is needed to assist retarded children. A more thorough understanding of language diagnosis and language remediation is required. The term "basic understanding" is an important one. Many SLPs have avoided this area because of insecurity regarding their knowledge and skills. There is no more need for the SLP to be a psycholinguist in order to function in the language area than there is for him to be a speech scientist to function in the area of speech defects. This is not to discourage a continuing upgrading of information and skills, which every SLP should engage in, but to encourage involvement in assisting children with language deficiencies. Whorf (1956, p. 222) states, "To strive at higher mathematical formulas for linguistic meaning while knowing nothing of the shirt sleeve rudiments courts disaster." The SLP needs the shirt-sleeve rudiments of language initially and should continually strive for greater sophistication in this important area.

Teachers of the Retarded

Teachers of retarded children, too, have paid minimal *specific* attention to language. A typical response to the question, "How do you improve language function?" has been, "I work it into all the activities throughout the day." Although this has been used successfully by some teachers, language too often is not sufficiently stressed if this is the sole method of aiding development and/or remediating. Commitment to a philosophy that highlighted the importance of language as a specific and critical aspect of the learning process was almost totally lacking in the field of mental retardation prior to the 1960s.

The special class teacher's task is clear. She must do all in her power to help the mentally retarded pupil acquire sufficient language skills so that he can interact successfully with his environment and use it profitably in the educational process. It is redundant by now to state that if the commonly held purposes and goals of a special class program are to be reached, the mentally retarded pupil must be helped to communicate to the limits of his capacity. Without reasonable language skills, it is difficult to imagine how any retarded pupil could become personally, socially, or occupationally competent. Through the acquisition of oral language skills that permit communication with others, retarded individuals may secure information about the world in which they live; maintain contact with friends, family, and employer; and, last but not least, develop the essential feelings of assurance and self-confidence that will help them relate effectively to others. The recent thinking that views mental retardation as a dynamic condition capable of positive change has resulted in a rethinking of previously held attitudes and beliefs about the mentally retarded and the nature of the programming provided for them. Habilitation programming of all kinds, including comprehensive language and speech programs, are increasing because it is believed that performance in personal, social, and intellectual areas can be markedly improved through such programs.

MAINSTREAMING

Although this text focuses on the special class teacher, teachers in "regular" classes are increasingly being assigned students with a wide variety of handicapping conditions. It is not unusual to find mentally retarded children spending all or part of their class days in regular classes. In such cases those teachers with special training in retardation and SLPs can provide much needed consultation to the "regular" teacher. Assisting these teachers in understanding the child's learning rate and limitations, learning style, social performance, emotional status, and, particularly important, communication system and needs can provide significant assistance to the teacher and benefit to the child. Much of the discussion and many of the suggestions in this book could be helpful for these teachers.

Improvement of the communication of the child diagnosed as mentally retarded is best accomplished by the involvement of all the persons of significance in the child's educational and home environments. In the educational environment, in addition to the teacher of the retarded, or regular class teacher, and the SLP, the school administrator, the child's classmates, and special subject teachers all play roles. In the home, the parents and siblings have important contributions to make.

The Home

Involvement of persons in the child's home environment is understandably dependent on their ability to successfully and comfortably make contributions. This is discussed in greater detail in Chapter Four. It is most helpful if the parents and siblings are aware of the goals of the child's communications program and are able to assist by encouragement and reinforcement at home. However, retarded children come from as varied backgrounds as do all children and the ability of home members to aid parallels this variability. It is important that those persons responsible for planning the child's program be able to assess the home and its potential contributions.

The Administration

"Team work" is probably the most overworked term and underworked concept in education. Planning, directed at improving the communication skills of the retarded child, offers a unique and critical opportunity for teamwork on the part of the administrator, the teacher of the retarded or regular class teacher, the SLP, and the special subject teachers. Without the support and cooperation of the administration, the program will likely flounder. The use of significant amounts of classroom time, the need for funds for special supplies and equipment, the need for the cooperation and involvement of the special subject teachers, and the need for the support of the superintendent and the board of education all dictate that the administrator immediately responsible for the program be fully aware of the goals of the program, the accomplishments that can be expected, the content of the program, the plan for conducting the program, and, most of all, that the administrator be "sold" on the program. Inviting the administrator to participate in some stages of planning, providing the administrator with reprints or articles that describe other programs and their success, sharing materials that are purchased for the program, and providing progress reports are all ingredients in enlisting cooperation. In addition, requesting time at an early staff meeting to explain the program and individual meetings with special teachers will assist in gaining understanding, support, and cooperation. These activities should be ongoing, year after year, but they are particularly important at the inception of a program.

TEACHER AND SPEECH-LANGUAGE PATHOLOGIST

The teacher of the retarded and the SLP should welcome opportunities to present information at PTA meetings and at meetings of the board of education. The greater the interest and acceptance by the school building personnel and the community as a whole, the more likely the success of the program. Enthusiasm breeds success, and the potential gains in the lives of the mentally retarded that can be expected with improvement in communication should provide a significant reason for enthusiasm.

The cooperation and joint planning on the parts of the teacher of the retarded and the SLP are the cornerstones on which the program must be built. In some school systems, joint planning and cooperation have been established practices; but unfortunately this is often not the case and these two specialists have gone their separate ways. This is regrettable, but understandable. The lack of flexibility in the schedule of the teacher of the retarded and the nature of scheduling for itinerant personnel such as the SLP make conferences difficult to arrange. In addition, the heavy case loads of SLPs have coerced many of them into spending almost all their time in providing speech therapy to the exclusion of other equally important activities such as cooperative planning with classroom teachers regarding individual children, speech improvement programming, or developmental language programs. Improved communication between the teacher of the retarded and SLPs is absolutely essential. The question of dialogue between the two specialists is one of "how" rather than "whether." Perhaps one way to improve the relationship is to examine briefly the factors that have caused inadequate communication and cooperation.

The most frequent message teachers of the retarded report receiving from SLPs is, "I have no room in my schedule for the children in your class." Thus, many teachers have come to view SLPs as disinterested and uncooperative. The reasons for the seeming elusiveness of the SLP are usually found to be related to factors other than the specialist's lack of interest in the communication problems of the retarded. For example, in some states laws prevent children from receiving more than one special service. In other instances school boards or school administrators question the appropriateness of providing assistance in the area of communication to retarded children. This is especially true where waiting lists include the names of "normal" children who, according to some misinformed persons, "can make faster progress and put the results to better use." Further, as previously stated, the professional literature of the SLP includes statements suggesting that it is fruitless to attempt to provide remedial assistance to the retarded. Finally, few training programs in the past have adequately prepared SLPs to understand the nature and learning needs of the retarded child or those special methods, materials, techniques, or alterations in therapeutic handling that enable the SLP to experience success in aiding the retarded child.

Frustrated by slowness of or even complete lack of progress, frequent regression, and the diversity of problems associated with retardation, the SLP has often withdrawn from contact with the teacher and her retarded pupils.

TIME AND THE SPEECH-LANGUAGE PATHOLOGIST

The SLP, already faced with providing programs of diagnosis and remediation for possibly 100 or more children, is understandably concerned about the additional responsibility of expending significant amounts of time providing consultation and services to the retarded population. Yet when one considers the relative merits of providing assistance to a child with a mild lisp so that he more closely conforms to society's standards of speech performance or of improving a child's language function so that his chances for educational, emotional, social, and economic success are improved, the choice becomes a relatively easy one. This does not mean that the child with the lisp does not need assistance. It means that he may merit a lower priority.

The teacher's attitude has not always been conducive to a spirit of cooperation either. Her frustrations over the lack of help provided the communication needs of her pupils have often led her to criticize the SLP's program in its entirety. One particular target among the SLP's activities lies in the area of scheduling. Since the SLP's program is often as flexible as the teacher's is inflexible, this is a logical place for misunderstanding. Working with small groups of children, a change of faces every half-hour, traveling from building to building, and the lack of a responsibility for a classroom must frequently look like "a snap" to a beleaguered classroom teacher. It is not. The professional, competent, and dedicated SLP puts in long hours under different, but not less trying, conditions than classroom teachers. Each profession is demanding, even if different.

Dialogue is the only real way to establish the necessary rapport between the SLP and the teacher. The teacher seeking consultation has often not recognized the necessity of *providing* consultation to the SLP. The teacher can provide a significant service by sharing his knowledge and experience regarding retardation. He can aid the SLP to better understand the nature of retardation, its effects on learning, and the adjustments necessary for success in learning. The teacher can also express his willingness to play a significant role in meeting the communication needs of the retarded. The teacher has not always done this in the past for reasons similar to those previously expressed for SLPs. Little in the way of training in this area has prepared the teacher for this responsibility, educational pressures have inappropriately given priorities to other areas of the classroom program, and demands of the management of the classroom have left little time for cooperation or cooperative planning.

PROGRAM ORGANIZATION

The SLP and teacher should agree on their relative responsibilities. This may vary from situation to situation depending on the abilities, training, and interests of the SLP and the teacher, and laws, rules, or regulations. Each of these specialists has something of value to offer in terms of knowledge in their field. Cooperative endeavor can lead to excellent results. Figure 3.1 presents a suggested organization for a complete program to meet the oral communication needs of retarded children. The explanation of this program will be more rigid than is necessary only to present

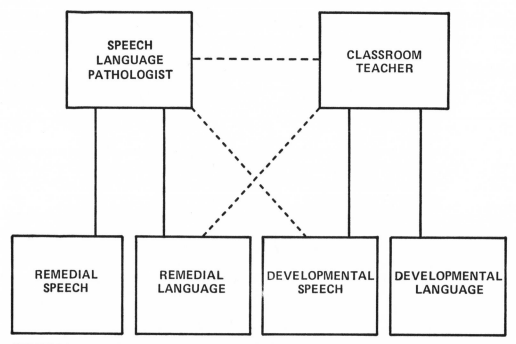

FIGURE 3.1   A complete program and responsibilities.

a suggested model. In reality, the actual program should be worked out cooperatively by the teacher of the retarded and the SLP to meet the specifics of their
situation and to take advantage of the particular skills and interests of the individuals involved. The specific assignments of responsibility is less important than the
determination that all aspects of the complete program are covered. The complete
communications program would include the four functions shown in Figure 3.1:

1. Developmental speech
2. Remedial speech
3. Remedial language
4. Developmental language

Developmental Speech

Speech, in this context, refers to articulation, voice, and rhythm. The developmental speech program is frequently referred to as speech improvement. It is the
joint responsibility of the teacher of the retarded and the SLP and may be administered by either one or administered jointly. Its goal is to speed the maturational
process or to prevent or minimize speech differences in children. It is aimed primarily at the articulatory process and its basic method is the development of
improved auditory discrimination through programs with major focus on listening.

Speech improvement programs are often planned on the assumption that the children have a mental age of 6-0 years. However, children functioning at younger levels can benefit from activities involving rhythmic activities, attending, listening, and gross motor activities.

Remedial Speech

Providing remedial assistance for children with speech defects has always been the responsibility of the SLP. This is no less true for children who are mentally retarded. Sommers (1969) has suggested that when therapy is of sufficient concentration, improvement does take place. It is likely that the speech problems of the retarded are indeed correctable once the appropriate methods for correcting them are employed.

Remedial Language

Specific deficits in language function that set certain retarded children apart even from their classmates require specific remediation. This is the major responsibility of the SLP. The same optimism is indicated for these children as is held for all children. Progress may be slower and the goals sometimes more limited; however, this does not reduce the SLP's responsibility nor, hopefully, her optimism.

Developmental Language

The teacher of the retarded has the responsibility for a daily, ongoing developmental language program, with assistance as needed from the SLP. The importance of a planned, continuing program cannot be overstated. Although the teacher should constantly be aware of the importance of language and attempt to develop it in all activities throughout the day, this is not enough. Each day the teacher should incorporate time for a scheduled, planned program. Such programs as those presented by commercial kits are helpful. It is probably more efficient and productive to have the teacher plan his program based on the specific needs he finds in the classroom. The SLP should provide consultative help in this process. It is on this latter area, developmental language, that the remainder of the material in this book will concentrate.

THE SPECIALISTS AND LEGISLATION

Legislation affecting exceptional children continues to expand at both state and national levels. Teachers of the retarded and SLPs should remain current in such matters. Professional associations such as the American Speech and Hearing Association (10801 Rockville Pike, Rockville, Maryland 20852) and the Council for Exceptional Children (1920 Association Drive, Reston, Virginia 22091) are very helpful in providing information and answering questions. The Education of All Handicapped Children Act, Public Law 94-142, is particularly important to all persons interested in educational programs for the handicapped. Signed into law by President Gerald Ford on November 28, 1975, this law became fully effective on October 1, 1977 for fiscal year 1978. This law requires states to provide special education and related services to children with special needs, provides financial assistance to states and local school districts for the development of appropriate programs and services, and establishes and protects substantive and procedural rights for children and their parents.

Both states and local school districts that meet certain requirements are entitled to federal funds according to a formula based on an escalating percentage of the national average expenditure per public school child, multiplied by the number of handicapped children between the ages of 3 and 21 being served in the school districts of each state. In the fiscal year 1978 the formula calls for 5 percent and escalates to 10 percent in 1979, 20 percent in 1980, 30 percent in 1981, and 40 percent in 1982. It remains at the 40-percent level in subsequent years.

Public Law 94-142 attempts to preclude mislabeling and overcounting of children by permitting no more than 12 percent of a state's children between the ages of 5 and 17 to be so labeled. Priorities assigned to the use of federal funding authorized by the statute describe the first priority as unserved children and the second priority as inadequately served children who are severely handicapped.

Beginning in 1979, the monies allocated to local education agencies (LEAs) will constitute 75 percent of the state's total entitlement. The state education agency (SEA) retains the other 25 percent. The state education agency is responsible for the achievement of the act's requirements and for ensuring that all education programs for the handicapped meet state education agency standards, and operates under the general supervision of persons responsible for the education of handicapped children. This includes programs administered under any other state or local agency.

A state education agency may refuse to pass on federal funds to a local district if the district fails to fulfill application requirements, the district's program for handicapped children is of insufficient size or scope, the district fails to conform to the state plan requirements contained in the new statute and preexisting laws, the district has achieved "full service" for its handicapped children with state and local funds, or the state determines that a district is unable to make effective and efficient use of its entitlement unless such entitlement is joined with another district. If the SEA withholds a district's entitlement for one or more of the above reasons, it must make certain that the funds are used to provide educational services for the handicapped children from the district from which funds are withheld. In order to participate, both state and local agencies must agree to:

1. Provide extensive child identification procedures.
2. Achieve a full-service goal according to a detailed timetable.
3. Provide a due process mechanism.
4. Provide an individualized educational program (IEP) for each handicapped child.
5. Assure the provision of services in the "least restrictive environment."
6. Have policies that protect the confidentiality of information.
7. Assure nondiscriminatory testing and evaluation.
8. Include parent, guardian, or surrogate consultation.
9. Conduct in-service training and other types of comprehensive personnel development.
10. Develop and maintain a workable policy guaranteeing the right of all handicapped children to free, appropriate public education. Children from 3 to 18 years must be served by September 1, 1980 unless this latter action conflicts with state law.

The policies and procedures describe due process safeguards available to parents and children concerning a child's identification, evaluation, or placement in an educational program. They must include prior notice to parents of any change in their child's program with a written explanation in the parents' primary langauge regarding the procedure to be followed in effecting that change. The parents must also be afforded access to school records and have the opportunity to obtain an independent evaluation of the child's special needs. Additionally, the parents must be provided opportunity for an impartial due process hearing, which must be conducted by the local district but not by an employee involved in the education or care of the child. In any hearing, the parents may be accompanied by legal counsel or expert consultation. Procedures available in a court of law are applicable and the parents may obtain a copy of the transcript and the written decision of the hearing officer. The parents may appeal the decision to the SEA and subsequently, if they desire, in federal or state courts. The parents have the right to have their child remain in her or his current placement, including a regular school program, until due process proceedings are completed.

The tests and procedures used to evaluate a child's special needs must be racially and culturally nondiscriminatory and must be in the primary language or mode of communication of the child, and no one test can be used as the sole determinant of a child's educational program.

The individualized educational plan (IEP) must include statements of the child's present levels of educational performance, short- and long-range goals, the educational services to be provided the child, and specific criteria to measure the child's progress. The plan must be reviewed annually by the parents, the teacher, and another designee of the school district, and records for each child must be maintained. If a state places a child in private school because public school programs are not available, it then assumes financial responsibility for transportation and room and board costs.

The law has been described as a bill of rights for the handicapped. It will only realize this potential if it is understood fully and used appropriately by school personnel and parents. The teacher of the retarded and the SLP have significant roles in the program planning for each mentally retarded child. The materials presented in Chapters Five and Seven may be helpful in planning short- and long-range goals.

APPLICABLE CHARACTERISTICS OF RETARDED CHILDREN

In further consideration of programming for the retarded, several aspects bear brief mention. For example, there is general agreement that the mentally retarded do not present unique speech problems although they do have a greater prevalence of defects of speech than persons with higher mental ability (Goertzen, 1957).

The importance of the parent's feeling regarding retardation also warrants attention. These matters are reflected in Chapter Four. As Friedlander (1961) notes, parents may withdraw from involvement with their child. Leberfeld and Nertz (1955) present the need to find means of helping parents learn to enjoy their children through participation in their training. They report that, when this occurred, children not only gained in specific abilities but became more secure. Leberfeld (1967) notes that parent attitudes improved when they were participants. Ezell (1960) states that retarded children receive from adults verbal responses that tend to perpetuate their retarded language performance. Siegel (1963) and Siegel and Harkins (1963) note that adult verbal behavior changes as a function of the child's retardation. Adults tend to reduce their language to the level of the retarded, become more redundant in their utterances, and become less stimulating. There is a reciprocal influence in which the child and adult affect one another.

As a result of either the retardation or the reaction of the environment to the retardation, the retarded child brings to the learning situation characteristics that mitigate against academic success. DiCarlo (1968) states that young retarded children are limited in the language models to which they are exposed and develop less divergence and elaboration in their thinking. They also have limitation in their ability to label, discriminate, categorize, and generalize and become less able to handle intellectual and linguistic tasks as they move through school. Finally, ego development may be immature and distorted, and weaknesses in auditory-vocal channels may be present.

Milgram and Furth (1963) indicate that the retarded performed as well as normals in solving problems in which perceptual rather than verbal modes of solution were assumed to be more suitable, but they performed more poorly in the discovery and application of a language-relevant concept that was within their realm of comprehension. The retarded were inferior in applying a concept to a transfer task. There is some evidence that the mentally retarded utilize a qualitatively different recall process for learning.

RESULTS OF PROGRAMMING EFFORTS

Retarded children tend to be behind in the development of communication. When they do begin to communicate they receive less reinforcement. They tend to have fewer sensory experiences and to be handicapped early by poor language. Their communication deficiency is cumulative and they are identified relatively early as possessing learning difficulty. In fact they are *taught* early that they are poor learners. They also may be identified as being poorly adjusted and/or as having poor social skills. They are talked to less and don't learn to listen. When they are talked to, it is frequently with questions that require only a "yes" or "no" answer. They often frustrate their early regular grade teacher and may even have a special class teacher who does not believe they can learn.

Early Intervention

The obvious question that emerges is, Will an elimination of these causative factors improve both the language ability and intellectual functioning of children? The effect of an improved environment in the early years is reported by the Milwaukee Project.

> This project attempted to measure the effects of early childhood stimulation and education of children from the disadvantaged area of Milwaukee.

> An initial survey of several hundred poor families with newborn babies revealed that high prevalence of mental retardation in American slums is not randomly distributed or randomly caused. It is concentrated in families with mothers of low intelligence.

> With the mothers' willing cooperation, the current program of enrichment started. Working with newborn babies of mothers whose I.Q. is below 70, a staff member of the Infant Education Center visits the home daily for several hours until the child is three or four months old, holding him, talking to him, fondling him and enriching his sensory perception.

> At about four months, the child comes in the Center every weekday for a slightly more structured, though highly flexible and individualized program.

> By 43 months, the children in the enriched environment are scoring an average of 33 I.Q. points higher than the control group, with some scoring to

an I.Q. of 135. Their intellectual development on the average is exceeding the norms generally established by peer groups of the majority culture. The superior performance is even more noticeable in language development. Children at the Infant Education Center are building an impressive vocabulary by 15 months, some even speaking in sentences. The control group has virtually no vocabulary at that age. A few of the control group children are not speaking at all by 28 months.

Both groups are composed of children who, because of their circumstances, were almost certain to be classified as mentally retarded during their school years. (Heber and Garber, 1971)

Classroom Programs

Many remedial classroom programs have been described in the literature during the past years. Reports of some of the pioneering efforts are reported here. Blessing (1965) selected remediation of vocal encoding as a means to test the hypothesis that teaching a specific deficit of a psycholinguistic nature to educable mentally retarded children would be feasible in small-group language classes. He presented lessons three times a week for 4 months. Although he felt that a specific deficit was amenable to remediation, he reports that the overall language age was not significantly enhanced by the remediation of vocal encoding. Olson, Hahn, and Herman (1965) conducted an 8-week program for mildly retarded children under 7 years of age. It centered around the strengths and weaknesses revealed from the Illinois Test of Psycholinguistic Ability (ITPA). They noted that the severely retarded benefited the least. Keehner (1966) tested the hypothesis that an intensive language program could significantly elevate language age as measured by the ITPA. Of her subjects, 68 percent did make significant gains. In 6 months the average gain was 18 months. Expressive language tested lowest at the beginning and most improved at the end.

Rittmanic (1958) presented a program to educables five times a week, 15 to 20 minutes a day for 3 months. Teachers presented the program. The results indicated that there was noticeable improvement in the use of oral language, and new word meanings were grasped sooner and retained longer. Smith (1962) matched sixteen pairs of educable mentally retarded children during a three-times-a-week program that extended for 3 months. The major purposes of the program were to increase the child's ability to receive visual and auditory clues, to associate, and to express verbally or through motor responses and linguistic symbols. Although the experimental group averaged a 6.75 gain, the control group lost 0.4 month. Mueller and Smith (1964) reviewed the results of this program a year later. Whereas before there had been a significant difference, they no longer found the difference significant. They concluded that the effect of language training was not stable and that a 3-month program was not sufficient for lasting effect.

Bereiter and Englemann (1966) presented their program 2 hours a day to fifteen disadvantaged children who had a median age of 4½ years. On the Auditory-Vocal Automatic and the Auditory-Vocal Association subtests of the ITPA, the children scored at about the 3-year level. Ten weeks later the children showed 3- to 4-month gains on reasoning and grammar tests and approximately a 1-year gain on the Vocal Encoding Test. At the end of 7 months of schooling, the children tested approximately normal on the verbal subtests of the ITPA except for vocabulary and were 6 months above average in decoding. At the end of 9 months, the children were administered the Wide-Range Achievement Test. The results indicated that although the children had not yet entered kindergarten they were ready in the areas of reading and arithmetic to enter first grade. Although these children were not labeled mentally retarded, some of these children would almost certainly have been assigned this label as they progressed through school.

More recently, Hammill and Larsen (1974) analyzed the results of thirty-nine studies emphasizing psycholinguistic training. They conclude that the training of psycholinguistic functioning has not been conclusively demonstrated. Their results seem to demonstrate the problem that exists when a specific test is given, a remedial program is undertaken to remediate the deficiencies found in the testing results, and then the test is repeated. Remedial measures should be aimed at correcting deficiencies but not concentrated on specific test results. The authors also note the frequent exclusion of training-receptive and automatic skills. If programming is not successful, it is likely because our methods and materials have not been appropriate. Several authors suggest reason for optimism in regard to the learning abilities of the mentally retarded. Lindsley (1964, p. 65) states, "It is not the population we train that is retarded, but rather our ability to design suitable environments." Ross (1974, p. 129) notes that "from the point of view of the applicability of learning principles, there are no inherent differences between the normal and the retarded." He acknowledges that genetic and physiological conditions set limits on the child's speed of learning and ultimate response repetoire but notes that retardation is a performance deficit and not a disease entity.

CONSIDERATIONS IN PROGRAM PLANNING

Program Management

The studies just reported point out that all language programs are not successful. We need to learn how best to provide assistance and which children are most able to benefit. We need to know if some areas are resistant to remediation and if there are variations in ability to improve based on etiology. When studying the programs yielding successful and unsuccessful results, several aspects of program management emerge as significant:

1. The program must be intensive. Daily periods need to be scheduled.
2. The program must be ongoing. Short periods of time may result in temporary gain but will not result in lasting improvement.
3. The classroom program at the preschool and primary levels should be predominantly a language program. At upper levels at least 40 minutes a day should be devoted to language.
4. It does not work only to "work language into all activities." The program needs to be planned and coordinated. It should not be a "cookbook" program but it must have continuity.
5. The program should have a developmental format, following the landmarks that "average" children display.
6. The SLP and the classroom teacher have joint responsibility for a complete communication program. Freeman and Lukens (1962) provide a good example of teacher-SLP cooperation and provide evidence that an effective program can be worked out between the teacher and the SLP.
7. The program should begin where the child or the group is found to be functioning.
8. Both imitation and spontaneous activity should be incorporated.

Program Content

In regard to the content of the language program, the following statements appear appropriate based on the literature:

1. The children must know how to attend, first, and then how to listen actively. Rankin (1954) studies the percentage of time a number of adults used in communication. He found that 70 percent of their waking hours were devoted 16 percent to reading, 9 percent writing, 30 percent talking, and 45 percent listening. For these children, listening is likely more important than it was to Rankin's adults.
2. The next step in the program should be to assist the child in establishing the grammatical system (syntax).
3. Following the establishment of an adequate syntax, all aspects of language function need to be included. Receiving, thinking, and expression all need attention.
4. Exposure to visual and auditory experiences is important.
5. Strengths in the visual and motor areas can be utilized, particularly initially.
6. Specific attention should be given to
   a. Remediation of the auditory-vocal channels and to memory tasks.
   b. Forming concepts and the use of transfer of learning.
   c. Moving the children from concrete to more abstract language behavior.

    d. Improving creativity and imagination in thinking.

    e. Learning to label, categorize, and differentiate.

    f. Learning to use gestures, not to substitute for communication but to enrich it.

7. The children will have to be taught what they need to know. They will profit less from vicarious learning.

The preponderance of available evidence suggests that most mentally retarded children possess more competence than performance. It also suggests that children labeled mentally retarded develop communication similar to others but at slower rates. The evidence also suggests that language performance can be improved resulting in increased ability to function intellectually, socially, and emotionally if time is taken to develop a careful and continuing language program.

The presentation in this book will not generally use the traditional category labels for the mentally retarded. This does not suggest that the results of intelligence testing are ignored. Accurate intelligence test results do indicate a child's current level of functioning and provide information about prognosis. This information should be considered. However, the focus here is on the child's current level of *language* function and programming aimed at improving language usage.

It is likely that prognosis will correlate with the child's intelligence level. However, evaluation of current language functioning may be more informative than I.Q. scores. Most improvement will be shown by children whose language deficiencies are related to socio-economic background and least by children with genetic restrictions in intelligence. It is further hypothesized that the earlier intervention begins the greater the improvement. Every child should be given the opportunity to develop communication to the limits of his ability. For some, realistic appraisal will result in the decision that assistance will not be beneficial and in other instances will result in interruption of assistance until more neuromuscular-social maturation takes place. To emphasize, it is not as likely that children diagnosed severely or profoundly retarded will benefit from programming presented here. It is more likely that mildly and moderately retarded will benefit.

If we are to err, it should be on the side of optimism. As Fitzgerald states (1954, p. 43):

> Think of no child as dull or subnormal. He may be so, but the teacher must not think of him as so. His mental process is stopped because your aspiration for him is not boundless. It is unfortunate for a pupil to feel, or say, "I can't," but it is still more unfortunate for the teacher to feel, or say, "You can't."

> Reason may say that somewhere there does exist a limit to mind development, but we cannot sense that limit because it is not yet located and because we have no unit for its measurement. . . . The larger truth is that the possibil-

ities of the human mind are boundless and that if limitations exist, the teacher should never think of them. . . .

FACTORS IN LANGUAGE DEVELOPMENT PROGRAMMING

A developmental language program for the retarded within an educational setting should give attention to four factors:

1. Establishment of a period or periods (a minimum of 40 minutes) in the school day for the direct teaching of a language development program.
2. Providing of experiences that can serve as a foundation for the development program; these experiences must be accompanied by preplanning so that the child will profit to a greater extent, a language-competent person to prove appropriate labels and descriptions, and follow-up activity to reinforce new knowledge.
3. Planning of a desirable physical and psychological environment in which language learning is to take place.
4. Use of a language model as a method of structuring activities.

Planned Time

Language activities such as reading, writing, and spelling have long been afforded a time in most daily classroom schedules for specific attention and direct teaching. It is generally recognized that these directly taught skills will be further utilized and reinforced throughout the school day in a variety of ways. The development of oral language skills has usually not been given the same important emphasis in the school program as reading, writing, or spelling. Oral language is ordinarily not taught as a subject area in the classroom curriculum; its development is often a product of chance, a secondary or incidental result of other activities.

It is suggested that a period or periods of time during each classroom day be specifically allocated to the development and direct teaching of oral language skills essential to optimum functioning of the retarded. This direct teaching period should, of course, be supplemented by the activities of the total school day to give practice for newly learned skills and consistent reinforcement to those already acquired. A defense of direct teaching of oral language skills should rest in the realization that once the retarded pupil leaves the school setting his acquisition of new information and knowledge will be, to a large degree, through his ability to listen and understand, to question and to effectively communicate orally with others in his environment. Any procedure that seems to offer opportunity to develop these skills to the highest levels should be utilized. Direct teaching of oral skills would seem to provide the method of choice.

Providing Experiences

Language is built upon the foundation of many varied first-hand experiences. Retarded children frequently come to a school setting with minimal background or experiences upon which to build language skills. Because of this limited experiential background they often come to school with limited vocabulary, immature forms of expression, a reduced reservoir of concepts, and meager knowledge. The net result of an impoverished fund of experience is a child who is not ready to participate in or assimilate fully the language experiences that the school provides.

The first step in developing a general language improvement program for the retarded should be providing pupils opportunities for many first-hand experiences. These should consist of visits to various parts of the school, to points of interest in the community such as parks, zoos, and stores. At advanced levels of the program, the locus of experience may shift to the community's institutions, industries, and service agencies. First-hand experiences within the classroom setting should also be included, such as having various people visit, caring for classroom pets, sharing toys and belongings, planning special events, and in general providing opportunities for play, exploration, and discovery. Obviously, the first-hand experiences that are provided should be appropriate to age and social maturity level of the pupils involved. However, these experiences should not be restricted only to younger children but should be used continuously through all levels of the program. Children provided with this type of program will have something to talk about and something that will serve as a basis for interrelating and expanding learnings. Such experiences will help pupils build vocabulary in a meaningful way, and this vocabulary will provide useful labels and descriptions that will also aid in the development of memory.

Desirable Classroom Environment

A language development program must take place in a positive physical and psychological setting if maximum gains are to be realized. The physical setting of the classroom should convey to the pupil an interesting, informal, and familiar atmosphere that provides natural opportunities for easy conversation. In addition, the physical environment of the classroom should provide colorful, interesting, and varied pictures, displays, materials, and objects that will stimulate the pupil to talk. The psychological climate in the classroom will be even more important. The teacher's role will be to create a nonthreatening, accepting, mutually respectful atmosphere that encourages children and teacher to listen and converse with each other. This kind of environment will be valuable in developing language skills because children will be permitted to talk freely, express opinions and ideas openly, ask questions, and learn to listen respectfully to others.

General suggestions for improving the atmosphere for language growth both in the classroom and in the therapy room are

1. The child must know that the specialist has confidence in her as a learner. She needs constant encouragement through verbal and visual praise and approval. She especially needs success experiences after her many experiences with failure. As Thorndike (1931) suggests, we learn by trial and success.
2. The specialist must phrase questions in such a way that answers other than simply "yes" or "no" are called for.
3. The specialist must not dominate with her own speech. She must allow significant opportunity for the children to express themselves.
4. The specialist must maintain language that is understandable to the children, but she must avoid totally accepting their language patterns so that there is no stimulation for growth.
5. The specialist should use short explanations and use frequent checks for understanding. Also, it must be determined that learning is perceptual, not simply imitative.
6. The specialist should use overlearning; also, many examples and recurrences rather than mere repetition.
7. The specialist should be certain that the child knows what is expected of her and the goals of the program at the child's level of understanding.

Use of Models

Finally, a language development program for the retarded benefits from a language model to guide in planning activities. Essentially, the model may be used by the teacher to structure language activities in the classroom so that all language processes receive attention. It is recognized that the language processes are complex and are interrelated in a complex manner. In most people the processes operate almost simultaneously. When people have marked deficiencies in one or more of these processes, reduced language efficiency results. Thus, an understanding and use of language models may alert the teacher to the importance of providing experiences and activities that will utilize each of the processes of receiving, thinking, and expressing. In practice, the teacher will help the retarded pupils be more attentive to what they see, hear, or feel; to help them assimilate, understand, and use these stimuli; and to talk about their experiences in a meaningful way. A model for remedial programming will be provided in Chapter Five.

Diagnosis

Following discussions between the SLP and the teacher of the retarded in which program rationale, goals, available resources, and plans for acquainting the administration and other school personnel are discussed, implementation of the program should begin. The first step must be methodology for assessing the status and needs of each child and for assessing the status and needs of the group. The chapter on diagnosis includes suggestions for the actual methods and materials. The strengths and weaknesses of each child must be determined and recorded and a program outlined for each child. This points out the need for discussion of responsibility in diagnosis, planning of time to complete the assigned tasks, discussion of test results, and agreement on the division of responsibility in programming and, particularly, the importance of a good method of record keeping.

Planned Conferences

After the preliminary diagnoses are carried out, the SLP should briefly outline to the teacher how remedial speech and remedial language activities will be carried out and the classroom teacher should outline plans for programming in the areas of developmental speech and developmental language. Following initiation of the programming, conferences should be held weekly to discuss progress, problems, and future activities. Face-to-face meetings and planning are essential to the success of the program. The conferences need not be lengthy but should provide the opportunity for ongoing cooperation and information sharing and ensure that each specialist will continue to particpate in planning.

The teacher of the retarded and the SLP who assist children labeled mentally retarded to better communication through improved speech and language function will reap rich rewards in the significant impact they have upon the lives of these children. The task is admittedly not an easy one; but the challenge is there. To learn new skills the retarded child must venture into new areas and attempt new ways. The teacher of the retarded and SLP can experience the same kind of discovery in initiating language programs and participating in experimentation.

chapter four
parent participation

The involvement of parents in planning their child's educational program mandated by Public Law 94-142 makes it essential that more efforts be made to help parents become more knowledgeable regarding their child's problem and needs. In addition, early detection and intervention is necessary if the child is to achieve to his or her potential. White (1975) emphasizes the importance of the first 3 years. Ironically, intervention seldom begins during this period. We must ensure it, and parents are the key to this.

Although not all parents have the abilities necessary for participation in preventative or remedial programming for their retarded child and it may not be advisable for others to participate for a variety of other reasons, parent involvement generally can provide dual benefits. First, assistance by parents can help to accelerate the development of more adequate communication. Second, and often overlooked, for some parents this provides a valuable cathartic experience. These statements are true for parents of all children and much of the information in this chapter is applicable to all parents. Also, the material is applicable for children traditionally labeled "preschool."

THE PARENTS AS FIRST TEACHERS

The school setting occupies only about one-fourth of a child's waking hours once a child begins school and none prior to that time. Exceptions occur when the child participates in a preschool program or is placed in a residential program. In residential programs, teachers or other attending personnel fill the roles of parents and should assist in the development of communication. However, for most children the home environment is the dominant factor in shaping early language development. The home provides a natural setting for fulfilling this role. The rooms, furniture, foods, utensils, family members, toys, and activities are the earliest vocabulary acquisitions of most children. Additionally, the parents and siblings can focus attention on one child and so the opportunity for interested, motivated, natural help is available covering considerable amounts of time.

Difficulties that exist at present in locating those children who may ultimately be labeled "retarded" in order to provide early assistance to them creates a serious problem. Hopefully, more recent advances and efforts in early detection will assist in this regard. It is possible that these children, who often will not receive the assistance they need during critical early stages of development, may never fully achieve the level of function they might have, had appropriate stimulation been provided them. Methods must be developed to locate parents of such children at as young an age as possible to aid the parents in providing assistance to their children. The previously cited Milwaukee project (Heber and Garber, 1971) is an excellent example of the efficacy of such an approach.

Parents' Desire to Help

The parents of retarded children are almost invariably affected psychologically by the experience. They feel responsible, in some way, for the condition. They may be embarrassed by the child's slowness or displays of behavior that nonthinking persons consider odd. In addition, it is frustrating enough to hear the physician say, "There is nothing I can do." It may be even more frustrating to hear, "There is nothing *you* can do." Most parents *want* to do something. They feel that, in some way that they don't understand, they helped to create the problem and so they want to contribute to the solution. If not guided to provide constructive help, they may innocently initiate counterproductive measures. "Trying to make it up to the child" by pampering, protecting from failure, by doing most things for the child or assisting in interpersonal relationships by acting as interpreter or spokesman are examples of such measures. If, on the other hand, the parent can aid in the diag-
    can contribute in some way in the planning and goal setting and can have an active role in the habilitative process, the parents' own mental health will be assisted, the parent-child relationships will be healthier and happier, and the child's development will receive a vital assist.

Conference

The first step should be a conference, hopefully involving both parents, a special educational specialist such as the primary teacher, and the SLP. The goals of such a conference should be to develop a better understanding of the child's home environment, to establish rapport with these important "team members," to help the parents develop the security of knowing that competent, interested help is available, and to begin the process of assisting the parents in the development of objectivity.

    One caution is appropriate in talking with parents. The professional is often tempted to use the innocent but shallow phrase, "I know how you feel." That is seldom true. We may have a sympathetic knowledge of some of the problems the parents face but we have not felt the actual fear, anxiety, frustration, anger, resentment, rejection, hopelessness, confusion, and/or basic emotional fatigue that parents often experience in varying degrees from living 24 hours a day with a seemingly unsolvable problem. We really don't know how *they* feel, even in those infrequent instances when we have experienced similar circumstances. A logical first step would seem to be to let them describe how they feel; even though we should be aware that they can likely only tell us part of it. A more desirable approach might be to listen to the parents and then to let them know the wide range of feelings other parents have expressed and encourage them to accept that their feelings are not unusual and are understandable.

Objectivity

The beginning of the development of objectivity begins with an accurate appraisal of how the person feels and thinks. We often separate our feelings from our thoughts. We know how we should feel so our mind develops these thoughts even though they do not represent the true emotions. Thus, bringing these two aspects together accurately is a prerequisite for improvement of both. Parents who cannot reduce emotionality to a manageable level will not be able to provide much help toward the solutions of the problems facing the child. In some instances, parents must be helped to understand that their excessive emotionality may well be a part of the child's problems.

The discussion should realistically and frankly recognize the existing problems, note the value of objectivity, discuss possible plans, and end the discussion on an optimistic note. For example, such statements as the following might be helpful. "Mr. and Mrs., the information we have available suggests that Billy will have some difficulty as he proceeds through school. He will probably be aided by a special class placement" (not "he probably will *have* to be placed in a special class," as though it were a sentence). "The first thing that we should try to do together is to develop as clear a picture of Billy as we can. The understandings that we can develop are going to be much more helpful than some of the labels that you may have heard or may hear in the future. Such terms as mentally retarded, mentally handicapped, or brain injured can be pretty disturbing if you view them as though they were labels for diseases. They're really not. They're intended to help us understand children so that we can plan for them. Actually, describing what children can and can't do works out much better than using labels. So, let's see if we can't find ways to describe Billy as accurately as possible. To do this we should learn to observe and report as accurately as possible the things that Billy can and can't do. As we improve in our abilities to do that we will also improve in our understanding of Billy and we will be better prepared to help him."

We should try to assist parents to become objective observers, competent in viewing, describing, and understanding behavior rather than reacting to it as a result of their own emotions. Often it is helpful to have the parents keep a log containing things you ask them to do. Early entries should be aimed more toward establishing methodology than securing information. Parents might be asked to report any vocalizations that the child produces, the manner in which the child makes his or her wants known, the times the child goes to sleep and arises, times of toileting activity. These things require only simple reporting. When the parent is able to accomplish this the next step might be to ask for information that requires the parents to separate out objective material from their own inferences. For example, the parent might be asked to list situations that seem to frustrate the child, situations in which the child seems handicapped by his or her inability to communicate adequately, the successes that are observed, or evidence that the child is ready for more difficult activity. It may be helpful to ask each parent to prepare a list of his and her own ideas and then examine them for differences in the content. On occasion, these differences may be used for discussion.

The parents' frustrations in not knowing exactly what to expect should be recognized. "We know that you would like to know exactly what Billy will be like in a year, or five, or ten. For now, let's concentrate on what he *is* doing and on our next goal for him."

Possible conflicts between parents should be noted. Such comments as "he has no patience with him" or "she thinks he's slow but I think he'll be o.k. in a year or two" spell potential difficulty not only for the child but for the parents' relationships as well. The additional expenses, time, emotions, and planning caused by the presence of any handicapping condition in a child place an added strain on a marriage. A decision must be made as to whether additional professional help is indicated. Additional professional help in the involvement of psychological or social work personnel may be required for a variety of reasons. However, the teacher and SLP should never underestimate the value of being objective, interested, and confidential listeners.

After efforts are made to aid the parents in the development of objectivity, the next step is to help the parents recognize the importance of the early years. We know that in the average child the shaping of character and personality occur in about the first 5 years. We do not know if the same time span is applicable for some or all of the retarded. Certainly the retarded child is developing in many ways during that period, even if at a reduced rate. Our safest assumption at this time is that this is also a critical period for the child.

Children learn both good and bad. They can learn to love and trust and feel secure but they can also learn the undesirable opposites. With retarded children the positive feelings of love, trust, and security are particularly important. For example, we all need to learn to succeed. We need to know that "we can!" We also must learn to fail gracefully and without injury to our basic adjustment. It is difficult to learn if we cannot handle failure. Unfortunately, children sometimes learn "I can't." Each new experience is preceded by an expectancy to fail. In retarded children we often see this resignation to failure. To counteract this we must assist parents to balance realistic demands with patience in the child's development. In other words, the child should have the opportunity to succeed but the child's environment should not be manipulated so that he or she always succeeds. Some parents try to help the child by not imposing any demands for performance whatsoever. This provides little incentive for growth. The child should be encouraged to try, rewarded for effort, and helped to accept failure as being acceptable behavior.

Much of this is based on the language behavior of the parents. Initially, the tone of their voices is as important as their words. It may be difficult, but parents should delay expressions of frustration at their child's failures or the anger that they may feel on occasion by their child's actions until the child is out of the range of seeing or hearing. Of course, the child needs to experience some of the parents' negative emotions, but not consistently. Creating an emotionally antiseptic world could in itself be harmful. If parents understand why it is necessary to control their feeling when dealing with the child and the realities of nonverbal communication, it is another step in developing the objective approach.

The Home as First Classroom

The parents are probably aware, to some extent, that those things the child learns first are based on what he feels, hears, and sees at home. They may not realize how important this is. This has implications for the kinds of things the child should see, hear, and feel. It also has implications about the manner in which this occurs. For example, children are assisted by a daily routine that is somewhat regularized. Although a total commitment to routine is neither necessary nor advisable, a somewhat regular routine contributes to a child's feelings of security and provides better opportunities for learning. Included in this learning process is the child's developing feelings and acceptance of belonging to a family group. This includes privileges, restrictions, and eventual responsibilities. The processes of sharing and assisting should not be violated because a child is handicapped in some way. All of us have observed those unfortunate situations in which an entire family unit is sacrificed to meet the needs of a handicapped child. This can lead to a "handicapped family" in which all members suffer. The handicapped child often does require extra time but every member of the family is worthy of consideration. The loss of status and loss of need fulfillment should be minimized in the presence of a handicapped child. Not only will family members benefit from this philosophy, but the child will live a more normal life and will grow in an environment more conducive to developing a realistic view of the world and her place in that world.

Guiding Parents

As the home is the first classroom, the family members are the first teachers. The mother is the most important figure in this process but all family members contribute. If family members can understand that the child is receiving stimuli from her environment even though reactions may not be noted to signal this, they will be more effective teachers. The retarded child needs to be stimulated by her environment even more than the average child. The child should be bombarded with sights and sounds and other sensory experiences. The child should be talked to constantly, even when persons are saying the obvious. The child should be talked to about what she is doing, about what family members are doing, about what has happened, and about what is about to happen. The process should be to say it, do it, and say it and then say it again. It is difficult to continue this activity when the child does not appear to notice or respond. It must be recognized that the child *is* responding but in ways we may not be able to identify.

REINFORCING EARLY COMMUNICATION

The parents should understand that developmental communication landmarks may be delayed. It is likely that retarded children, in varying degrees, are behind in the age levels at which they babble, say first words, add additional vocabulary, combine words, speak clearly, and so on. Parents should not give up on reinforcing their child. It is likely that the child needs more reinforcement over a longer period of time. This is difficult for parents because *they* are not reinforced. The language must be simple but parents need to talk, talk, talk and praise communication efforts effusively.

As an example, let us examine the periods of language development when these landmarks are translated into the rate of development for the three defined types of retardation. At present, this has no scientific validity but it may serve as a helpful illustration. As described in Chapter Two, prelinguistic activity includes the early behavior that serves as the early basis for later oral-verbal communication and that has previously been described as the first stage. Stage two, or development of the basic linguistic system, has been described as including the purposeful use of the sounds to form words, enlarging the repertoire of words, improving understanding of the meaning of words, and using such things as stress, pitch changes, phrasing, etc., to change the meanings of the words the child uses or to shade meanings. Stage three, or refining and expanding the linguistic system, includes enlarging further the store of available words and developing greater complexity in the aspects of language. The age levels are expressed in months as ranges. As emphasized in Chapter Two, all children do not develop at exactly the same rate and ranges of expectancy are more appropriate:

	Average child	*Mildly retarded*	*Moderately retarded*	*Severely retarded*
Prelinguistic activities	0–18	0–36	0-54	0-?
Developing the linguistic system	18–48	24–96	36–144	54-?
Refining and expanding the linguistic system	48-?	64-?	96-?	144-?

The question marks reflect the fact that the process may continue indefinitely or reflect the fact that we are not certain as to when the development of the skills ends. Consideration of these figures is meant to highlight what delays imposed by intellectual restrictions could mean to the development of communication. Consider what could occur with even a mildly retarded child. The child is relatively quiet early and babbles very little. The parents are initially pleased by the lack of disturbance created by the "good baby." As time goes by the parents become discouraged as they receive no response to their attempts at interaction with the child through their use of words, babbling, and cooing. The parents may continue this behavior until the child is past his or her first birthday. Experiencing no success and receiving no reinforcement from the child, the parents withdraw into a caretaking role, becoming increasingly nonverbal in their interactions with the child. The child, in turn, is subjected to an increasingly nonverbal environment, lacking in the samples of verbal behavior he or she needs at an increased, not reduced, level.

It is likely that the child does experience a later beginning to verbal behavior, goes through a longer period of prelinguistic behavior, and exhibits early some indistinct attempts at verbal behavior that may not be recognized as such and may not be appropriately reinforced. Repeating a child's "ba-ba-ba" at 3 years of age may seem unimportant to some parents and ridiculous to others. Parents need encouragement to continue trying, continue listening, continue observing, continue noting behaviors, and continue feeling optimistic. The specialists must function as the reinforcers. Waiting is not enough. It cannot be a passive process; rather, this period must be filled with activities and actions designed to improve comprehension, assure the function of the articulators, and reward any communication efforts.

THE PARENT AS CLINICIAN

Helping the parent to better play the role that all parents play but adjusting it to the needs of the retarded child is a logical first step. However, we must make certain that we have provided the child with every possible advantage. This involves the provision of planned assistance. Some parents, mothers in particular, do many of the things that will be recommended but others will need varying degrees of guidance.

In addition, the parents will need advice as to the manner of assisting the child. For example, suggestions for stimulation should be carried on throughout the day. Yet, for some mothers this is impossible. Nothing is accomplished by having the mother feel guilty if she is not able to spend as much time as she would like to because of other responsibilities, the limits of her own patience, or failure of the child to respond. The parents should be commended for interest and effort. They should be told that when the child responds they should be encouraged; when not, they should be patient. They should be assisted to be pleased with success but not discouraged by failure. They should not dwell on possible mistakes and should recognize that their best efforts and their desire to assist are the more important things.

As the child grows older the development of a specific work place and work time are desirable. The work area should be relatively quiet and free from distraction and include furniture and materials that are comfortable for the child. The time used should be when the child is relatively calm and not being taken from some other activity she enjoys. A place should be provided to store materials. The parents should review materials that will eventually be utilized well in advance so that they may obtain those less expensive things they need should they happen to locate them on shopping trips.

The professional should guide the parents by helping them to determine appropriate goals and activities. Observing the parent or asking for descriptions or examining and discussing the log that the parents keep can be of value. Evaluation such as, "Don't you think that's a little too difficult for him right now?" or "Do you suppose we might be more successful if we tried this right now?" or "Would it be better if we tried simpler words?" or "Don't forget to talk in complete sentences" are examples of appropriate guidance. No matter how objective the parents may become, the professional will be more objective. Another thought, another idea, another ear is always helpful.

DECIDING "WHAT TO DO"

Probably the most difficult aspect of all is deciding which activities are appropriate for the child and when to move on. Since retarded children are more varied in their developmental patterns, the decisions are even more difficult for them than for other children. Certainly the parents should begin to stimulate the child as early as possible. What to do after that is difficult to describe and even more difficult for the parents to know. The wisest course is for the parents to have a general understanding of the sequencing of assistance and then to occasionally try certain of the recommendations for the next steps to see if the child appears ready to learn in that area. The SLP can make more specific suggestions based on the needs of each child.

The general sequence of assisting the child will be

1. Stimulating the child throughout the day in activities in the home.
2. Providing specific exercises aimed at developing the functioning of the articulators.
3. Providing listening experiences to aid in the development of auditory processing.
4. Providing activities that are basic to later learning.

STIMULATING THE CHILD THROUGHOUT THE DAY IN ACTIVITIES IN THE HOME

Following are suggestions for parents to use in the home environment. Suggestions are taken from several sources including suggestions for parents distributed at the University of Pittsburgh Cleft Palate Center (1975). Teachers and SLPs may wish to reproduce such suggestions for distribution to parents. These guidelines are stated as though they are addressed to parents. They are for parents to use under professional guidance:

In the Kitchen

Let the child watch you prepare meals. Let him watch you move items about, open cans, tear foil and paper, stir food, boil liquids, fry meat, pour water, wash and dry dishes. Describe everything you do as you do it. Look at the child as you talk to him. Use a pleasant voice. Speak loudly, clearly, and in short, complete sentences.

Let the child hear the water running, the water boiling, the meat frying, the toaster pop up, the dishes and pans clacking. Attach verbal sounds to these sounds such as "pop" when the toaster pops up or "Shhh" for the running water. Let the child feel soap suds, cereals, jams, margarine, cooking oil, bread, peanut butter, ice cubes, cake mix.

Keep a mirror about 4 inches by 6 inches handy so that the child can see himself, the frosting on his face, the chocolate on his bib, the milk on his tray, the bread crumbs on the table (and the jam in his hair). Tell the child where things are kept, how big or little things are, how high or low things are, how heavy or light they are, how hot or cold they are, how long or short they are. Describe the shape of things, such as round or square, the texture of things, such as soft or hard, the color of things. Describe where things are in terms of on, in, under, over, between, beside, next to, on top of, etc.

Develop the concept of questions and answers. "Where did mother get the water? Mother got the water from the faucet in the sink." "Where is the waste basket? Is the waste basket under the sink? Yes, the waste basket is under the sink." "Where are the spoons? Are the spoons in this drawer. No, the spoons are not in this drawer. Where are the spoons? Are the spoons in this drawer? Yes, here they are. The spoons are in this drawer."

In the Eating Area

Talk about foods, silverware, dishes, pots and pans, chewing, swallowing. Describe colors, tastes, hot and cold, sweet and sour, hard and soft, big and little, hungry

Shaw University Library

and full. Point out the lips, the tongue, the teeth, and the mouth. Say things such as, "I put potatoes *on* Billy's spoon. Here comes the potatoes up to Billy's mouth. Billy opens his mouth wide. In Billy's mouth go the potatoes. Billy chews the potatoes. Now Billy swallows the potatoes. The potatoes go down Billy's throat to Billy's tummy." Then do the same with something from your plate. Say such things as, "Daddy cuts his meat with his knife. Daddy picks up the meat with his fork. Daddy puts the meat in his eye. In his eye? That's silly. Daddy puts the meat in his mouth, not in his eye."

In the Bathroom

Let the child hear the water running, the electric razor, the toilet flushing, the water draining, and tooth brushing. Play "this little piggy" with toes, "peek-a-boo" with the wash cloth.

Play with the child as he blows bubbles off your hand, feels the soap and lets it slip through his hands, squeezes the tooth paste out, floats toys in his bath. Discuss all these things and make sounds for the actions. Let the child feel warm and cool water, the wet wash cloth, the bath towel, the baby oil or lotion, the baby powder, the comb. Let him see himself in the mirror while you point out body parts. Describe body parts as you dry him off.

In the Living Room

Let the child listen to the radio, the television, the clock, the vacuum cleaner, the record player, the sweeper, the doorbell, the fan, the furnace going on, someone knocking on the door, the door opening and closing, the phone ringing, sirens outside, dogs barking outside, birds singing outside. Always attach verbal labels. When the sound is outside say, "What's that? Do you hear that? That's the doggie barking, woof, woof. Hear the doggie barking, woof, woof." Take him to the window and see if you can see the action described.

Have the child feel the rug, the sofa, the chairs, the table, the windows, pillows. Stress words such as pretty, big, heavy, new, old, thick, long, short, high, low.

In the Car or Outside

Talk about the weather. Use words such as sun, clouds, rain, snow, warm, ice, cold, hot, wet, lightning, thunder, wind, moon. Let the child feel the rain, the snow, the rock warm from the sun, the breeze, the icicle. Go to the grocery and department store, a farm, the zoo, the woods, a lake. Talk about what you see, hear, smell, and feel.

Play Activity

Play "all gone," "patty cake," dance while holding the child in your arms, laugh and go "boom" to the thunder. Let her play with the mirror, labeling the facial parts she sees and the emotions she displays (crying, laughing, smiling, frowning). Give her a can or a pan with a spoon and let her bang it. Give her soundmakers such as blow toys, harmonicas, and pull toys that produce sound. Blow a bubble pipe for her or let her try.

Show her picture books, naming the pictures. Play with a ball describing it as it bounces, rolls, is thrown, and is caught. Bathe a doll and name the body parts as you do so. Do the same naming with a toy dog, toy cat, toy horse, toy cow, toy lion, toy tiger, or toy turtle.

Hide one of her wind-up toys that makes a sound and help her find it. Hide some other object that doesn't produce sound. Help her at first and later see if she can find it. Fill a lid with cereal, marbles, or popcorn and let her play with it. Put salt, pepper, sugar on a plate and let her play with it. Put a little to her mouth. Put several amounts of different colored Kool-Ade on a plate and let her play and taste.

String beads. Use crayons to scribble and water colors to paint. Find easy form boards or puzzles for her to solve.

PROVIDING SPECIFIC EXERCISES AIMED AT DEVELOPING THE FUNCTION OF THE ARTICULATORS

Production of speech to convey language is dependent on human systems designed for breathing and eating. In particular, development of chewing, sucking, and swallowing is a first step in preparing for speech production.

Sucking

Sucking is one of the first natural acts of the child. For a short time after birth almost any stimulus such as taste, touch, or temperature will elicit a sucking response. Shortly after birth it becomes necessary to stimulate the mouth for a response.

If the child reveals the ability to suck normally as evidenced by the use of a nipple without the hole enlarged or nursing at the mother's breast, no suggestions are indicated except that, even if not breast feeding, the mother should be encour-aged to hold the child. The normal nipple size can be defined as one that will allow twenty drops of liquid per minute when the bottle is held upside down.

Sucking includes good lip and tongue exercises and should be continued until the limits of normal nursing are reached somewhere between the ninth and eighteenth months, depending on the child. After this, sucking can be continued by having the child suck through a straw. At first a plastic straw may be used to overcome the initial difficulty the child may experience. If the child has difficulty holding the straw because of its small size, the straw can be wrapped with transparent tape to increase its size and make it easier for the child to hold with her lips.

The child should sip liquids that are cold and sweet with a pleasant odor. Where liquids do not have prominent odors, mint, small amounts of ammonia, or oil of cloves can be rubbed on the outside of the glass. As time goes by the size of the taping can be reduced. The process should not be rushed and the entire experience should be made pleasurable and without critical comment. If the child experiences difficulty using this method the parents should obtain a plastic transparent straw. So that the child will know what to do, wait for the jaw to relax then apply pressure on the lower jaw to raise it so that the teeth close lightly. Hold the straw between the lips, just touching the closed teeth. After this has been repeated five or six times so that the child has learned to relax his jaws and close his lips so the lips hold the straw, some colored and pleasant tasting liquid is drawn into the straw by immersing it and then closing one end with a finger to hold an amount about one-third to one-half the length of the straw. The straw is then placed between the lips, the liquid just touching so that the child tastes it. This usually succeeds in getting the child to swallow and after several trials he will suck it all the way up. The tube can be tilted on successive trials so that greater effort is required. When the child has learned to sip from the straw it is placed in a glass and the child sips from the glass. The use of stick candy, suckers, and popsicles can also be helpful.

Swallowing

In addition to sucking, swallowing is very beneficial. Difficulty in swallowing may be evidenced by drooling. In very young children this is normal behavior; however, neuromuscular maturation usually eliminates this before the end of the first year. Delay past this time may be due to the child's inability to use his tongue to work food or liquid to the back of the mouth. Giving the child liquids he enjoys in small amounts on a spoon and then tilting the head slightly backward may be of assistance initially. The child should then be encouraged to do this without tilting the head backwards. The next step is to have the child take several small sips from a glass. Then, being careful that the child does not choke, continue the liquid so that the child must continue to both suck and swallow. The child should be moved through foods as normally as possible, following the physician's recommendations in going from the bottle to baby foods to junior foods to table foods. The child should not eat only soft foods and should be taught to chew food carefully and completely.

Speech Articulators

When the child is about 3 years of age, imitative activities can be begun in using the articulators. Playing follow-the-leader with lip protrusions and retractions, smiles and frowns, tongue activity and jaw movements encourages articulatory activity. Use the mirror so that the child can observe herself as well as you. Hold the child whenever possible when pursuing these exercises. At times imitation can take place while both of you look into the mirror. Effort should be rewarded more than success and activities should be filled with fun and laughter.

Place jam, jelly, peanut butter, or honey at the corners of the mouth and on the upper and lower lips. Have the child lick them off. Move from the edges gradually outward so that the child has to reach a little more. Do this two or three times at each meal time. Place a sucker in these positions and have the child lick it. Lip smacking should be utilized and loud pressure sounds made by drawing in the lips and then releasing them. Play with a toy in the bathtub that talks to the child by going /ap/, /apa/, and /pa/. The child should continue to blow soundmakers and bubble pipes. See if the child can blow up an "easy" balloon, one that a parent has blown up first. Blow feathers across a table or have the child on one side of the table and you on the other and play "ping pong soccer" by blowing it off the other person's side of the table. Blow a piece of tissue across the table in the same manner.

As the child becomes older, efforts should be made to have all such activities become slightly more formal. Try to lengthen the periods of activity during which the child sits and participates. Attention span may be assisted by this and the beginnings of the educational program rooted here. Occasionally the training program should be completely abandoned for a short and specified period of time so that all can have a rest.

PROVIDING LISTENING EXPERIENCES TO AID IN THE DEVELOPMENT OF AUDITORY SKILLS

Much of this is worked on in previous suggestions. The child should hear the activity around the house and have her attention called to it with verbal labels applied. Encourage the child to listen to the radio or television. Say, "What's that?" when a new sound is heard on television or outside. Put your finger in front of your mouth and say "shh" when you want the child to listen for a sound such as a bird call or an airplane or helicopter overhead.

Play "where is it?" by having the child point to the source of sound when he is able. Obtain various whistles, horns, and other sound makers and produce sound behind the child to see if he turns to it. Then see if he can imitate you in pointing to where the sound came from. One parent can have the child face her while the other moves about behind the child producing sound.

Have one parent hide in a room or closet and say, "Sandy, where am I?" Have the child locate you and reward with hugs and laughter. Take two sound makers and place them in front of the child. Have the child close her eyes or cover the two with a piece of cardboard. Make a sound on one and then have the child point to the one that made the sound. Increase to three, then four, and then five.

Obtain records or record sounds outside on an inexpensive cassette recorder. Make a sound and then look through books to find an animal or object that makes the sound. Read to the child while she sits on your lap. Embellish the stories by making the sounds the animals make, or the car makes, or the boat, the truck, the drill, and the like. Continue to fill the child's world with sound and see if the child can match sounds, or match the sound maker to the sound, or begin to note differences in sounds (loud, soft, high, low, near, far, and so on).

PROVIDING ACTIVITIES BASIC TO LATER LEARNING

4 to 8 Years

When the Child is 4 to 8.   Again, it is difficult to know exactly when the child can benefit from the following suggestions. For higher functioning children, they will probably benefit when they are about 4 years of age, for other children the appropriate age will be 5 to 8 years. The best procedure is to try some of the exercises with the child. If the child can attend and participate, she is ready. Parents should check periodically for readiness. Basic learning is a process of observing, imitating, comparing, contrasting, matching, discriminating, and noting similarities and differences. Up to this point we have tried to expose the child to basic aspects of her environment. Informally, she has compared and contrasted sights, sounds, tastes, odors, and the way things feel. Now we begin by more active exercises.

Again, the teacher may wish to prepare a ditto of suggestions for parents. Following are samples of activities.

Matching

Matching Colors
1. Cut out two squares of red, yellow, and blue paper. Put one square of each color in front of the child, naming the colors as you lay them down. Then hand the child a square and say, "Here's a red one. Where is another red one? Put this on the other red one." Do the same with other colors. Remember to talk to the child and reward effort.
2. Assemble objects of red, yellow, and blue. Such items as buttons, toy cars, combs, plastic bottle tops, yarn, plastic spoons, forks and knives, boxes, pieces

of cloth and leather can be used. Again, put squares of each color in front of the child, give the child an item and say, "This is a blue car. Put the blue car on the blue paper." Proceed with the other colors and items.

3. Paint a board about 16 inches long and 4 inches wide in 4-inch squares of red, yellow, and blue. Repeat the exercises in steps 1 and 2 with the board.

4. Cut out outlines of fish, cars, dogs, houses, and chairs out of red, yellow, and blue paper. Have the child place each item (all the dogs) on the appropriate color. Go through each item.

5. Paint three of the same kind of cans red, blue, and yellow. Have the child place the objects in step 4 in the appropriate can.

6. Paint snap clothes pins the three colors and have the child snap them on the appropriate can.

7. Have the child take the objects in step 4 and snap in the clothes pins.

8. Add the colors of green, orange, white, and black and repeat steps 1 through 7.

9. Cut out stars, circles, squares, and triangles. Have the child put them in the appropriate can.

Matching Forms

10. Use the items in step 4. Place one of each in front of the child. As you hand the child additional forms, have the child place them on the appropriate form, disregarding color. If the child errs by using color say, "Yes, they are the same color. They are both red. Now we want to put all the *cars* together. See, here is another car. Put it here."

11. Use the items in step 9 and repeat.

12. Cut out items of felt or some other coarse material (items in step 4). Have the child sort by forms.

13. Cut out and have the child sort items of felt or other coarse material (items in step 9).

14. Cut out three sizes of items in step 4. Have the child match by form.

15. Cut out of wood and paint, or buy commercially, stars, triangles, squares (blocks), and circles. Have the child match the others to those you place in front of him.

Matching Types

16. Have the child match toys such as dolls, cars, trucks, teddy bears, boats, fish, dogs, and so on.

17. Have the child match clothing such as shoes, socks, hats, belts, aprons, shirts, trousers.

18. Have the child match silverware such as spoons, forks, and knives.

19. Have the child match cupboard items such as soup and vegetables.

20. Put salt, pepper, chili powder, and the like in small clear envelopes. Have the child match them. Be sure to continue to talk and describe activities.

Matching Drawings

21. Draw squares, circles, crosses, and triangles on plain paper. Place one of each in front of the child and have her match as before.
22. Draw stars, moons, rectangles, and ovals and proceed as in step 21.
23. Combine steps 21 and 22. If the child becomes confused by likeness of squares and rectangles, circles and ovals, eliminate them.
24. Draw simple line drawings of chairs, tables, cars, plates, and cups. Place one of each in front of the child and have her match.
25. Draw forks, knives, dogs, boats, and houses and proceed as in step 24.
26. Combine steps 24 and 25.

Matching Pictures

27. Use old magazines to find two pictures of grass, butter, doors, cars, and guns. Have the child match as before.
28. Find more objects such as dogs, cats, lions, snakes, bears, horses, and have the child match.
29. If possible find various kinds of fish, flowers, birds, and have the child match.
30. Use Old Maid cards and have the child match cards.
31. Place Old Maid cards face down. Start with two pairs, then three, four, and as many as the child can tolerate. Play the game of pairs in which the child can keep the cards if he finds a pair; if not he replaces them. If the child cannot succeed after trial, eliminate.

Matching Size

32. Use the items in step 14 and match by size.
33. Draw three sizes of items in steps 24 and 25 where possible. Take four to start and match (sort) by size.
34. Proceed to other items in steps 24 and 25 in the same manner.
35. Find pictures of big and little dogs, horses, houses, cars, and have the child sort by size.
36. Find pictures of mothers and babies. Match babies to mothers.

Differences

37. Take the items in steps 1, 2, 4, 5, 15, 16, 17, 18, 21, 22, 24, 25, 27, 28, and 29. This will be used to constitute many lessons. Use three items initially, then enlarge to four, five, and six. Each time lay all but one of one item and one other. Have the child tell you what doesn't belong. Alternate the placing of the incorrect item such as first, second, third, etc.

Puzzles

38. Take some of the shapes and cut them in two. Have the child put them back together.

39. Take some of the shapes and cut across them irregularly into two parts. Have the child reassemble.
40. Cut into three pieces and then four and see if the child can succeed.
41. If the child succeeds, find simple commercial puzzles and work with the child in solving them.
42. Take a picture and cover it with a piece of paper. Ask the child to guess what it is. Remove the paper a little at a time and ask the child to guess what it is.
43. Cut a piece of paper in two parts. Cover a picture and remove one part and have the child guess what it is, then the other. Increase the number of pieces in the covering paper to three, four, and five, and repeat as before.
44. Put two different items from earlier exercises in front of the child. Have her close her eyes. Remove one and ask her to guess what is missing.
45. Increase the number to three, four, five, and repeat.
46. Play "guess what I am thinking of." Take a picture, have the child examine it, and give the child clues, one at a time, until he guesses correctly.
47. Play "Simon says." You will remember that the child only performs the act if Simon says it. Simon says raise your hand; the child does so. Touch your nose; the child doesn't or she loses.
48. Ask the child to listen for something specific in a sentence. "Mary had a new doll—what does Mary have?" "Andy broke his wagon—what did Andy break?"
49. Place two objects from previous exercises in front of the child. Ask the child to tell you how they are alike and how they are not alike.
50. Ask the child to perform two acts. "Touch the car, then the dog." "Put the circle on the lion and the square on the bear."
51. Increase the items to three and see if the child can succeed. If not, eliminate.
52. Add another factor. "Put the green square on the horse and the red square on the chair."

Description

53. Show the child pictures and ask her to describe. Give hints and prompt as needed to aid in the child's description.

Providing those parents who can profit with appropriate reading materials is still another way of assisting them.

Use of these suggestions likely overlaps the time that the child enters school. Allow the parents to observe and keep them informed of progress.

PARENTS AND LEGISLATION

Chapter Three includes a section on Public Law 94-142, which has significant meaning for parents of handicapped children. Assisting parents to understand the content, ramifications, and appropriate utilization of the law is an important responsibility of specialists working with parents of retarded children. As mentioned previously, the requirement that parents participate in the planning of their child's educational program again emphasizes the need for early parental involvement and the need for assisting parents to become more knowledgeable regarding the educational process, special programming, and the nature and needs of their child.

OTHER RESOURCES

A language kit and a community program are available that may provide additional assistance for parents. The language kit is designed for home use to assist parents in aiding in the development of language. It would require guidance on the part of the specialist for application to retarded children. It is aimed at children between the ages of 3 and 5 years:

Karnes, M., *Learning Language at Home*
The Council for Exceptional Children
1920 Association Drive
Reston, Virginia 22091

The community program was developed cooperatively by professionals, parents, and volunteers under the sponsorship of the Philadelphia Association for Retarded Citizens and Special People in the Northeast with support from the Bureau of Education for the Handicapped, the U.S. Department of Health, Education and Welfare. This program, Parents are Effective Early Education Resources (PEERS), is designed to provide early intervention services to infants, birth to 3 years, who are described as developmentally delayed. PEERS is a community program that, the developers state, can be replicated in any community at minimal cost. Additional information can be obtained from

Executive Director, Special People in the Northeast
8040 Roosevelt Boulevard
Philadelphia, Pennsylvania 19152

or

Director, Motivating Agency Department
Philadelphia Association for Retarded Citizens
1211 Chestnut Street
Philadelphia, Pennsylvania 19107

chapter five
diagnosis for program
planning

Consideration of the many facets of language cannot help but impress the teacher and SLP with the difficulties in completely and accurately assessing the child's language performance. In fact, this has often been a barrier to the provision of programming. In an attempt to present a relatively simple basis for diagnosis, an approach has been chosen directed toward a basic understanding of the child's language performance and primarily toward placement in the program presented. The important thing is to use a method whereby cooperative decisions can be made as to where to initiate habilitative measures and how to proceed from that point.

Cooperative Diagnosis

The cooperative diagnosis by the SLP and the teacher of the retarded involves determining the present status of the child's communication abilities, determining the goals for the individual child, determining whether there are organic or functional factors that will impede or prevent the child from achieving the goals established for her, determining whether barriers that exist can be removed or reduced, and deciding on how to help the child move from her present level of functioning. After these decisions have been made, the decision remains as to which problems each individual child displays are relatively unique and which will be dealt with through group programming in the classroom. The problem need not be universal in order to justify classroom programming. In fact, unless some members of the class are able to assist the classroom teacher by their competence in a given area, programming will be extremely difficult.

Case History

Some of the desired information is best obtained by a case history, a history of the child's development. Although it is not unusual for various specialists to compile extensive case history information that is later filed and not used, certain basic information is essential in understanding the child and in program planning. The teacher of the retarded and the SLP may wish to develop a short-answer questionnaire to be sent home and returned. The specialists should determine whether the school district has a preferred form and whether there is a policy governing materials sent home for return. In addition, an individual face-to-face meeting with the parents is desirable. This offers the opportunity to get to know the parents, gain additional information, assess their potential for cooperation, explain the program to them, and enlist their cooperation.

The information to be obtained should include the child's early developmental background, particularly in the prelinguistic area, the child's health history, the quality of the language in the home, the language proficiency of the parents and the siblings, the child's motivation for communication, the parents' interest in the quality of communication, foreign language usage or background that may interfere with the child's use of the English language, and the child's opportunity to use communication for expression of ideas, information, emotion, and recreational purposes. Particular attention should be given to obtaining information that focuses on the child's physical ability to communicate (auditory, visual, neuromuscular, dental), psychological ability to communicate (intellectual, motivational, environmental, social), and the present status of communication. Figure 5.1 presents a possible format.

SPECIAL CONSIDERATIONS FOR CHILDREN LABELED "NONVERBAL"

Particular attention should be given to clarifying the problems of children who are labeled "nonverbal." For children who reveal no communication, an assessment should be made as to whether the child appears to be prelinguistic, preverbal, or nonoral.

The representation of the communication process in Figure 5.2 attempts to provide a general ordering of this behavior in order to establish a diagnostic framework particularly applicable for nonverbal children and to provide a basis for remedial consideration. In this model, an incoming stimulus is received (sensation) through one of the sensory channels, noted by the receiving organism (attention), and examined in comparison with other stimuli and past experience (perception). The stimulus is then understood (comprehension), reacted to immediately for response or stored momentarily or for lengthy periods of time (association-processing). In association-processing lies the link between reception and expression. In the formulation process, an original expression is created if the reason for expression is motivated internally by the organism's desire to express thoughts, feelings, or emotions, or—in the case of the previous processes being operative—a response is generated. Following determination of the response, three possible modes of communication are utilized: oral production alone; gestural activity alone; or, often, a combination of the two.

It is important to note whether gestural activity is used to enhance oral production or is used to replace oral communication. Where gestural activity is used to

NAME OF SCHOOL DISTRICT

Dear Parent: To help us better understand your child we would like to have the following information which we hope you can provide. Some of the answers may be difficult because you are not certain of the correct informa-tion We know how hard it is to remember some of these things, so just do the best you can. We will call you if we need more information. Thank you for your help.

(Name of Administrator or Teacher)

NAME OF PERSON FILLING OUT FORM _____

_____

CHILD'S NAME _____

DATE OF BIRTH _____

PRESENT ADDRESS OF CHILD _____

_____

MOTHER'S FULL NAME _____

ADDRESS _____

MOTHER'S PHONE _____ AGE _____

OCCUPATION _____

HIGHEST GRADE MOTHER COMPLETED IN SCHOOL _____

FATHER'S FULL NAME _____

ADDRESS _____

FATHER'S PHONE _____ AGE _____

OCCUPATION _____

HIGHEST GRADE FATHER COMPLETED IN SCHOOL _____

IF CHILD DOES NOT LIVE WITH PARENT, NAME OF ADULT

WITH WHOM CHILD LIVES_____

PHONE _____

FIGURE 5.1   Suggested case history form.

OTHERS LIVING IN THE CHILD'S MAJOR PLACE OF RESIDENCE:

NAME _____ RELATIONSHIP_____

_____

_____

_____

(USE THE BACK OF THIS PAGE IF MORE ROOM IS NEEDED)

WHAT DO YOU THINK THE CHILD'S MAIN PROBLEM IS?

_____

HOW DO YOU FEEL ABOUT THE CHILD'S ABILITY TO TALK? _____

_____

BIRTH HISTORY

DID THE MOTHER HAVE ANY PROBLEMS DURING PREGNANCY? _____

_____

DID THE MOTHER TAKE ANY MEDICATIONS/DRUGS?

_____

WAS THE PREGNANCY NINE MONTHS OR MORE OR LESS?

_____

WHAT DID THE CHILD WEIGH AT BIRTH? _____

WERE THERE ANY PROBLEMS AT BIRTH (BREATHING, FEEDING, HEALTH)?

_____

WHAT ILLNESSES, ACCIDENTS, OR OPERATIONS HAS THE CHILD HAD? _____

FIGURE 5.1 (cont.)

DATE   DESCRIBE   TREATED BY   PRESENT STATUS
_____

_____

(USE BACK OF PAGE FOR MORE INFORMATION IF NECES-
SARY)_____

AT WHAT AGE DID THE CHILD: BABBLE OR MAKE FIRST

SOUNDS? _____ BEGIN TO WALK? _____ SAY MAMA? _____

DADA? _____ BYE-BYE _____ TAKE FIRST STEP? _____

PUT TWO WORDS TOGETHER (E.G., GO BYE-BYE)? _____

COMPLETE TOILET TRAINING? _____

HOW ARE SISTERS AND BROTHERS DOING IN SCHOOL?

_____

IN THEIR TALKING? _____

WHAT ARE YOUR BIGGEST WORRIES? _____

_____

WHAT WORRIES YOU MOST ABOUT THIS CHILD?_____

_____

PLEASE RETURN TO: _____

replace oral communication it may reveal the presence of some degree of reception and thinking.

It is suggested that children be described as prelinguistic, preverbal, or nonoral rather than simply nonverbal. Although there is no particular magic to these particular labels, they hopefully would reduce the pessimism attached to some children based on the nonverbal label.

Prelinguistic

The term "prelinguistic behavior" is used here to describe the individual who engages only in very rudimentary behavior. No real expressing of feelings or thoughts

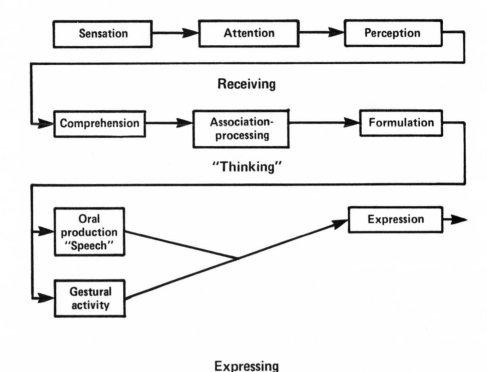

FIGURE 5.2   Schema of sequencing of language use.

is noted and the only receiving behavior may consist of startle responses. The "normal" child exhibits such behavior during the first month or two.

Preverbal

"Preverbal behavior" is used to describe the child who appears to be arrested in some stage of early behavior, prior to the initiation of verbal behavior. Thus, the child might be arrested at the level of sensation, revealing the ability to turn toward sound (3 months); the child may be arrested at the level of attention, including abilities up to the 4-0 year level such as watching television programs; the child may be arrested at the level of perception, being able to signal recognition of differences in sound discrimination at the 4-0 year level; the child may be arrested at the level of comprehension, revealing the understanding of her environment at almost any level of maturity. It is sometimes difficult to determine whether a child is preverbal or nonoral. In general, preverbal suggests that the child is not progressing in communication development and it appears unlikely that the child will without specific help, perhaps not even after help is provided.

Nonoral

In contrast to preverbal, "nonoral" suggests that the child is at one of the previously mentioned levels but possesses inner verbal behavior. Such children often reveal some basic vocabulary.

In diagnosing children who are not exhibiting oral language, prognosis is critical, particularly with lower functioning individuals. Some such individuals have intellectual limitations that prevent the development of communication, limit the development, or allow only rudiments of communication behavior to develop. A balance must be found between realistic appraisal and undue pessimism regarding the child's language ability. Undue pessimism may deprive a child of remedial assistance that could lead to some means of communication.

ASSESSING ATTENDING BEHAVIOR

If the teacher of the retarded is confronted with children who do not attend or attend poorly, referral for hearing testing and psychological diagnosis is indicated. In regard to those children who do attend but poorly, the teacher should also attempt to note whether the quality of attending is variable. If so, under what conditions does the variability occur? Is the variability related to time? Does the child attend well in the morning but more poorly as the day progresses? This could suggest inadequate rest at home. Does the child attend more poorly as various breaks in scheduling occur? This could suggest alteration of programming to accommodate this. Does the child attend more poorly based on which peers she is seated near or working with? Does the child attend more poorly in dictated material? Even though hearing tests within normal limits, this could suggest difficulty with other aspects of auditory processing.

There are many different types of attending and many levels of attending in the classroom and outside. Noting the loci of difficulty is a logical first step in planning remedial measures. Attending is basic to many educational and social skills. The child must function within acceptable limits before other skills are developed.

USE OF BEHAVIORAL LANGUAGE LANDMARKS

A large number and variety of studies have been undertaken to gather information on the "normal development of speech and language" referred to here as behavioral language development landmarks. In addition, many checklists and other measures have been used by SLPs to check the child's level of performance. Approximately thirty of these studies, tests, and checklists were examined to develop the behavioral language landmarks presented here.

Using the Chart

In the behavior language development chart (Figure 5.3), years and months are reported (years–months). For example, 0–6 represents 6 months and 2–3 represents 2 years and 3 months. The child's performance should be located on the chart for each of the three areas of "receiving," "thinking," and "expressing."

Recommendations are also included as to where to place children in the program for the development of syntax as presented in Chapter 6. Generally, the child should begin where it is certain she can succeed before proceeding to items where she will experience difficulty.

It is assumed that the child has inadequate language performance if this chart is used. If she has an adequate vocabulary for her age level and adequate basic syntax, she need only participate in the classroom program.

The specialist must recognize that this is not a precise instrument and the results obtained are to be considered approximations. It offers the advantage of using spontaneous language use for evaluation, if available, or informal testing if it is not. The arbitrariness of placing various behaviors under receiving, thinking, and expressing is recognized. Almost any judgment we make about a child's language behavior is based on expressing skills. We have not determined ways to clearly isolate receiving skills or thinking skills or, as a matter of fact, expressing skills. However, behaviors are classified as being *primarily* one of the three. Even so, there are twenty landmarks under receiving, thirty-three under thinking, and the majority, seventy-seven, under expressing. Language experts indicate that we have more inner abilities or competence than we use in expression (performance). This is not only demonstrated in the chart, it is the major factor underlying the philosophy of the programming presented.

As mentioned previously, where spontaneous language (observe) cannot be used for judgments, situations can be contrived (test) for evaluation.

Items in this chart may be helpful in developing IEPs for the child.

Keeping Records

It is recommended that the SLP and teacher of the retarded ditto forms for each child and maintain these to note progress. Figure 5.4 presents a sample recommended form. The child's name and birthdate are recorded for identification as well as the date of evaluation, mental age, chronological age, and other tests' results.

The name of the evaluator is recorded at the top and the results are noted at the bottom. A check denotes passing, a cross denotes that the child is incorrect or weak

FIGURE 5.3 Behavioral language landmarks.

RECEIVING

Behavior and Age	Assessment
1. Is aware of presence of sound (0–1)	Startles with loud sound
2. Hears sound (0–2)	Produce loud sound
3. Turns to loud sound (0–3)	Produce sound and observe
4. Attends in acquiring manner (0–6)	Observe
5. Perceives value of communication (0–6)	Observe
6. Stops activity when name is called (0–9)	Observe
7. Correct response to "no-no" (0–9)	Observe

Child Fails Below Here—Begin at Step 1

8. Discriminates among gross sounds (1–0)	Response to bell, door, close, etc.
9. Responds to simple instructions (1–1)	Observe
10. Comes to name (1–6)	Observe
11. Recognizes names of three body parts (1–7)	Observe
12. Responds to "show me a dog, a man, a hat" (2–0)	Show appropriate pictures
13. Stays in chair for 1 minute (2–0)	Observe
14. Attends to activity for 3 to 5 minutes (2–0)	Observe
15. Identifies action in pictures (2–8)	Observe
16. Selects situational cues (3–0)	Observe
17. Discriminates among gross verbal sounds (3–0)	Show child two pictures with one sound difference (hat, cat) "Show me _____"

Child Successful to 7, Fails 8–17—Begin at Step 15

18. Works in three- to four-children group, 15 minutes (3–6)	Observe

FIGURE 5.3 (cont.)

19. Discriminates finer verbal sounds (4-0)	More difficult judgments than 17
20. Attends for pleasure (radio, T.V.) (4-0)	Observe

Child Successful to 17, Fails 18–20—Begin at Step 23

THINKING

21. Comprehends vocabulary appropriate to age	Peabody Picture Vocabulary Test
22. Looks at object named (1-0)	Observe
23. Points to object named (1-6)	Observe
24. Points to picture named (2-0)	Observe
25. Indicates yes or no to short questions (2-0)	"Do you like ice cream?"
26. Matches like objects (2-0)	Use several cars, boats, cups, etc.
27. Obeys simple commands (2-0)	"Stand up," "Sit down"
28. Formulates thoughts (2-0)	Observe
29. Classifies by function (2-3)	Use spoons, pencils, glasses, etc.

Child Successful to 20, Fails 21–29—Begin at Step 15

30. Listens to nursery rhymes (3-0)	Observe
31. Listens to story and imitates action (3-0)	Observe
32. Points to stimulus picture of "ball, boat, baby, car, cat, shoe" (3-0)	Observe
33. Comprehends a basic vocabulary of "ball, boat, baby, boy, bird, book, bed, cat, car, coat, chair, dog, girl, fish, horse, fork, spoon, glass, man, cow, table, bicycle, pencil" (3-0)	Determine by testing or observing (no more than two incorrect)
34. Comprehends verbs "eat, sit, run, jump, hit" (3-0)	No errors. Observe or test
35. Comprehends "big/little" and "fast/slow" (3-0)	Observe or test
36. Comprehends "who, what"	Observe or test
37. Comprehends "on, under, in"	Observe or test

38. Comprehends "he, she, they" (3-0)	Observe or test
39. Comprehends simple noun-verb "dog runs" (3-0)	Observe or test
40. Comprehends simple commands "Show me the cat" (3-0)	Observe or test
41. Comprehends simple modifiers "big ball, red table" (3-0)	Observe or test

Child "Talks," Successful to 29, Fails 30–41—Begin at Step 63
Child Doesn't "Talk," Successful to 29, Fails 30–41—Begin Step 45

42. Comprehends "tall/short" (3-6)	Observe or test
43. Comprehends "orange, black, green, yellow" (3-6)	Observe or test
44. Comprehends "him, her, them" (3-6)	Observe or test
45. Comprehends concept of "two" (4-0)	Observe or test
46. Comprehends "when" and "where" (4-0)	Observe or test
47. Comprehends "his, her, their" (4-0)	Observe or test
48. Comprehends plurals "cats, babies" (4-0)	Observe or test
49. Comprehends "er," "farm/farmer" (4-0)	Observe or test
50. Comprehends plural verbs "is/are" (4-0)	Observe or test
51. Comprehends "that" and "this" (5-0)	Observe or test
52. Comprehends noun/verb agreement in plurals "dogs run"	Observe or test
53. Comprehends "alike/different" (6-0)	Observe or test

Child Talks, Successful to 41, Fails 42–52—Begin at Step 96
Child Doesn't Talk, Successful to 41, Fails 42–52—Begin Step 51

EXPRESSING

54. Phonation, involuntary (0-1)	Observe
55. Phonation, voluntary (0-2)	Observe

FIGURE 5.3 (cont.)

56. Produces random sound (0-3)	Observe
57. Laughs aloud (0-4)	Observe
58. Babbles (0-5)	Observe
59. Vocalizes to toys (0-6)	Observe
60. Articulates syllables (0-6)	Observe

Child Fails Below 20 and 54-60—Begin at Step 1
Child Successful to 20, 29, 41, but Fails 54 on—Begin at Step 15

61. Says "dada, mama" in babbling (0-3)	Observe
62. Imitates sound (0-9)	Observe
63. Shakes head for "no" (0-10)	Observe
64. Says "dada, mama," one other word (1-0)	Observe

Child Fails 1-20 but Succeeds 54-64 Test Hearing Then Go to Step 1
Child Successful to 64, Fails Beyond—Begin at Step 15

65. Produces four or five words (1-3)	Observe
66. Holophrases (1-6)	Observe
67. Names objects—"ball, baby" (1-6)	Observe
68. Favorite expression is "all gone" (1-6)	Observe
69. Vocabulary of ten words (1-6)	Observe
70. Produces "big, hot" (1-9)	Observe
71. Produces "go, run" (1-9)	Observe
72. Produces "mine" (1-9)	Observe
73. Vocabulary of twenty words (1-9)	Observe
74. Noun/noun phrases, "boy-car" (1-9)	Observe
75. Noun/verb phrases, "baby-go" (1-9)	Observe
76. Uses prepositions (1-9)	Observe
77. Uses adjectives (1-9)	Observe
78. Uses pronouns (1-9)	Observe

Child Succeeds to 78, Fails Beyond—Begin at Step 96
If Child Succeeds to 78 but Fails 13-20, Do 1-36 before 96

79. Discards jargon (2-0)	Observe
80. Produces two-syllable words or phrases (2-0)	Observe
81. Vocabulary of fifty words (2-0)	Observe
82. Names familiar objects, "ball, dolly" (2-0)	Observe or test
83. Answers, "What is your name?" (2-0)	Test
84. Adjective–noun phrase, "big doggy" (2-0)	Observe
85. Uses gestures for meaning (yes-no) (2-0)	Observe
86. Uses verb-object, "go car" (2-0)	Observe
87. Uses possessive, "my ball" (2-0)	Observe
88. Concept of "more" (2-3)	Observe or test
89. Produces simple sentences (2-6)	Observe
90. Uses "I, me" correctly (2-6)	Observe
91. Uses "ing," "jumping" (2-6)	Observe or test
92. Asks questions of adults (3-0)	Observe
93. Names one color (3-0)	Observe or test
94. Tells whether "boy" or "girl" (3-0)	Observe or test
95. Uses fifty words in conversation (3-0)	Observe
96. Has vocabulary of 500 words (3-0)	Observe or test
97. Concept of "more/less" (3-0)	Observe
98. Engages in conversation (3-6)	Observe
99. Alludes to objects, persons, events (3-6)	Observe
100. Describes events with recall (3-6)	Observe or test
101. Concept of "many/few" (4-0)	Observe or test
102. Tells street name and number (4-0)	Observe or test
103. Describes experiences within last 8 hours (4-0)	Observe or test
104. Counts to 5 (4-0)	Observe or test

FIGURE 5.3 (cont.)

105.	Identifies three colors by name (4-0)	Observe or test
106.	Speaks in complete sentences (4-0)	Observe or test
107.	Says full name (4-0)	Observe or test
108.	Vocabulary of 1,500 words (4-0)	Observe, estimate
109.	Intelligible speech (4-0)	Observe, test if not

Child Fails Below 109—Begin at 96
Use Other Steps as Needed for Attention, Listening
Following Items Are to Estimate Level. Beyond This Point Child
Probably Does Not Need Syntax Program, Only Developmental Program

110.	Tells street name and town (4-6)	Observe or test
111.	Tells month of birth (4-6)	Observe or test
112.	Can repeat twelve-syllable sentence (4-9)	Test
113.	Verbal responses appropriate to situation (5-0)	Observe
114.	Tells weather (5-3)	Observe or test
115.	Describes action in pictures (6-0)	Test
116.	Names penny, nickle, dime (6-1)	Test
117.	Tells a familiar story (6-5)	Test
118.	Tells differences between common objects, "car-boat; cat-boat" (6-6)	Test
119.	Counts from 1 to 50 (6-8)	Test
120.	Describes past events, "yesterday" (7-0)	Test
121.	Names quarter, half-dollar, dollar (7-3)	Test
122.	Can repeat five digits (7-7)	Test
123.	Names the days of the week (7-11)	Test
124.	Can repeat sixteen-syllable sentences (8-3)	Test
125.	Can rhyme words (9-0)	Test

126.	Can repeat four digits reversed (9–5)	Test
127.	Can repeat six digits (10–5)	Test
128.	Can repeat twenty-syllable sentence (10–11)	Test
129.	Can repeat five digits reversed (12–0)	Test
130.	Can repeat five one-syllable words (13–5)	Test

in the item, and a minus denotes failure. Marking should be strict to aid consistency and performance should be without doubt. At the bottom the assumed age for receiving, thinking, and expressing should be entered with the mean of the three noted as the assumed functional language age. Scores can be determined by taking the age level of the last correct item before three consecutive failures. Comments on specific aspects of the child's language functioning should be noted on the back as an anecdotal record.

Classroom Summary

Figure 5.5 presents a classroom summary for the teacher. The children's names are followed by the chronological age, mental age as determined by a standardized intelligence test (not a language test), and each child's scores for receiving, thinking, and expressing. "Comments" might include more information on language, speech, or hearing problems or behavioral notes. Assessment is recommended at the beginning and end of each semester so that four scores during the year can be obtained to note language growth.

PUBLISHED TEST MATERIALS

Many teachers and SLPs will wish to enlarge their understandings of certain children through more formal testing. Following are a number of measuring instruments for this purpose. The instructions should be read carefully and, where administration is limited to specifically trained examiners, untrained persons should not

Tests of Development and Intelligence

Frankenberg, W. and Dodds, J., *The Denver Developmental Screening Test,* Ladaco Project and Publishing Foundation, Inc., Denver, Colorado, 1968. Measures early development in infants.

NAME _____ DATE OF EVALUATION _____

BIRTHDATE _____ CHRONOLOGICAL AGE ___ MENTAL AGE ___

OTHER TESTS RESULTS _____

HEARING AND OTHER AUDITORY _____

ARTICULATION _____

VOICE QUALITY _____ RHYTHM _____

EVALUATION BY: _____

√ = CAN DO   X = NEAR SUCCESS   − = CANNOT DO

RECEIVING							
1	17	32	47	62	71	81	91
2	18	33	48	63	72	82	92
3	19	34	49	64	73	83	93
4	THINKING		50	65	74	84	94
5	20	35	51	66	75	85	95
6	21	36	52	67	76	86	96
7	22	37	53	68	77	87	97
8	23	38	EXPRESSING		78	88	98
9	24	39	54	69	79	89	99
10	25	40	55	70	80	90	100
11	26	41	56	SCORE CONSECUTIVELY. STOP AFTER THREE FAILURES. CONSIDER AGE LEVEL OF LAST ITEM AS AGE FOR THAT FUNCTION.			
12	27	42	57				
13	28	43	58				
14	29	44	59				
15	30	45	60	ESTIMATED RECEIVING AGE ____			
16	31	46	61	ESTIMATED THINKING AGE ____			
				ESTIMATED EXPRESSING AGE ____			

FIGURE 5.4   Recommended data sheet for each child.

TEACHER _____

CLASSROOM LEVEL _____

	NAME	CA	MA	RECEIVING	THINKING	EXPRESSING	COMMENTS
1							
2							
3							
4							
5							
6							
7							
8							
9							
10							
11							
12							
13							
14							
15							
16							
17							
18							
19							
20							

FIGURE 5.5   Recommended classroom data sheet.

Mardell, C., and Goldenberg, D., *DIAL/Developmental Indicators for the Assessment of Learning,* Childcraft Education Corporation, 20 Kilmer Road, Edison, New Jersey 08817. Designed to help locate children in need of special education and who are between 2½ and 5½ developmentally or chronologically.

Nihira, K., Foster, R., Shellhaas, M., and Leland, H., *Adaptive Behavior Scales,* American Association for Mental Deficiency, 5201 Connecticut Avenue N.W., Washington, D.C. 20015, 1970. Assesses adaptive behavior in children 3 to 12 and adults 13 years and older, particularly mentally retarded and emotionally maladjusted.

The Santa Clara Inventory of Developmental Tasks (IDT), Richard L. Zweig Associates, Inc., 1974. Described as being useful for a kindergarten screening device, a basis for parent conferences, and a record of a child's performance.

Terman, L., and Merrill, M., *Stanford-Binet Intelligence Scale* (Forms L-M), Houghton Mifflin Company, Boston, 1960. Tests children's intellectual progress for class placement and estimate of school success.

Wechsler, D., *The Wechsler Intelligence Scale for Children,* The Psychological Corporation, 304 East 45th Street, New York, New York 10017, 1949. Measures child functioning level in intellectual areas for class placement and prediction of school success.

General Basic Tests

Boehm, A., *Boehm Test of Basic Concepts,* The Psychological Corporation, 304 East 45th Street, New York, New York 10017, 1971. Assesses children's ability in the area of conceptualization. K through second grades.

Doll, E., *Vineland Social Maturity Scale,* American Guidance Service, Inc., Circle Pines, Minnesota, 1936. Provides a measure for social development from birth to 25 years. Seems most applicable for children under 5 years of age.

Engelmann, S., *The Basic Concept Inventory,* Follett Educational Corporation, Chicago, 1967. Uses a checklist to assess the child's basic concepts that are involved in new learning situations in the first grade (Preschool and K).

The Magic Kingdom: A Preschool Screening Program, Southeast Mental Health and Retardation Center Preschool Program, 700 First Avenue South, Fargo, North Dakota 58102, 1975. A screening program that provides a gross assessment of children ages 3-0 to 6-0 in motor, visual, auditory, language, conceptual, and social-emotional areas.

Tests of Language Development

Anderson, R., Miles, M., and Matheny, P., *Communication Evaluation Chart,* Educators Publishing Service, Cambridge, Massachusetts, 1963. Tests the development of language and some nonlanguage factors in young children (3 months to 5 years).

Bangs, T., *Language and Learning Disorders of the Pre-Academic Child,* Appleton-Century-Crofts, New York, 1968. Includes several methods of assessing children, particularly through kindergarten.

Bzoch, K., and League, R., *Receptive-Expressive Emergent Language Scale,* The Anhinga Press, P.O. Box 13501, Gainesville, Florida 32604, 1973. Developed to measure language skills in infancy.

Crabtree, M., *The Houston Test for Language Development,* Houston Test Company, Houston, 1963. Tests receptive and expressive language skills from 18 months to 6 years.

Lenneberg, E., *Biological Foundations of Language,* John Wiley and Sons, Inc., 1967. Includes information on the developmental landmarks in language development to 4 years.

Mecham, M., *The Verbal Language Developmental Scale,* American Guidance Service, Inc., Circle Pines, Minnesota, 1971. Extends the items dealing with communication on the *Vineland Social Maturity Scale* to 15 years.

Mecham, M., Jex, J., and Jones, J., *The Utah Test of Language Development,* Communication Research Associates, Box 11012, Salt Lake City, 1967. Compiles items from a variety of other sources to measure language from 1 to 15 years.

Zimmerman, I., Steiner, V., and Evatt, R., *Preschool Language Manual,* Charles E. Merrill Publishing Company, 1969. Provides for determination of an overall language quotient from 1½ to 7 years.

Auditory Comprehension

Carrow, E., *Screening Test for Auditory Comprehension of Language,* Learning Concepts, 2501 N. Lamar, Austin, Texas 78705, 1973. Screens comprehension of English and Spanish.

Carrow, E., *Test for Auditory Comprehension of Language,* Urban Research Group, 306 West 16, Austin, Texas 78701, 1973. Tests the child's ability to comprehend representative language patterns.

Miller, J., and Yoder, D., *The MY Test of Language Comprehension,* University Book Store, 711 State Street, Madison, Wisconsin 13706, 1974. Measures language comprehension through use of stimulus pictures.

Auditory Discrimination

Goldman, R., Fristoe, M., and Woodcock, L., *Goldman-Fristoe-Woodcock Test of Auditory Discrimination,* American Guidance Service, Inc., Circle Pines, Minnesota, 1970. Assesses auditory discrimination under quiet and noise conditions.

Lindamood, C., and Lindamood, P., *Lindamood Auditory Conceptualization Test,* Teaching Resources Corporation, 100 Boylston Street, Boston, Massachusetts 02116, 1969. Assesses ability to recognize differences in speech sounds as well as in sound patterns.

Mecham, M., and Jex, J., *Picture Speech Discrimination Test,* Brigham Young University Press, Provo, Utah, 1962. Tests speech discrimination using pictures of Thorndike list words.

Templin, M., *Short Test of Sound Discrimination* from "A Study of Sound Discrimination Ability of Elementary School Pupils," *Journal of Speech Disorders* 8, 127-132, 1943. Can be administered individually or in small groups to pupils in grades 2 to 6. Child must decide whether syllables are the same or different.

Pronovost, W., and Dumbleton, C., *The Boston University Speech Sound Discrimination Picture Test,* Boston University School of Education, Speech and Hearing Center, 332 Bay State Road, Boston, Massachusetts, 1958. The child chooses among three sets of two pictures each, to reveal skills in discrimination. Grades 1 to 6. (In "A Picture-Type Speech Sound Discrimination Test," *Journal of Speech and Hearing Disorders* 18, 258-266, 1953.)

Templin, M., *Certain Auditory Skills in Children,* University of Minnesota Press, Minneapolis, 1957. Includes a fifty-item syllable test to measure auditory discrimination in children 3 to 9 years.

Wepman, J., *Wepman Test of Auditory Discrimination,* Language Research Associates, 175 East Delaware Place, Chicago, Illinois 60611, 1958. Tests children's ability to determine whether words are same or different. Grades 1 to 6.

Vocabulary Tests

Ammons, R., and Ammons, H., *Full Range Picture Vocabulary Test,* Psychological Test Specialists, Missoula, Missouri, 1958. Can be used to measure recognition vocabulary from approximately 2 years to adult.

Dunn, L., *Peabody Picture Vocabulary Test,* American Guidance Service, Inc., Circle Pines, Minnesota, 1965. Measures recognition vocabulary from 18 months to 18 years.

General Language Tests

Berry, M., *Language Disorders of Children: The Diagnosis,* Appleton-Century-Crofts, Inc., 440 Park Avenue South, New York, New York 10016, 1969. Presents several language tests of other authors and some original language tests.

Foster, R., Sidden, J., and Stark, J., *ACLC: Assessment of Children's Language Comprehension,* Consulting Psychologist Press, 577 College Avenue, Palo Alto, California 94306, 1973. Assesses children's comprehension of language in four elements.

Kirk, S. A., McCarthy, J. J., and Kirk, W. D., *Illinois Test of Psycholinguistic Abilities,* University of Illinois Press, Urbana, Illinois, 1968. Designed as a diagnostic test to assess nine separate linguistic functions of children between 2½ and 9 years.

Monaco, J., and Dillon, L., *Inventory of Language Processes*, from *Hey I Got Sump'n to Tell You an It Cool*, Board of Education, Montgomery County, Rockville, Maryland, 1972. Comprehensive guide for the assessment of children's language.

Wolski, W., and Lerea, L., *The Michigan Picture Language Inventory,* University of Michigan, Ann Arbor, 1958. Attempts to measure various aspects of language from 4 to 6 years.

Aspects of Language—Syntax, Morphology

Berko, J., *Berko Test of English Morphology (The Wug Test)*, see "The Child's Learning of English Morphology" in S. Sapora, *Psycholinguistics*, Holt, Rinehart and Winston, New York, 1961, pp. 359–376. The purpose of the test is to examine children's use of morphological rules of different types and under different phonological conditions.

Carrow, E., *Carrow Elicited Language Inventory,* Learning Concepts, 2501 N. Lamar, Austin, Texas 78705, 1974. Aimed at providing a means for measuring a child's productive control of grammar.

Lee, L., "Developmental Sentence Types: A Method for Comparing Normal and

Deviant Syntactic Development," *Journal of Speech and Hearing Disorders* 31, 311–330, 1966. Measures syntax of children's sentences.

Lee, L., "Developmental Sentence Scoring: A Clinical Procedure for Estimating Syntactic Development in Children's Spontaneous Speech," *Journal of Speech and Hearing Disorders* 36, 315–340, 1971. Measures children's sentences for syntactic development.

Lee, L., *The Northwestern Syntax Screening Test,* Northwestern University Press, Evanston, Illinois, 1969. Measures comprehension of morphologic and syntactic structures in children from 3 to 8 years.

Menyuk, P., *Sentences Children Use,* The M.I.T. Press, Cambridge, Massachusetts, 1969. Tests syntax through sentence repetition.

Visual Perception

Frostig, M., *Marianne Frostig Developmental Test of Visual Perception,* Consulting Psychologist Press, 577 College Avenue, Palo Alto, California, 1966. Designed to measure five operationally defined perceptual skills.

chapter six
developing basic syntax

Programming recommendations are presented in three sections. This chapter outlines a program for developing syntax, intended for individual or small-group (two to six children) use. Chapter Seven offers suggestions for classroom use. The material in Chapter Seven repeats several aspects introduced in this chapter for use in classroom activity. Chapter Eight presents supplemental material for the classroom program.

IMPORTANCE OF SYNTAX

The importance of syntax in the total language process cannot be overstated. Obviously it must be preceded by the possession of concepts and a knowledge of vocabulary meaning and usage. However, without syntax, language remains only a word-naming process with limited application. Mentally retarded children are often particularly deficient in this area. Several studies have shown that improving syntax improves a child's achievement levels in school (Bereiter and Englemann, 1966; Bonnell, 1972). Many retarded children have concepts that they are unable to express and the development of syntax will aid in further concept formation. Also, development of syntax will aid the child from a minority background develop academic language.

Presenting the Program

This is a structured developmental program. The material should be supplemented by the use of much free conversation. An attempt has been made to initiate the program at a level at which a child considered nonoral can benefit and to provide exercises up to a basic level of syntax. Obviously, no one program could suffice for all children. The teacher or SLP should use the recommendation in the developmental chart and professional judgment in determining initial placement and the pacing, moving some children ahead more rapidly and adding additional but similar material for other children. The children should receive the program in this chapter daily in 20- to 30-minute segments. Social reinforcers are preferred but other methods may be used consistent with the philosophy of the presenter. In teaching activity, those things tend to work best in which the presenter has confidence. Totter (1975) has used this material with moderately and severely retarded children and recommends not skipping material. Actually it is probably beneficial to include material that the children find relatively easy. It sometimes seems that we believe children are only learning if they are failing. It is more likely that the opposite is truer. During the therapy session the children should be encouraged to speak in full sentences. This introduces a mild amount of artificiality to the work period but it is intended that way. The exception is with the lower functioning children. Telegraphic speech may be used if that will aid them in being successful. Although this is preferable to no speech at all, it should be considered only a step in the total communication habilitation process.

After determining the starting point it is recommended that the teacher or SLP copy the material on 4-inch by 6-inch cards for easy accessibility. The work area should be reasonably quiet and free from auditory or visual distraction. A section of the regular classroom isolated by screens may be used satisfactorily if distractibility can be minimized. The specialist should be seated close to the children and at their level. The use of a tray for materials is recommended so that materials can be quickly presented or removed. Materials not in use should not be in the children's vision. At the beginning of each lesson, steps from the previous lesson should be repeated. Children who cannot keep pace should be given additional instruction.

Materials used should be as large as possible while still remaining manipulable. With lower functioning children brighly colored objects may interfere with the child's attention on the exercises if placed, for example, with a black shoe and a white chair. In other words, the child may fail to respond appropriately if one stimulus presents stronger appeal. This is not always avoidable, but it should be minimized.

The program generally follows the sequence of the model presented in the preceding chapter; sensation and attending behavior, perception, comprehension and association, formulation, and production. Some items will occupy several· therapy periods; others will fill only a part of a therapy period. The teacher or SLP should move at a rate that is beneficial for the children. This section can be completed in a year; it may take considerably longer.

SYNTAX PROGRAM

The method used for teaching syntax is a "hear it–repeat it" approach. The child is given a correct model and told to repeat it. The tone of voice should be loud and firm. The attitude should be "you can." Pacing within each lesson should be as rapid as the children can tolerate. Reinforcement should be frequent with nodding, smiling, and the phrase, "good talking." Children should be required to speak loudly and clearly. Part of the system used is based on aspects of programming recommended by Bereiter and Englemann (1966).

(Note: In the activities that follow only the teacher's actions and remarks are included. It is assumed that the teacher will know the expected response of the child.) The assumption is that the child has a mental age of 2-0. At the beginning of each lesson repeat one or two steps, or parts of steps for about 5 minutes. Always attempt to end a lesson with success, even if contrived.

Improving Attending

Lack of attending behavior reveals the child's inability to attend to a given task but also reveals the child's difficulty in excluding intruding stimuli. Lack of attending is usually not an effort to be "bad," although it may represent manipulative behavior. More often the child is exhibiting difficulty in controlling her central nervous system to remain with a given stimulus. Training in attending should begin where the child is and move the child toward quiet sitting for increasing periods of time.

1. Have the child attend to something that interests her (for example, a favorite toy). The child may stand or sit, whichever is easier for her. The important thing is that the child look at or respond to something for 1 minute. Try to lengthen the time when the child can accomplish this. Each minute is progress.

2. Have the child sit in a chair (armed chairs are helpful for this). Show the child something of interest to her and try to extend the length of time she is able to sit. As long as she remains in the chair she should be rewarded, even if she moves about.

3. Show the child something of interest. Control the stimulus and try to reduce her activity. Whereas she was allowed to use her hands or move her legs previously, try to encourage her to sit quietly. Advise her or assist her in holding her hands and crossing her legs at the ankles. In addition to rewarding the child say "Good" when the child sits quietly, even for 30 seconds. Goals should be 1 minute, then 2, then 3.

4. Have the child sit quietly. Say "Be quiet" and then "Shhh," gesturing with finger to mouth. If child sits quietly, immediately say "Good. You are quiet." If child moves say "Shhh, sit quietly." Be stern in tone when ordering and nodding, pleasant and smiling when rewarding. Try to extend quiet sitting to 5 minutes.

5. Allow the child to sit without hands folded and legs crossed. Again tell the child "Shhh" and then "Good" when she responds adequately. Try to get the child to sit this way for periods up to 5 minutes.

Improving Receiving

6. Show the child large, interesting pictures but have him sit quietly for 5- to 10-second intervals. After each picture reward the child and say "Good." If the child moves, gently restrain him and say "Shhh."

7. Try to increase the number of pictures the child will observe to four or five. Say to the child, "Look at me." Point to your mouth and name each picture.

Accept no response from the child except quiet sitting. Say "Good" or "Shhh" as appropriate.

8. Have the child sit quietly. Say "Shh" with finger to mouth and say "Listen" with finger to ear. Have someone stand behind the child and clap hands hard or blow a whistle. If the child turns to the sound say "Good" and reward. Have the child come to a rest position and then repeat three or four times.

9. Have the child sit quietly. Say "Listen" with your finger to your ear. Have someone stand behind the child and loudly say his name. If the child turns say "Good" and reward. Repeat three times decreasing the loudness of the name.

10. With the child sitting quietly, say "Listen" with your finger to your ear. Have someone stand to the child's left rear and then right rear. Say the child's name or clap. If the child localizes say "Good." If the child turns incorrectly gently direct the child's face correctly and point saying "See. There."

11. Place something of interest to the child at the periphery of his vision. If the child attends to the pictures presented in steps 6 and 7 as they are presented again, say "Good" and reward. Move the distraction more into the visual field of the child and continue to reward if he avoids the distraction.

12. With the child sitting quietly, say to the child "Listen to me," point your finger to your ear and say "Watch me," pointing to your mouth. Show the child the pictures and have someone clap softly behind the child. If the child turns toward the sound say "No. Listen to me." If the child is not distracted say "Good" and reward. Do not use clapping for the sound localization following this.

13. Bring a child who is at a similar stage into the activity and seat the two side by side. Use new pictures and repeat steps 11 and 12. Reward both and say "Good" to each if they participate successfully.

14. Have the children sit quietly, side by side. Have someone stand behind them. Say "Listen," say one of the children's names. Only that child should turn to the name. Reward appropriate turning and not turning. Add the child's name. "Good, (child's name)."

15. Place a cup and a playhouse bed on a tray in front of the children. Say, "(child's name), touch cup." Alternate children and use of the items. Reward success verbally. Show the correct item if failure.

16. Add a spoon and repeat the exercise with three items.

17. Add a doll shoe and repeat the exercise with four items.

18. Add a playhouse chair and repeat the exercise with five items.

19. Remove the above items and replace with, first, a pencil and a book. Then add a kitchen knife (as in step 16) and then a dollhouse table (as in step 17).

20. Combine items from steps 15 to 18. Say to the child "Touch cup, touch bed." Expand to two, three, and four items. See how many items the child can sequence. Correct errors and repeat. Reward effort as well as success. Do the same with items in step 19.

21. Repeat the "touch" activities with body parts. Say to the child "Touch eye," and then ear, nose, mouth, hair.

22. Repeat with the step 15 items using "Give me—." Start with two items and expand until all items up to step 18 are used. Repeat with step 19 items.

23. Say to the child "Do this." Encourage the child to imitate while you clap your hands, tap knees, tap feet, close and open eyes, put hands on ears, fold arms, put hands on head, put hands on eyes, open and close mouth. This should constitute *several* lessons.

24. Say to the child "Say this" and then babble, "Ba, ba, ba," then "Pa, pa, pa," then "Ma, ma, ma." Reward *any* attempt child makes. Spend almost no time on this if the child already produces words. Spend more time if the child does not but cooperates in babbling. Add other sounds such as ta, da, ma, ka, ga. If the child makes no sounds, move on for now.

25. Use the items previously used and ask "Is this—" as one of the items is lifted off the tray. Some of the time the appropriate response should be "Yes" and sometimes "No." Accept any yes or no type of response. Reinforce by verbally repeating the answer and using the appropriate head gesture.

26. Ask the child "Are you—?" Use the child's name then: (a) Nonsense names such as Mickey Mouse; (b) Real but fictitious names; (c) Names of classmates.

27. Secure a whistle, a small drum, a bell, and a rachet. Demonstrate the sound each one makes several times. Demonstrate the sound that one makes and then place the child's hand on the item. Make a sound on one of them and motion for the child to put her hand on it. Say "Which one?" Do this several times.

28. Use a piece of cardboard to hide two instruments. Make a sound on one of them and then reveal them and gesture for the child to place a hand on it. Also say "Which one?" Do this several times.

29. When the child is successful with some consistency, add another sound maker and repeat the procedure.

30. Continue to add using the same procedure until all the sound makers are in use.

31. Use several other sound makers. You can use similar but different ones. Start with two of them using the procedure above. Add others as described above.

32. Have two verbal children stand several feet away from the child. Have them say "I am (name)." Use a boy and a girl initially. Then have the child close her eyes and have one of the two say "Hi (name)." Say to the child "Who?" and have the child point.

33. If the child succeeds, add another child and then another following the same procedure. Repeat using all boys or all girls. It is assumed that the child is still being rewarded for sitting, attending, and attempting. Use "Good," nod, a smile, and a reward. At this point add the child's name after "Good." "Good, (name)."

34. Have two children stand about 7 feet away and about 7 feet apart. Have one say "Hi, (name)." Either shield the child's eyes or have her lower her head. Say "Where?" and have her point to the voice. When the child succeeds add a third and then a fourth.

35. Use the sound makers. Have a child make a sound and say "Where?" Have the child point. Start with two and increase as long as the child can succeed.

36. *Try,* and then abandon if confusing, having two children say "Hi, (name)" and have the child point in succession. If the child succeeds, add a third.

Improving Thinking

37. Use a large picture from a magazine or draw a ball, house, or the like on a piece of paper and then paste it on a piece of poster board. Cut into two pieces and have the child piece it together. After success with two pieces use pictures cut into three (the same picture initially is helpful). Then cut into four, five, and six (this step can be introduced earlier if desired).

38. Find or draw two identical pictures of things of which you have objects (two shoes, two chickens, two balls, two dogs, two cups, two beds, two spoons). Put two different pictures in front of the child. Show one of the two and say "Where?" When the child succeeds, add more, and so on.

39. Find pictures of the objects that are slightly different than the first ones. Show one of each and repeat the procedure in step 38.

40. Place the objects in front of the child on the tray and show a picture and say "Where?" Add items as before.

41. Find or draw pictures of the sound makers. Place two pictures in front of the child. Make a sound and say "Which?" Match the correct picture and the object when the child succeeds. Add items as before.

42. Place one picture in front of you and the sound makers in front of the child. Point to a picture and say "Where?" Expand to include all the pictures and all the items. Initially guide the child to the correct choice and have her make the sound.

43. Place the sound makers in front of the child. Say "You do" and encourage her to make a sound while you cover your eyes and then select the correct one. Make occasional errors.

44. Find pictures with several items in them including the previous pictures (shoe, for example). Show the child a picture and say "Where?" Have her point to the object in the picture.

45. From colored paper, cut out five balls of one color, five cups of another, five beds of another, five shoes of another, five spoons of another, and five dogs of another. Mix them together (two items such as balls and spoons). Pick up a ball and say to the child "Where?" Guide her to picking one up and placing it aside. Repeat "Where?" and have her put another one on the pile. Add a third item and repeat. A fourth, and so on.

46. Place two items together and encourage her to sort into two piles. Demonstrate and then say "You do." Help as needed. As you add each item to a pile say "Yes."

47. Make two piles of balls and beds. Place one of each in the other pile. Say "No" and return it to the correct pile. Have the child do the same. Then do it with three piles.

48. Use the pictures of items. Put two correct and a third wrong one. Point and say "No" and take out the wrong one. Have the child repeat.

49. Use two whistles and another sound maker. Blow all three. Say "No" and set the wrong one aside. Have the child repeat. Vary the sound makers and repeat several times. The idea is to have the child sort out the different sounds.

50. Use Old Maid cards and start with four cards. Place the cards face down and try to pick up matching pairs. As the child succeeds, add cards. When a pair is picked up say "Yes." When a pair is not picked up say "No" but not in a reprimanding tone.

Improving Expressing

51. Show the child five picture cards of basic words which the child may be able to say (mama, car, doggie, baby, and so on). Show one at a time for 20 to 30 seconds and then encourage the child to name each one. Reward all vocal responses by the child and reward eye contact. Do this for 3 minutes and repeat after rest. If child is successful go to step 55. If not go to step 52.

52. Emit a simple vocal demonstration (ba-ba-ba) at 10-second intervals and reinforce the child for emitting any vocal response within 6 seconds.

53. Reinforce the child if the vocal response is similar to yours.

54. Same as previous step but use ma, ma, ma. Then use pa, pa, pa. Then use ka, ka, ka.

At this point the clinician may have to intervene to develop vocabulary. Try the following. If the child cannot succeed, enter her in therapy and return to this point later if and when she is able to produce "ball, cup, spoon."

55. Use the ball and the cup. Hold up the ball and say "What this?" Immediately say "ball." Encourage the child and reinforce for imitating the sound. Lengthen the time between "What this?" and your production of the word. Do the same with "cup."

56. Hold up the ball and say "See ball." Place it with the cup, hold out your hand and say "Where ball?" Have the child point. Say "Give ball" and accept it. Say "Throw ball" (and duck). Say "Want ball" and then "Give ball" as you hold out your hand. Repeat step 55.

57. Hold up the cup and say "See cup." Place it with the ball and say "Give cup" and accept it. Say "Drink cup" and have child perform the action. Place it down again and say "Want cup" and then "Give cup."

58. Alternate the objects (ball, cup) and the commands "Where," "Give," "Throw," "Drink," "Want."

59. Using the procedure in step 55 teach "spoon" (accept 'poon).

60. Repeat step 56 with "spoon."
61. Repeat steps 57 and 58 with "ball" and "spoon."
62. Repeat with "cup" and "spoon."
63. Hold up the ball and say "This is a ball, you say." Say "What this?" Use the same procedure with "cup" and "spoon." Hold up the cup and say "This is cup, you say" and then "What this?" Hold up spoon and say "This is spoon, you say" and then "What this?" Accept poor articulation as long as it is recognizable.
64. Display "ball," "cup," and "spoon" on a tray. Point to the tray and say "Where ball?" Pick up ball and say "This ball. Where cup? This cup. Where spoon? This spoon."
65. Pick up cup. Say "This ball? No, not ball." Pick up spoon. "This ball? No, not ball." Pick up ball. "This ball? Yes, this ball."
66. Repeat for "cup" and "spoon."
67. Repeat 65, 66. After saying "No, not ball" add "You say" and get response.
68. Place ball, cup, and spoon on the tray. Say "Where ball? Show me ball." After the child locates the ball say "This ball? Yes, this ball." Then "You say." Point to the cup and say "This ball? No, not ball" and then "You say." Point to the spoon. "This ball? No, not ball. You say."
69. Say "Show me one *not* ball?" Pick up one and say "Not ball" and then repeat saying after "Not ball. You say." Repeat with other items.
70. Go back to step 56 and repeat entire procedure with "dog," "boy," and "chair" to step 69.
71. Repeat steps 56 to 69 with "kitty," "knife," "girl."
72. Show the "ball," "baby," and "bed." Say "This is a ball, say it." Say "This is a what?" "This is a baby, say it." Then, "This is a what?" "This is a bed, say it." Then, "This is a what?"
73. Point to the ball "Is this a ball? Yes, this is a ball. You say it." Point to the baby. "Is this a ball? No, this is not a ball. You say it."

Note: (Accept approximations and contractions but encourage use of syntax.)

Point to bed. "Is this a ball? No, this is not a ball. You say it."
74. Repeat with "baby" and "bed."
75. Repeat steps 72 to 74 with "spoon," "kitty," "boy."
76. Repeat steps 72 to 74 with "dog," "chair," "girl."
77. Use "ball," "baby," "bed." Say "Show me ball." Then ask, "Is this a ball? Yes, this is a ball. You say it." Then point to the baby "Is this a ball? No, this is not a ball. You say it." Then point to the bed. "Is this a ball? No, this is not a ball. You say it."
78. Repeat for "baby" and then for "bed."
79. Repeat using "spoon," "kitty," "boy."

80. Repeat using, "dog," "chair," "girl."

81. Use "ball," "baby," "bed." Point to the ball and say, "Is this a ball? Yes, this is a ball, you say it." Hold up the ball and say "What is this?" Do not prompt but expect response. Hold up baby and then bed and do the same.

82. Ask again (holding up ball) "What is this?" Then ask "What is this not?" If the child has difficulty, ask "Is this a baby? No, this is not a baby. You say it." "Is this a bed? No, this is not a bed. You say it." Try again to have the child say "This is not a—" without help.

83. Repeat for "spoon," "kitty," "boy."

84. Repeat for "dog," "chair," "girl."

85. Repeat steps 56 to 69 with "car," "fork," "shoe." Then repeat steps 72 to 74 and then 77 to 82.

86. Repeat these items with "pencil," "table," "truck."

87. Have a child talk or point out a child who is talking in the group or in the classroom. Say "What is (name) doing. (Name) talk. You say it." "Show me someone talk. Yes, (name) talk, you say it." Look in a magazine. "Let's find a picture of talk. Man talk, you say it." Continue to use the word.

88. Have a child eat or point out a child who is eating. Say "What is (name) doing? (Name) eat, you say it." "Show me someone eat. Yes, (name) eat. You say it." "Show me how you eat. You do it." "Now you say it. Say, 'I eat.' You say it." Look in magazines and find a picture of someone eating (a scrapbook representing common verbs may be helpful). "He talk? No, what is he doing? No, he eat."

89. Do the same with "walk," "run," "sit," "stand," "cry," "sleep," "laugh."

90. Find combinations of nouns and verbs used to this point. Say it first and then have the child repeat. "Baby sleep, you say it."

91. Have several children participate. Pass out the "ball," "bed," "baby," and "cup." Say, "Who has ball? (Name) has ball. You say it." Do the same with "bed," "baby," and "cup." Also say, "Does (name) have ball? No, (name) has ball. You say it." Use other items and repeat.

92. Say to the child. "You say, Who has ball?" Have the child ask the question and you respond. Repeat with other items.

93. An important concept for the child to acquire new knowledge is the phrase "What's that?" Place objects in front of the child, point to the ball, and say "What's that?" After the child responds, say "You say." Encourage the child to point to items and say "What's that?" Accept "What that" without comment but with your correct pronunciation following, "That's correct, we say what's that."

94. Place the items in front of the child and say "I want ball. What I want?" "(Name), say, You want ball?" Repeat with other items. Now say, "What you want? (Name), say what you want." Hand the child the item he requests.

95. Say to the child "What you want me do? You want me stand? Say, You stand." Follow the child's commands. Always precede by "What you want me do?" and suggest one of the verbs.

Production

The child with a minimum behavioral language age of 3 years and/or a basic vocabulary of fifty words begins here. With others, it will first be necessary either to return to an appropriate previous step or to attempt to develop the following vocabulary: mama, daddy, bye-bye, ball, water, milk, cup, dog, shoe, cookie, man, pretty, mine, all gone, thank you, boy, big, car, truck, house, chair, table, rug. T.V., look, no, yes, run, hot, cold, sleep, see, at, the, and, eat, give, go, desk, floor, book, shoe, knife, spoon, fork, hat, coat, block. Production of words should be recognizable but need not be completely accurate.

The next unit deals with personal identity. Remember that the format is to ask the question and model the answer for the child with the child repeating after you. Give praise verbally, with voice, nodding and smiling. Use "good talking" to let the child know that he is using good language. In the following steps it is hoped that the child will develop a better sense of personal identity and personal worth. The retarded child is so often plagued by a history of failure that he develops a resignation to failure. Such phrases as "I know I can't," "I know I won't get it right," "I don't know how to do this," and "I can't do anything right" all lead to a feeling of inadequacy in any learning situation. An attempt must be made to break this often deeply rooted failure syndrome by replacing it with success experiences. The language program provides a unique opportunity for this with most children if presented correctly. The child does not need "to know," only to imitate. Failure should be met only by another attempt or a return to easier material. Also, reward effort as much as success. As previously, except where stated, it is understood that the specialist will know the expected response.

96. Begin with: "What is your name? Say, My name is (name), you say it." "Say it again, My name is (name), you say it." "That is your *first* name, say, My first name is (name), say it." "Now say your first and last name. Say, My name is (full name.)" "That's your first and last name, (full name). Say again, My name is (full name), you say it." (If a group) "Ask (name of another child) what her name is, say, What is your name? Say it." "Did she tell you her first and last name?" "Ask her again, What is your name?" (Repeat with other group members.)

97. "Are you a boy or a girl? Say, I am a boy, say it." "Say it again, I am a boy. Say it." "Is (name) a boy or a girl? She is a girl. You say, (Name) is a girl, say it." "Now ask, (Name) are you a boy or a girl. Say, (Name) are you a boy or a girl? Say it." (Repeat with other group members.)

98. "Where do you live? Say, I live at 1142 Main Street, say it" — "Say it again, I live at 1142 Main Street, say it" — "(Name) you ask (name) where he lives. Say, Where do you live? Say it." "(Name) answer (name), say I live at 1142 Main Street, say it" —. "Now you ask (name) where she lives. Say, (Name), where do you live? say it" — "(name), you say, I live at 414 Canal Street, say it." (Repeat with other group members.)

99. "Who lives with you?" (Use appropriate response.) "My mother, my father,

and (name) live with me, Say it." "Say it again, My mother, my father, and (name) live with me. Say it." "Ask (name) who lives with her. Say, (Name) who lives with you? Say it." "(Name), say my mother and (name) and (name) live with me, say it." (Repeat with other group members.)

100. "Say, (Name) who is (name)?" You say, (Name) is my brother. You say it." (Repeat with other family names. Keep a record of family names including pets. Check for accuracy with parents or school records.)

101. "How old are you, (name), Say I am eight years old. Say it." "Say it again, (name), Say I am eight years old. Say it." "(Name) ask (name) how hold she is. Say, how old are you, (name) Say it." Say, I am nine years old, say it." (Repeat with other group members.)

102. The following is dependent on ability level. The goal would be for the child to say, "My name is Sally Smith. I live at 1142 Main Street. I live with my mother, my father, and Joy. I am eight years old." Do only what the child can succeed at. Start with, "Say, my name is Sally Smith. I live at 1142 Main Street. You say it." (At this point discourage the use of "and.") Use individual statements. Continue in this manner having all children participate to the limits of their abilities. Always attempt to end a lesson with success. Retreat to an earlier lesson to accomplish this, if necessary.

Personal Identify-Body Parts

103. "(Name), where is your head? Put both hands on your head and say, this is my head, say it." "(Name) where is your head? Put both your hands on your head and say, this is my head, say it." "(Name) ask (name) where her head is. Say, (name) where is your head? Say it" "(Name), answer him. Say, this is my head. Say it." (Repeat with other group members.)

104. "(Name), where is your nose? Touch your nose like this. Now say, this is my nose, say it." "(Name), where is your nose? Touch it like this and say, this is my nose, say it." "(Name) ask (name) where his nose is, say, (name), where is your nose, say it." Always insist on complete statements. Remind the child if the physical activity is forgotten.

105. "(Name), where is your mouth? Say this is my mouth and then open it wide, say this is my mouth, say it." Make certain children talk at a strong conversational level, not in a whisper. "(Name), ask (name) where her mouth is. Say, (name), where is your mouth? Say it." "(Name) you say, this is my mouth, and then open it wide. Say this is my mouth, say it." (Repeat with other group members.)

106. "(Name), where is your eye? Point to your eye and say, this is my eye, say it." "(Name), where is your eye? Point to your eye and say, this is my eye, say it."

"(Name), ask (name) where her eye is. Say, (name), where is your eye? Say it." "(Name) say, this is my eye, say it." (Repeat with other group members.)

107. "(Name), where is your ear? Hold your ear and say, this is my ear, say it." "(Name), where is your ear? Hold your ear and say, this is my ear, say it." "(Name), ask (name) where her ear is. Say, (name), where is your ear. Say it." (Repeat with other group members.)

108. "(Name), hold up your chin. Rub your chin and say, this is my chin, say it." "(Name), where is your chin? Rub your chin and say, this is my chin, say it." "(Name), ask (name) where his chin is. Say, (Name) where is your chin. Say it." (Repeat with other group members.)

109. "(Name), where is your cheek? Pat your cheek and say, this is my cheek, say it." "(Name), where is your cheek? Pat your cheek and say, this is my cheek, say it." "(Name), ask (name) where her cheek is. Say, (name), where is your cheek, say it." (Repeat with other group members.)

110. "(Name), where is your hair? Feel your hair and say, this is my hair, say it." "(Name), where is your hair, feel your hair and say, this is my hair, say it." "(Name), ask (name) where his hair is. Say, (name), where is your hair, say it." (Repeat with other group members.)

111. "(Name), where is your hand? Hold up your hand and say, this is my hand, say it." "(Name), where is your hand? Hold up your hand and say, this is my hand, say it." "(Name) ask (name) where her hand is. Say, (name) where is your hand, say it." "(Name), show (name) where your hand is and say, this is my hand, say it." (Repeat with other members of the group.)

112. "(Name), where is your arm? Squeeze your arm and say, this is my arm, say it." "(Name), ask (name) where her arm is. Say, (name) where is your arm, say it." "(Name), you squeeze your arm and say this is my arm, say it." (Repeat.)

113. "(Name), where is your knee? Slap your knee and say, this is my knee, say it." "(Name), where is your knee? Slap your knee and say, this is my knee, say it." "(Name), ask (name) where his knee is. Say, (name), where is your knee, say it."

114. "(Name), where is your foot? Wiggle your foot and say, this is my foot, say it." "(Name), where is your foot? Wiggle your foot and say, this is my foot, say it." "Now, (name), ask (name) where her foot is, say, show me your foot, say it." (Change in wording) "(Name), you say *here* is my foot, say it."

115. "(Name), where is your leg? Pat your leg with both hands and say, here is my leg, say it." "(Name), show me your leg. Pat your leg with both hands and say, here is my leg, say it." "(Name), ask (name) where her leg is. Say, show me your leg, say it." (Repeat.)

116. "Who can show me her arm and her hair? Good, (name), show me and say, this is my arm. This is my hair." "Who can show me her eye and her mouth. Good (name). Say, this is my eye. This is my mouth." (Involve group and randomize any two items.)

117. "Listen carefully. Who can show me his nose, his hand, and his foot? Good

(name). Say, this is my nose, this is my hand, this is my foot." (Involve group and randomize. Work for success. Encourage to say in order.)

118. "(Name), you be the teacher. Ask someone to show you two things. Say, show me your _____ and show me your _____ . Say it." (Prompt with items if necessary.)

119. "(Name), stand up, pat your chair and say, this is a chair, say it." "Say it again, this is a chair, say it." "This is a what? Tap your foot on the floor and say, this is a floor, say it." Teacher taps foot on the floor and says, "This is a what?" Teacher holds up pencil and says, "This is a pencil, say it. This is a what?" Place a pencil, cup, and doll house chair on a tray. Point to the chair and say, "Is this a chair? Yes, this is a chair. Say it." (Obvious nod during the statement.) Child says, "Yes, this is a ball."

120. Point to the cup. "Is this a chair? No, this is not a chair" (shake head in obvious manner). Say it." Child says, "No, this is *not* a chair." Point to the pencil. "Is this a chair? No, this is *not* a chair. Say it." (Repeat each item several times using all children if working with a group.)

121. Go through procedure with one child at a time. "Show me the chair, (name)." After success, "Is this a chair?" Child responds, "Yes, this is a chair." Point to the cup. "Is *this* a chair?" Child responds, "No, this is not a chair." Point to the pencil. "Is this a chair?" Child responds, "No, this is not a chair."

122. Say, "Show me one that is *not* a chair." Child points and verbalizes. "This is not a chair." Then point to other objects, "Is this a chair?" Child responds, "No, this is not a chair." If children have difficulty, prompt with, "This is not a *what*?" so that child will respond, "No, this is not a chair." Use this procedure with groups of three from dog, desk, book, table, shoe, spoon, knife, car, ball.

Production Without Imitation

(In this series children are expected to produce the desired response without imitating. If they cannot, previous sections must be reviewed.)

123. (Show the chair) "What is this?" Child responds, "This is a chair." "What is this not?" Child responds, "This is not a cup. This is not a pencil." If child experiences difficulty say, "Is this a cup?" eliciting the response, "No, this is not a cup." "Is this a pencil?" "No, this is not a pencil." Then ask, "What else is this not?" Accept appropriate responses such as, "This is not a door." "What *is* this?" Child responds, "This is a ball." Other nouns for this action: ball, book, shoe, car, table, desk, window, coat, dog, cat, sock, pin, pie, block.

124. Find pictures of two chairs of distinctly different sizes or draw them on the board. First point to one and say, "This is a chair. What is this?" Child responds. "This is a chair." Ask, "Is this a pencil?" Child responds, "No, this is not a pencil." "What is this?" Child responds, "This is a chair." Then point to the bigger one and say, "This chair is big, say it." Child responds, "This chair is big." Then

say, "Is this chair big?" (pointing to the same chair). Child responds, "Yes, this chair is big." (Point to the smaller other chair) "This chair is *not*-big, say it." Child responds, "This chair is *not* big." Then ask, "Is this chair big?" Child responds, "No, this chair is not big." Remember to have the children speak in full voice and to reinforce through verbal praise, particularly "good talking" and nodding and smiling. Repeat the above sequence with other words from the list. Describe the items as "big" or "not big." Do not use these words preceding the noun at this stage ("big ball") and if the child says "little," say, "That's correct but we are talking about 'big,' is this chair big? No, this chair is not big." At this time only one of a pair of polar opposites is dealt with.

125. Now say, "Find the chair that is big." The child should point to the bigger chair. Then say, "Is this chair big?" Child responds, "Yes, this chair is 'big.' " Then, "Find the chair that is not big." Child points to the smaller chair. Say, "Is this chair big?" Child responds, "No, this chair is not big."

126. Now cross off the chair that has been referred to as big and draw a chair smaller than the remaining one. Then erase the bigger chair. If using pictures, first show all three chairs and then remove the former big one. Say, "*Now* show me the chair that is big." Have the child point and say, "This chair is big." Then say, "Show me the chair that is *not big.*" Redraw the chair that was erased and draw a bigger one. Then erase the smaller two. If using pictures, show all four and then eliminate the smaller one. Say, "Now show me the chair that is big." Child points and responds, "This chair is big." Then say, "Show me the chair that is not big." Child points and responds, "This chair is not big." Repeat this entire sequence with (127), long; (128), high; (129), tall; (130) dark; (131), cold; (132), hot; (133), straight; (134), hard; (135), loud; (136), heavy; (137), rough.

Opposites

138. Show two chairs as before and say, "This chair is big, say it." Child responds. "This chair is big." Then say, "This chair is not big, say it." Child responds, "This chair is not big." Then, "Is this chair big?" Child responds, "No, this chair is not big." Point to the smaller chair and say, "This chair is not big, say it." Child responds, "This chair is not big." Then say, "When a chair is not big we say it is little. Little is another way of saying not big. When something is not big we say it is little. This chair is little, say it." Child responds, "This chair is little." Point to the big chair and say, "Is this chair little?" Child responds, "No, this chair is not little." Then say, "Find the chair that is big." Child points and responds, "This chair is big." Then, "Find the chair that is not big." Child points and responds, "This chair is not big." Then, "Find the chair that is little." Child points and responds, "This chair is little." Then, "Find the chair that is not little." Child points and responds. "This chair is not little." Repeat for all other polar statements.

139. Hold up pictures of three chairs, or three dollhouse chairs, or draw three chairs on the board. Say, "This is a chair. This is a chair. This is a chair. Say it." Child responds as indicated. Point to all three slowly saying, *"These are chairs."* Repeat, "These are chairs, say it." Child responds. "These are chairs." If a child has difficulty point to each saying, "Chair, chair, chair, say it." Child responds. Then, "Chair*s*, say it." Then, "These are?" Child responds, "Chairs." Then point and say, "This, this, this, say it." Then, "These are chairs, say it." Then point to all three saying, "What are these?" Child responds, "These are chairs." Then go to the beginning of this section and repeat. Use the plural statements with two chairs that look identical, with three chairs that look identical, with two chairs of different sizes, and with three chairs of different sizes.

140. Repeat with other items such as cups, blocks, spoons, balls, knives.

141. Show the chair and say, "What is this?" Child responds, "This is a chair." Say, "How many chairs?" *"One* chair." "Say, this is a chair." Child responds. Add a chair and say, "Now how many chairs are there? One, two. Two chairs. So we say these are chairs." Child responds, "These are chairs." If child says "these is," say, "If there is more than one we say, *'these are,'* say, 'these are chairs.'" Now attempt to elicit unmodeled correct responses. "What am I showing you?" (Point to one chair.) Child responds, "This is a chair." Then, "Now what am I showing you?" (two chairs). Child responds, "These are chairs." Present one and more than one chair in varying order. Use variations in questions such as "What do you see?" "What am I pointing to?"

142. Repeat with ball, book, shoe, car, table, desk, window, coat, dog, cat, sock, pin, pie, block.

143. Hold out one hand and say, "What is this?" Child responds, "This is a hand." Hold out both hands and say, "What are these?" Child responds, "These are hands." Then say, "Show me a hand." Child responds and says, "This is a hand." Then, "Show me hands." Child responds and says, "These are hands." Repeat with eyes and ears.

144. Say, "I am going to ask you a question. What is this?" (hold up a chair). Child responds, "This is a chair." Say, "Good, you gave me the *answer*. Now I'm going to ask another question. What are these?" (hold up two chairs). Child responds, "These are chairs."

145. Give the child one chair and say, "Sally, you be the teacher. Ask the question, What is this?" Child responds, "What is this?" Then say, "I will give the answer. This is a chair." If in a group let each child ask the question and give the answer. Prompt each time with "Sally, you ask the question. Susan, you give the answer." Then give the child two or three chairs and say, "Sally, ask the question." Repeat with the child, "What are these?" Then say, "I will give the answer, these are chairs." Then, "Now I will ask the question a different way, are these chairs? Answer *with me*—these are chairs." Ask one child to ask the question, "Are these blocks?" Ask a child to respond. Then ask a child to ask another child (or you if individual), "Sandy, are these blocks?" Child should respond, "These are blocks."

146. Use with other words on list or use other words as long as they do not have irregular plurals such as foot, mouse, and so on.

147. In this exercise, more than one polar statement is used with an object. For example, show four books: (1) big and thick, (2) big and thin, (3) small and thick, (4) small and thin. Use big and fat. Book 1. "Is this book big?" Child responds, "Yes, this book is big." Then, "Is this book fat?" Child responds, "Yes, this book is fat." Then, "Is this book big and fat?" Child responds, "Yes, this book is big and fat."

148. Book 2. Say, "Is this book big?" Child responds, "Yes, this book is big." Then, "Is this book fat?" Child responds, "No, this book is not fat." Then, "Is this book big and fat?" "This book is big and not fat. You say it." Child responds. Ask again, "Is this book big and fat?" Child responds, "This book is big and not fat."

149. Book 3. "Is this book fat?" Child responds, "Yes, this book is fat." Then, "Is this book big?" Child responds, "No, this book is not big." Then, "Is this book big and fat? This book is fat and not big. Say it." Say again, "Is this book fat and big?" Child responds, "This book is fat and not big."

150. Book 4. Say, "Is this book big?" Child responds, "This book is not big." Then, "Is this book fat?" Child responds, "This book is not fat." Then, "Is this book big and fat? This book is not big and not fat. Say it." Child responds, "This book is not big and not fat." Say again, "Is this book big and fat?" Child responds, "This book is not big and not fat." Ask a child to show you one that is big and fat, big and not fat, not big and fat, not big and not fat. Have the child repeat the statement as she points. "This book is big and not fat." Where there is a negative and a positive statement always place the negative statement second to avoid the ambiguity of "not fat and big."

151. Then say, "We want to find a book that is big and not fat." (Point to book 1) "Is this the book?" Child responds, "Yes, this book is big." Then, "Is this book fat?" Child responds, "Yes, this book is fat." Then say, "Remember, we wanted to find a book that was big and not fat. Is this book big and not fat?" Child responds, "No, this book is big and fat." Then say, "Is this the book?" Say, "No, this is not the book. Say it." Say, "This is not the book so let's cross it out." Child responds.

152. Point to book 2 and say, "Is this book big?" Child responds, "Yes, this book is big." Then, "Is this book fat?" Child responds, "No, this book is not fat." Then, "Is this book big and not fat?" Child responds, "Yes, this book is big and not fat." Say, "We want a book that is big and not fat. Is this big and not fat?" Child responds, "This book is big and not fat." Ask, "Is this the book?" Child responds, "Yes, this is the book." Say, "Yes, this is the book."

153. Book 3. "We are looking for a book that is big and not fat. Is this book big?" Child responds, "No, this book is not big." Say, "Is this book fat?" Child responds, "Yes, this book is fat." Say, "This book is fat and not big. We want the book that is big and not fat. Is this the book?" Child responds, "No, this is not the book." Then, "Good, this is not the book."

154. Book 4. Say, "We are looking for the book that is big and not fat. Is this

book big?" Child responds, "No, this book is not big." Say, "Is this book fat?" Child responds, "No, this book is not fat." Then say, "We are looking for the book that is big and not fat. Is this the book?" Child responds, "No, this is not the book." Say, "Good, this is not the book." Then say, "Show me the one we were looking for." Child points and responds, "This one is big and not fat."

155. Show pictures of two trees or draw on the board. One should be tall and fat, the other short and fat. Point to the tree that is tall and fat and say, "This tree is tall, say it." Child responds, "This tree is tall." Say, "This tree is fat, say it." Child responds, "This tree is fat." Point to the other tree and say, "This tree is fat, say it." Child responds, "This tree is fat." Then, "This tree is not tall, say it." Child responds. "This tree is not tall." Point to the two trees and say, "This tree is fat and this tree is fat. Say *these* trees are fat." Child responds, "These trees are fat." Say, "These trees are what?" Child responds, "These trees are fat."

156. Say, "Tell me about this tree." Child responds, "This tree is tall and fat." Then, "Tell me about this tree." Child responds, "This tree is fat and not tall." Then, "Tell me about these trees." Child responds, "These trees are fat."

157. Repeat the segment using long and fat books, long and thin worms, rough and smooth paper.

Prepositions

158. Use a cigar box with a cover and a block. Keep the cover closed for the "on" lessons. Begin by identifying each. Say, "What is this? Say it." "That is correct, this is a box. What is this? Say it." "That is correct, this is a block. This is a block and this is a box. Say that."

159. Place the block on the box. Say, "The block is on the box, say it. (Name), tell me again, where is the block?"

160. Place the block under the box and say, "Where is the block? Is the block on the box? No, the block is not on the box." Then say, "The block is not on the box, say it." "Tell me again, where is the block?"

161. Put the block on the floor and say, "Where is the block? The block is on the floor, say it." Then place the block on a chair and say, "Where is the block? The block is on the chair, say it."

162. Then place the block on the floor and ask, "Where is the block?" Then place the block on the chair and ask, "Where is the block?" Place the block on a desk, book, etc., and ask where is it.

163. Then place the block under a chair and ask, "Where is the block? Is the block on the chair? No, the block is not on the chair, say it."

164. Place the block to the side of or in front of objects and ask, "Where is the block?"

165. Do the same with several other objects. Using the block, box, chair, ball, dog, cat, sock, table, car, and shoe. Practice "on the —" and "not on the —."

166. Use pictures of these objects in various spatial relationships and elicit these responses. Follow this by drawing the objects in various relationships (on the board).

167. Alternate placing the block on the box and over the box and have the child answer the question, "Where is the block?" Prompt as needed and repeat to establish the concept that touching is "on" and not touching is "over." Place the block on the box and cover with your hand. Ask, "Where is my hand? My hand is *over* the block, say it."

168. Alternative "on," "over," and "under" by using yes and no responses. Progress to other objects, then pictures, and then board drawings.

169. Put the block on the box and ask, "Here is the block?" Open the box cover and place the block in the box and say, "Where is the block? The block is in the box, say it. Say it again, the block is in the box." Then place the block in the box and say, "Is the block on the box? No, the block is not on the box, say it" "Is the block under the box? No, the block is not under the box, say it." "Is the block over the box? No, the block is not over the box, say it." Then, "Where is the block, tell me." Prompt if the child does not respond correctly. Then hold the block above the box and say, "Is the block in the box? No, the block is not in the box, tell me."

170. Place the block on, under, and to the side, and ask if the block is in the box. Then place the block in the box and say, "Tell me where the block is." Prompt as needed. Follow the procedure with pictures and board drawing. Also expand to, "Sandy, where are we? Are we in school? Yes, we are in school, tell me, We are in school, say it." "Tell me again, where are we?" Prompt as needed.

171. If appropriate ask, "Where is your mother? Is your mother in your house? Yes, your mother is in your house. Say, Mother is in the house, say it."

172. Repeat with sisters, brothers, and father using in the house, in the store, in school.

173. Then show pictures of milk in a glass, a dog in a house, a bird in a cage, etc., and question.

174. Review "on, under, over." For example, "Is the dog on the house?" "Is the milk under the glass," etc.

175. Say, "Sandy, point to the ceiling. Where is that? That is *up,* say it." "Tell me again, it is up. Where is the light? It is up, say it." "Where is the sky, it is up, say it." "Tell me where the sun is, it is up, say it." Add other items.

176. Say, "Susan, where is the floor? Is it up? No, it is not up, say it." If the child says, "It is down," say, "That's correct, it is down but we are talking about up now. It is *not* up."

177. Place one or two objects on the floor and ask, "Where is the block?" (etc.) Then place objects on the floor and hold up above the children. Vary the "upness" and "not upness" to aid in establishing the concepts.

178. Say, "When something is not up we say it is down." Place a block on the floor and say, "The block is down, say it." Then, "The floor is down, say it." Add other items and questions as indicated.

179. Place two objects on the floor and say, "The block and the ball are down, say it." Then vary "up" and "down" questions. Prompt as needed. Involve the child or children in the questioning process. "Where is the block?" "Where is the ball?" "Where is the eraser?" Then, "Where are the ball and the eraser?", etc.

180. Place the block under the box and ask, "Susan, where is the block?" The child should respond, "The block is not on the box." Say, "That is correct, the block is not on the box. The block is *under* the box, say it." Then say, "Where is the block? Tell me." Then, "Tell me again, where is the block?" Then ask, "Is the block on the box? No, the block is not on the box, say it." Say, "Tell me again, is the block on the box?"

181. "Tell me the answer, is the block on the box?" Then, "Now tell me the answer" (place the block under the box), "is the block under the box? Yes, the block is under the box, say it." "Answer me, is the block under the box?"

182. Continue to develop the concept by varying yes and no responses by then introducing other objects, then by using pictures, and then by drawing on the board. If children experience difficulty, give several successive illustrations: under my foot, under the chair, under my chin, under your leg.

183. Although "under" means something is beneath something else or something is resting on something else, and "below" has an almost identical meaning, the prepositions "on" and "over" have similar but distinctively different meanings. "Over" means above and sometimes covering while "on" means placed on or situated on. This makes this concept slightly more difficult. Hold the block over the box and say, "Where is the block? The block is *over* the box, say it." "Say it again, the block is over the box." "Is the block under the box? No, it is not under the box, say it."

184. Place the block on the box. "Now the block is on the box, say it." Lift the block up noticeably and say, "When it is like this I say the block is not on the box. Say, the block is not on the box, say it." "Where is the block? It is over the box, say it." If children experience difficulty, give several successive illustrations.

185. Perform several reversal tasks in which the block is first under the box, then the box is under the block, in which the block is first over the box and then the box is over the block. For example, put the block on the box. "Where is the block? Where is the box?" Put the box on the block. "Where is the box?" "Where is the block?"

186. "Put your hand on your knee. Where is your hand?" "Place your hand under your knee. Where is your hand?" "Place your hand under your chin. Where is your hand?" "Place your hand on your shoulder. Where is your hand?" Continue.

187. Repeat exercises from step 158 using plurals with prepositions. For example use two blocks and the box. "Where *are* the blocks?" "The blocks *are* on the box, say it." Continue with other prepositions.

188. Perform several "point to" tasks. Have the children give "point to" commands.

189. Place the block in the box. Take it out and say, "I take the block *from* the

box." Now say, "I give the block *to* Steve." Put the block in the box, take it out and say, "What do I do? Tell me." "That's correct. I take the block from the box. Then what do I do? I give it to Steve." Repeat putting the block in the box and taking it out. Say, "What do I do?" (give to Steve). "Now what do I do?" Then take the block from Steve. "What do I do now? I take the block from Steve." Give the block to another child. "Now what do I do?" Prompt as necessary as you do this and have the children give and take the block.

190. Say, "Shari, go to the board." When the child gets there say, "Now come to me *from* the board." Have the children give each other commands to go to the board and come from the board or other parts of the room.

191. Stand at the board and say, "Jesse, come to the board. Now go to your seat." "Jesse, come to the board. Now you ask someone to come to the board." "Now tell them to go to their seat." Repeat with other children.

192. Hand a child the box. "Jesse, where did you get the box from? You got the box from me. Where did you get the box?" (If children can respond without third sentence prompt, don't use it.)

193. Ask questions to elicit "to" responses. For example, "Where do we go to buy groceries? Where do we go to learn? Where do we go to buy gasoline? "Make certain full sentences are used in reply.

194. Elicit "from" responses. Where do we get our mail? Where do we get milk? Where do we get a glass of water? Where do we get shoes?

195. Say to a child, "Shari, go to your desk." Then say, "Where is Shari? Shari is at her desk. Jill, where is Shari?" Repeat with other children. Then vary places such as the board, the door.

196. Ask questions to elicit "at" responses. "Where is your mother? Where is your father? Where is the gas station man? Where is the man who owns the store?"

197. Use full sentences in this exercise including the intial clause. Say, "Joyce, why do we go to school? We go to school because we want to learn. You say it." Then, "Gail, why do we wear shoes?" Make certain the children use a why-because answer. Continue with other questions.

198. Use with if-then response even though the "then" is usually omitted in conversation. Ask, "What would happen if birds didn't have wings, Scott?" Expect, "If birds did not have wings, *then* —" Repeat with many such questions. Prompt as necessary.

199. Develop and practice exercises for "by, near, off, out of, through, between, before, behind, away from, with, of, for, like."

200. Say, "Sandy, I want to play a game with you. I am going to say something but I will leave out one word. I want you to fill in the word I leave out. I will say 'blank' instead of the word. Listen, Jack blank Jill went up the hill. You say it right." Prompt as necessary. "Now try this. Tom blank Ann like flowers." Try several more until the concept of "blank" replacing a word is established and until the group is found to use "and" successfully.

201. "Here is a different one. Listen. Everyone is going blank me." If the child

says "but" accept it. If the child says "except" say, "That's a very good one. You could also have said, 'Everyone is going *but* me.' " Then, "Alice likes cats, blank I don't." Add as many exercises as needed to establish "but."

202. Alternate "and" and "but" responses.

203. Say, "Now listen. I have blank of the blocks." Give to a child, "Now Susan has blank of the blocks." Expect "all" responses. "I ran blank of the way home." "He ate blank of the candy." Continue to competence.

204. Play a "what am I doing" game to test competence. Begin by standing and saying, "What am I doing? I am standing." Sit down and ask, "Sally, what am I doing?" Demonstrate from sitting, running, jumping, crying, laughing, talking, singing, thinking, taking, eating, calling, cutting, finding, giving, playing, making, seeing, saying. Have children demonstrate and the others guess. Vary by choosing up sides and timing as in **charades**. Make certain all participate by having one acting and one guessing.

205. If children have difficulty with specific words, work on it by saying, "What am I doing? I am walking, say it." Then, "See I walk and we say I am walking." Walk again, "What am I doing? I am walking." Then, "Sandy walk. What is Sandy doing? That's right, she is walking." Repeat with other words as needed.

206. Say, "Now we will play another game. I will say a sentence and you say the next one. For example, if I say, The car belongs to my dad, you would say, It is dad's car." Question understanding. Then use sentences such as, "The ball belongs to Steve. It is —. You say it. The bike belongs to Shari. The bat belongs to the boy. The nest belongs to the bird."

207. Continue with above exercises on possessives to competence. Then say, "We are going to play the same game. However, now you can only use the words 'his' and 'hers.' " Add more sentences.

208. Say, "Now you can use four words, his, her, its, and my." Use appropriate sentences.

209. Produce sentences using "him, her, me, it." For example, the book is his. It belongs to_____ ?

210. Show a picture. Ask the child questions that can be answered in single sentences. Correct errors and have the child repeat.

211. Show a picture. Ask the child to describe. Correct errors.

Depending on the group and possible other factors such as geography, age level, and special interests, some of the language functions recommended may not be appropriate and others that are important may have been omitted. Using the suggestions should enable the specialist to prepare lessons to compensate for omissions. Judgment can aid in omitting material considered unnecessary. In addition, some material may need considerable expansion and other need shortening. The SLP or classroom teacher will be able to make these adjustments.

A number of English books provide suggestions for continuation of syntax development, for example, *Speak English, a Practical Course for Foreign Students,* Durel (1972).

BASIC VOCABULARY

The following is a recommended basic vocabulary to use either in roughly determining the child's vocabulary development or in planning programming. These are 280 of the words most frequently used by children and would appear to represent logical words to use in developing vocabulary.

a	brown	feet	hold	money	please
about	but	few	home	more	pretty
afraid	bye-bye	find	horse	morning	put
after	call	fire	hot	most	rain
again	came	fish	house	mother	read
all	can	five	how	much	ready
along	car	floor	I	must	red
always	carry	for	if	my	right
am	child	fork	in	myself	room
an	children	found	into	name	run
and	cold	four	is	never	said
any	come	friend	it	new	saw
are	could	from	jump	next	say
arm	cry	full	just	nice	school
around	cup	gave	keep	night	see
as	cut	get	kind	no	sew
ask	daddy	girl	knife	not	shall
at	day	give	know	now	she
away	dear	go	last	of	shoe
baby	did	good	laugh	off	should
back	do	gone	left	old	show
bad	dog	got	let	on	sing
ball	dolly	great	letter	once	sit
be	done	had	light	only	sleep
because	door	hand	like	open	small
bed	down	happy	little	or	some
been	each	hard	live	other	something
before	eat	has	long	our	soon
best	enough	hat	look	out	spoon
big	ever	have	made	over	stand
black	every	heard	make	own	start
blue	eye	help	man	page	stay
book	fall	her	many	people	still
both	far	here	may	place	summer
boy	fat	him	me	plate	sure
brother	father	his	men	play	table

take	there	together	use	well	will
talk	these	told	very	went	wish
teacher	they	too	walk	were	with
tell	thing	took	want	what	work
than	think	truck	warm	when	would
thank	this	turn	was	where	write
that	those	under	watch	which	year
the	thought	until	water	while	yes
their	time	up	way	white	you
them	to	upon	we	who	your
then	today	us	week		

chapter seven
group language
program planning

I. THE MODEL AND GOALS

Increased academic achievement, improved social functioning, and better emotional adjustment for many mentally retarded children can be accomplished by the provision of carefully planned and executed programming. The type of language program presented should be dependent on the current functioning of the child and the goals established for the child's ultimate level of communication. Four general basic levels of communication can be identified among the retarded. These are, from the lowest to the highest level: (1) the ability to make basic wants known through gestures or signs, (2) limited verbal communication or the use of a few basic words that may be augmented by gestures or signs, (3) the use of speech and language even though there may be errors of language or speech usage, and (4) the correct use of at least a basic linguistic system with correct speech performance. Obviously there are many gradations of these basic levels, but at some point decisions must be made as to expectations for each child so that programming can be planned.

The material in this chapter is primarily for children who are assumed to have capabilities at the third and fourth levels. If the child is at level 1, it is recommended that a program be utilized such as that included in Kent (1974), the chapter entitled "Sign Language and Total Communication" by Martha Snell. An alternative is use of the Bliss Symbols (Vanderheiden et al., 1975). Other parts of the Kent book plus those presented in *A Language Program for Nonlanguage Children* by Gray and Ryan (1974) are applicable for suggestions to achieve level 2. For some children, a ladder concept may be indicated in which the child moves on to a higher level of verbal function after succeeding at one level. Children should attempt the syntax program if they have the entry behaviors described and then enter the program presented in this chapter if they display those entry behaviors. If they cannot succeed, the previously mentioned sources as well as other suggestions at the end of this chapter may provide assistance.

At the primary level, the daily classroom program should include at least two periods of 30 minutes and at the intermediate and secondary levels a minimum of one daily period of 40 minutes. The teacher should plan a basic program that is supplemented by activities aimed at ameliorating any unusual deficits found in the performances of her pupils.

Preparation of the behavioral outcomes and program activities was coordinated by Norman J. Niesen, Ph.D., Department of Special Education, Eastern Michigan University, Ypsilanti, Michigan.

115

Basic Structure

This chapter presents a basic structure for classroom programs at three levels: primary, intermediate, and secondary. The communication behaviors at each level are divided into receiving, thinking, and expressing. Thus, first receiving is presented at each of the three levels, then thinking, and then receiving. The same format is followed in each process but the sophistication increases. For example, item 1 deals with sound discrimination at three levels of sophistication or complexity. The program outcomes are based upon the language model illustrated on pages 118–121. The material is presented in *outcomes* or *goals charts.* An outcome is defined as a level of behavior that must be achieved in order to successfully meet the demands of one's environment. An outcome may be thought of as an objective or a goal, stated in behavioral terms. The outcomes are an attempt to delineate minimum speech and language performance necessary for successful adjustment of the mentally retarded at particular age levels.

The outcomes, therefore, may be used to give direction to the daily classroom language program. In addition, they may give an overview of the sequence of long range expectancies for speech and language development of mentally retarded children.

Requirements for Participation

In order to succeed in the group program planned at the primary level, each child should have a minimal behavioral language age of 4–0 years except for vocabulary. Specifically, the child should be able to participate in group activity for 30 minutes (at the onset), be able to count to 5, be able to say her full name and speak in complete sentences. The child only needs a vocabulary approximately equal to the basic vocabulary presented in Chapter 6. This is about the vocabulary level of the average 2- to 3-year-old child but should suffice for entry into the program.

Entry into the program outlined for the intermediate level should be based on the child's ability to fulfill the outcomes listed for the primary level. Similarly, entry into the secondary program should be based on the child's ability to fulfill the outcomes of the intermediate level.

This does not suggest that children must be excluded from the program if they do not meet these suggested levels. It does indicate that success is more likely if a child is able to perform at the recommended levels. For illustration, to accommodate teachers accustomed to using traditional labels, a child with a reported I.Q. of 75 could begin the program when she is about 5-1/2, a child with a reported I.Q. of 50 could begin at 8, a child with a reported I.Q. of 33 could begin at 12 years. It should be remembered that the author prefers to utilize language performance rather than the child's I.Q. On this basis the program is more appropriate for children labeled mildly (educable) retarded, would have application for moderately (trainable) retarded, and would have limited application for the severely retarded.

Following the outcomes overview charts, the remainder of the chapter is organized around sections for instructional program levels: primary, intermediate, secondary. The age levels presented refer to chronological ages. Primary level includes a chronological age range of 6 to 9 years, intermediate includes a range of 10 to 12 years, and secondary includes a range of 13 to 18 years. Each contains materials devoted to the development of the communication processes of receiving, thinking, and expressing. Each section contains a restatement of the speech and language behavioral goals and suggested activities designed to achieve the goals at those age levels.

The suggested activities represent only samples of the instructional experiences that may be used by the teacher of the retarded to attain the specified goals. Teachers may wish to develop additional activities to help pupils attain these important language goals. In such situations, in order to be effective, the activities should meet the following criteria:

1. They should be of interest and appropriate to the chronological age and social maturity level of the children for whom they are designed.
2. They should provide for active participation of the child in the learning experience.
3. They should have meaning, purpose, and utility to the child.
4. They should be considered an important part of the curriculum offerings for the mentally retarded.

Suggestions for supplementary activities are presented in Chapter Eight. Additionally, the equipment and materials presented in Chapter Nine may provide added assistance.

LISTENING

Regardless of other program considerations, attention to two specific needs of retarded children are indicated based on reports of teachers and research results. These are listening and methods of responding.

Mentally retarded children need to attend and listen. If children cannot attend, material from Chapter Five may be helpful. Following are some suggestions for building a listening program:

1. Have the children remain silent. Listening does not mean merely being quiet although this is a logical first step in training.
2. Have the children describe what they hear when they are silent.
3. Have them repeat a word, a sound, a noise the teacher makes.
4. Have them repeat the question the teacher asks.
5. Have a child make up a question after the teacher gives an answer.

6. Have the children formulate and ask questions based on a topic the teacher provides.
7. Have the children play guessing games in which they must ask questions.
8. Help the children learn improved ways to ask questions. The importance of appropriate questioning cannot be overstressed. Not only is it necessary to academic success but much of our internal problem solving is done as we respond to questions we ask ourselves.

RESPONDING

The children must know how to formulate answers. Semmel (1968) feels that mentally retarded children can better answer questions if they know how to formulate a response. Questions beginning with "why" are usually responded to with "because." Questions beginning with "if" usually require a "then" concept. "When" questions require "when," "before," or "after" answers. "Where" questions require one of several prepositions. The words the child needs to trigger her response are often not known to her. These could well be called "tactic" (*the answer-connoting terms in communication*) words because they provide the child a "tactic" for answering the question and solving the problem. Helping the child to frame a response in complete sentence forms with appropriate tactic words will have far-reaching benefits.

Grammar has been described as the logical and necessary place to begin a language program. Whether it is the child's first or second language learning, she must develop the prevailing grammar of the society in which she will function.

After the child reveals appropriate attending and listening and produces a basic vocabulary and syntax, she can both begin to use these skills in appropriate social situations, in this case the classroom, and expand existing skills. This is the purpose of the classroom program.

LANGUAGE FUNCTIONS—THE MODEL

The language model prepared by Niesen (1969) is presented in Figure 7.1. The language functions of receiving, thinking, and expressing are interrelated in a complex manner. In most people these processes operate almost simultaneously. When people have marked deficiencies in one or more of these functions, reduced language efficiency results. Thus, an understanding and use of this language model may serve as a means of providing experiences and activities that will utilize each of the functions of receiving, thinking, and expressing in the language program. The children will be assisted to be more attentive to what they see, hear, or feel; to assimilate, understand, and use these stimuli; and to talk about their experiences in a meaningful way.

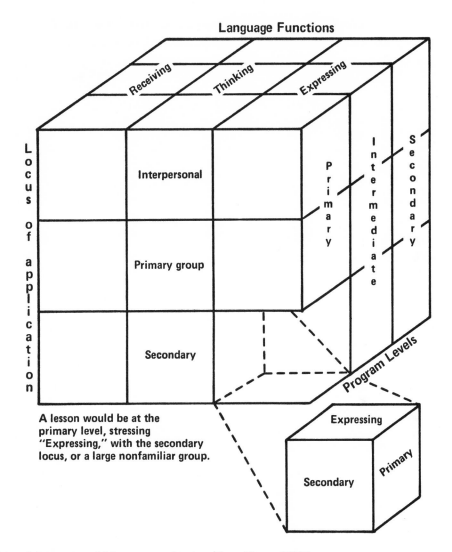

FIGURE 7.1   A language model for program planning. (From Niesen, 1969.)

The first dimension of the language model is concerned with the three major language functions utilized by children. These processes are

1. Receiving of language through auditory, visual, or tactile-kinesthetic channels

2. Thinking or the use of language stimuli to conceptualize, classify, organize, and analyze

3. Expressing of language through speech, gestures, and other communication methods

Each of these functions, for the purpose of this model, is subdivided into several distinct but closely related categories of language activity. By subdividing the language functions into categories, a more manageable and definitive language program is possible.

Receiving

The language function of receiving is subdivided into six categories of language activity. These are

1. Discriminating between environmental sounds
2. Attaching meaning to and using environmental sounds in daily living
3. Developing behavior that facilitates effective listening
4. Acquiring the ability to follow verbal and gestural directions
5. Understanding verbal conversation and communications in a wide variety of settings
6. Attaching meaning to nonverbal events (such as people hurrying, seeing a dark cloud in the sky, or a scowl).

Thinking

Similarly, the thinking function, which involves the internal relating and manipulating of ideas, is subdivided into several categories of language behavior. These categories are

1. Associating correct labels with persons, places, things, and feelings
2. Developing the ability to categorize by noting similarities and differences in size, color, shape, form, function, and feeling tone
3. Developing an understanding of cause and effect in events
4. Understanding the sequence of events
5. Developing an ability to effect closure of such things as filling in the missing parts of pictures, sentences, and events
6. Developing some basic problem-solving techniques such as formulating pertinent questions, recognizing absurdities, choosing acceptable and best courses of action, and engaging in convergent and divergent thinking processes.

Expressing

Last, the expressing function is subdivided into four categories of language activities. These are

1. Responding with correct verbal labels to those things and events in one's environment

2. Accurately describing persons, places, events, and feelings encountered

3. Adapting and modifying one's environment through relating personal needs, giving personal information, asking questions, and using conversation for developing social relationships

4. Using acceptable language forms and patterns to assure free and easy communication.

PROGRAM LEVELS

The second dimension of the model pertains to the level of the program: primary, intermediate, or secondary. The child's language needs and skills become more complex as she matures and advances through her school program and life. This dimension of the model provides for a systematic means of classifying language goals and activities according to the pupil's developmental level. This aspect of the model also provides for scope and sequence in a language development program.

LOCUS OF APPLICATION

The third dimension of the model is concerned with the locus of application of the child's language skills. These loci are interpersonal, primary group, and secondary group. Interpersonal locus involves the application of language on a one-to-one basis, the primary group locus involves communication within the family and small, familiar social groups, and the secondary locus involves communication with individual, small, and large nonfamiliar groups. It is assumed that language skills may vary according to their loci of application. In short, a more complex use of language skills may be required by the child when talking to a group of unfamiliar people than when talking to a friend.

In summary, this chapter attempts to present some behavioral outcomes necessary for the development of an effective clinical and classroom speech and language improvement program for the mentally retarded and activities intended to assist in reaching this objective.

GOALS FOR COMMUNICATION BEHAVIORS

Following are the goals by age level and by receiving, thinking, and expressing listed as behavioral outcomes:

Receiving

Primary Level (6-9 Years)
1. Discriminates between gross sounds

A. Discriminates between gross environmental sounds (e.g., fire sirens, car horns)
B. Discriminates between gross speech sounds

2. Continues to develop basic listening skills to guide behavior in both individual and group situations
    A. Listens to and follows single verbal instructions (one- to two-step)
    B. Listens to and enjoys simple short stories, poems, rhymes
    C. Listens when others speak in both group and individual situations
    D. Listens attentively to records, radio, and television appropriate to age level
    E. Comprehends simple social language amenities (e.g., please, thank you, etc.)
3. Attaches meaning to actions, nonverbal activities, and conversation
    A. Understands simple gestures
    B. Listens to and understands the interpersonal verbal communications and those of his primary group
    C. Begins to attach meaning to the nonverbal events and situations such as people hurrying, a cloudy sky indicating rain, a siren, an accident
4. Utilizes sound
    A. Locates the direction from which sound came
    B. Judges distance between source of sound and self (knows if sound is near or far, approaching or diminishing, etc.)

Intermediate Level (10–12 Years)
1. Develops fine discrimination of speech sounds
    A. Discriminates between most speech sounds (e.g., f from th; s from sh)
    B. Makes fine discrimination in pitch, quality, intensity, and rhythm of speech, music, and nature
2. Develops appropriate listening skills and behavior
    A. Understands two- to three-step verbal directions
    B. Listens for specific information (e.g., information in a story, a weather forecast, an announcement)
    C. Maintains eye contact with speaker
    D. Listens attentively to members of peer group in conversation or formal class participation (e.g., student oral report, show and tell)
    E. Listens attentively in formal group situations (e.g., theatre, church, school assembly)
    F. Begins to respond appropriately to social amenities
3. Attaches meanings to more complex actions, nonverbal activities and conversation
    A. Understands complex gestures such as motions, pantomime, hand signals
    B. Attaches meaning to facial expressions
    C. Understands the verbal communication of those in primary group and some from secondary group

    D. Attaches meaning to a wide variety of events and situations that he encounters
4. Attaches meaning to a variety of environmental sounds. Knows that certain sounds mean danger, that certain sounds require specific action, such as school bells, fire bells, alarm clocks, etc.

Secondary Level (13-18 Years)
1. Uses fine sound discrimination functionally
    A. Hears and evaluates his own speech performance
    B. Hears and evaluates speech performance of others
    C. Recognizes feelings conveyed by voice, intonation, and the subtleties of speech, e.g., Look out! (danger); Look out (watch)
2. Uses good adult listening skills, habits, and courtesies
    A. Listens attentively when others are speaking
    B. Listens for the purpose of remembering
    C. Understands four- and six-step verbal directions
    D. Remembers verbally described people, places, pictures, events, and objects in a sequential order
    E. Responds appropriately to common social amenities
    F. Demonstrates appropriate listening behavior and skill as a part of an audience
3. Understands a wide variety of verbal and nonverbal cues that enable him to meet situations adequately
    A. Appraises the intent of strangers through their facial expressions, gestures, and voice intonations
    B. Understands a technical vocabulary to satisfy vocational and social needs
    C. Understands the verbal communication of those in his secondary group in a wide variety of situations

Thinking

Primary Level (6-9 Years)
1. Begins to label, associate, and categorize familiar people, places, animals, and events
    A. Categorizes and labels at the level of utility (Daddy's work, people talk, crayons color)
    B. Begins to differentiate between opposites (big–little, up–down)
    C. Begins to understand that different words have the same meaning (synonyms such as cat–kitty, town–city)
    D. Begins to notice similarities and differences in size, shape, color, and form
2. Begins to associate words with feelings (happy, surprise, cry, hurt)

3. Begins to arrange experiences into sequential order
   A. Develops elementary time and space concepts
   B. Arranges events and pictures into sequence
4. Begins to develop problem solving techniques
   A. Recognizes auditory and visual absurdities
   B. Solves simple every day problems by beginning to use elementary suppositions, evaluative, predictive, and inferential thinking (e.g., what would you do if, what do you think will happen next, how did this happen)
   C. Recognizes missing parts in pictures and in simple sentences
   D. Begins to ask simple questions
5. Begins to develop elementary grammatical forms and concepts
   A. Attaches meaning to prepositions, endings, plurals
   B. Usually recognizes the differences in tense and gender
6. Begins to memorize simple rote information
   A. Recites finger plays and verses for enjoyment
   B. Memorizes some vital information (e.g., name, address)

Intermediate Level (10–12 Years)
1. Categorizes, labels, and associates names and symbols of people, places, and events
   A. Categorizes familiar symbols into classes (bananas, oranges, and apples are fruit; baseball and football are games, etc.)
   B. Differentiates between opposites
   C. Recognizes synonyms
   D. Notices similarities and differences
   E. Knows that there are words that sound the same but have different meanings (blue–blew; red–read, etc.)
2. Associates a wider variety of words with feelings (sorry, worry, angry)
3. Continues to develop the ability to arrange experiences into sequential order
   A. Extends understanding of time and space relationship (e.g., past, present, future, days, weeks, months, seasons, far, near)
   B. Finishes incomplete sentences, events, and stories logically
4. Increases in the development of problem solving techniques
   A. Asks questions to gain information to solve problems
   B. Begins to discriminate between relevant and irrelevant information, fact from fantasy
5. Understands some of the basic grammatical forms that govern language usage
   A. Correctly formulates statements comparing two objects
   B. Correctly formulates negative statements
6. Increases ability to memorize simple rote information
   A. Recites poems and songs of six to eight lines for enjoyment

B. Knows important and vital information (such as bus schedules, birthdate, etc.)

Secondary Level (13-18 Years)
1. Expands ability to categorize and classify meaning-symbols
    A. Categorizes symbols into larger more abstract categories (e.g., milk, water, tea, coke, and coffee are all liquid; or policeman, sheriff, governor, principal, and bosses are all authorities)
    B. Uses language to make assumptions
    C. Formulates generalizations
    D. Draws conclusions
2. Associates subtle language expressions with feelings and emotions (reacts to voice tone and inflection, facial expression, choice of words, gestures)
3. Develops systematic methods for organizing and retaining information
    A. Evaluates information to select relevant data
    B. Develops methods for learning new words (prefix, suffix, compound words, rhyming words)
    C. Retains several ideas simultaneously
        1. Formulates and gives directions
        2. Sees cause and effect relationships; understands sequence of events
        3. Sees interrelationships of ideas, events, and feelings
4. Uses language to solve problems effectively
    A. Knows how and where to ask questions when help is needed for clarification and information
    B. Interprets and analyzes unfamiliar situations, makes correct responses (meeting new people, emergency situations)
5. Continues to understand and use more of the basic grammatical forms important to standard language and speech
    A. Uses more verbs, adjectives, and adverbs than nouns in daily conversation
    B. Rewords ideas when not understood
    C. Can elaborate on ideas
6. Memorizes and recalls automatically pertinent information
    A. Knows important dates such as school graduation, birthdate, dates of employment
    B. Knows telephone numbers of family, friends, place of employment
    C. Knows social security number, zip code, address
7. Is aware that one's behavior may be influenced by persuasive language
    A. Recognizes some of the ways that advertising may influence him, for example, "Be a He-Man"; "Only 2 left—Hurry!"; "Join the 'in' group"
    B. Becomes aware that people do not always mean what they say when there is personal gain involved, for example, "I'll do this only for you"; "I love you"; "I won't tell anybody"

C. Is aware that slogans are used to communicate ideas, for example, "Equal Opportunity," "Uncle Sam Needs You," "Safety First"

Expressing

Primary Level (6–9 Years)
1. Responds with correct verbal forms to his immediate environment
    A. Uses appropriate labels for people, places, and things (choo-choo becomes train; bye-bye becomes goodbye)
    B. Gives simple description of familiar objects
    C. Describes function of familiar objects, places, and people (e.g., what do you do with a spoon?)
    D. Verbalizes personal experiences (show and tell)
    E. Responds appropriately to simple questions
2. Begins to use language to adapt to his environment
    A. Verbalizes personal needs and feelings
    B. Uses simple social amenities
    C. Relates personal information (name, address, etc.)
3. Begins to use correct enunciation, grammatical form in self-expression
    A. Uses simple sentences correctly
    B. Asks simple questions correctly
    C. Attempts to say words clearly when corrected
4. Begins to use language for enjoyment
    A. Recites simple nursery rhymes and sings simple songs
    B. Converses with others

Intermediate Level (10–12 Years)
1. Responds verbally to meet the demands of an expanding environment
    A. Increases vocabulary
    B. Describes experiences more accurately and completely
    C. Begins to use elaboration in his conversation, i.e., uses more detail in relating events and ideas
    D. Begins to gain and give information through questioning and discussion
2. Uses language to meet social needs
    A. Gives vital information accurately (name, address, birthdate, parents' name, etc.)
    B. Responds appropriately to questions
    C. Begins to use the telephone for communication
    D. Verbalizes feelings and emotions
    E. Delivers simple messages
    F. Extends use of social amenities (handles simple introductions, excuse me, I am sorry)
3. Begins to use acceptable language patterns

    A. Uses correct elementary grammatical constructions

    B. Speaks comfortably and intelligibly in interpersonal and small-group situations

    C. Gives oral reports using four to ten sentences

4. Uses language for enjoyment

    A. Participates in role playing and simple skits

    B. Recites poems and songs of several verses

    C. Converses with friends freely on topics of mutual interest

Secondary Level (13–18 Years)

1. Uses appropriate speech and language to meet social and occupational demands

    A. Increases vocabulary to include many work-related terms such as foreman, check, time clock, double time, etc.

    B. Uses socially acceptable speech and language forms in a variety of situations, for example, doesn't swear in mixed company, chooses acceptable topics for conversation, doesn't dominate conversations, etc.

    C. Regulates pitch, rate, and volume appropriately to the demands of specific situations

2. Uses language as an adaptive manipulative and modifying tool of his environment

    A. Gives personal information effectively in interviews

    B. Responds verbally without tension or undue hesitation

    C. Asks questions to obtain information or assistance

    D. Responds appropriately to unfamiliar or stress situations (police, fire, accident)

    E. Expresses respect, admiration, friendship, and apologies through appropriate language forms.

    F. Expresses disagreement in an acceptable fashion

3. Speaks intelligibly, fluently, and comfortably with strangers in large-group situations

4. Uses language for enjoyment

    A. Uses telephone effectively for social and business needs

    B. Exchanges ideas, information, and interests freely with others

    C. Participates in choral speaking, dramatic skits, role playing, etc.

    D. Meets and relates well with others

II. SUGGESTED PROGRAM ACTIVITIES

Preceding each section is a restatement of speech and language behavior goals in the appropriate area. Following each of the goals are several suggested activities, which have been developed by age level. The suggested activities included in each section represent only a sample of the kinds of instructional experiences that may be used by the classroom teacher to develop specific goals.

II. THE PRIMARY LEVEL

Development of Receiving Skills
Primary Level (6–9 Years)

Receiving

1. Discriminates between gross sounds
    A. Discriminates between gross environmental sounds (e.g., fire sirens, car horns)
    B. Discriminates between gross speech sounds
2. Continues to develop basic listening skills to guide behavior in both individual and group situations
    A. Listens to and follows single verbal instructions (one- to two-step)
    B. Listens to and enjoys simple short stories, poems, rhymes
    C. Listens when others speak in both group and individual situations
    D. Listens attentively to records, radio, and television appropriate to age level
    E. Comprehends simple social language amenities (e.g., please, thank you, etc.)
3. Attaches meaning to actions, nonverbal activities, and conversation
    A. Understands simple gestures
    B. Listens to and understands the interpersonal verbal communications and those of his primary group
    C. Begins to attach meaning to the nonverbal events and situations such as people hurrying, a cloudy sky indicating rain, a siren, an accident
4. Utilizes sound
    A. Locates the direction from which sounds come
    B. Judges distance between source of sound and self (knows if sound is near or far, approaching or diminishing, etc.)

SUGGESTED LANGUAGE AND SPEECH
PROGRAM FOR PRIMARY
GROUP (6–9 YEARS)

Receiving

GOAL 1. Discriminates between gross sounds
    A. Discriminates between gross environmental sounds (e.g., fire sirens, car horns)
    B. Discriminates between gross speech sounds

Suggested Activities

Play records that emphasize environmental sounds, such as car horns, motors, bells, and so on. Encourage children to listen for, identify, and recognize differences and similarities in specific sounds. Talk about the sounds they hear, let the children attempt to imitate them, and encourage children to listen for similar sounds at home, school, and in the neighborhood. (Use record *What Do I Say* by Utley or the *Listening Time Series.*) (1A)

Take listening walks around the school, on the playground, and in the neighborhood. Have children listen for as many different sounds as they can hear. Discuss the sounds after the walk; talk about whether they were loud or soft, what made the sound, etc. (1A)

Read or tell stories that provide the opportunity for the teacher to use many different sounds. Use as many real objects for making the sounds as possible, for example, a clock, a bell, a whistle, or a balloon bursting could be reproduced in the classroom. After the children have become familiar with the story, assign children roles that will require them to fill in the sound at the appropriate time as the story is read. (1A)

Play musical records. Have children keep time to the music by tapping, clapping, marching, or running. Change the tempo and volume of the music, and have the children change their actions to match the changes in the music, e.g., clap softly when music is loud, march fast or slow as the music dictates, etc. (1A)

Record children's voices on a tape recorder. Have them listen to the tape and identify the speakers. Talk about the beginning sounds of the names of the children and the words that they hear (e.g., That was Billy, the next voice was Betty. Betty and Billy begin the same way. Listen and see if you can hear that.). (1B)

Play a variety of simple listening games such as, "That sounds like —" Have children take turns making a single, isolated sound, and have the other children suggest what the sound could be. The child who is "it" chooses the next child to be "it" depending on which answer he liked best, e.g., child who is "it" makes an "s" sound. Other children suggest that it sounds like a snake hissing, air coming out of a tire, or a mad cat. Child who is "it" decides that the sound was most like a mad cat and chooses the child who made that suggestion to take his turn to be "it." Initially, the teacher should suggest sounds for the children to make and should guide the class with the suggestions. (1B)

GOAL 2. Continues to develop basic listening skills to guide behavior in both individual and group situations
    A. Listens to and follows single verbal instructions (one- to two-step)
    B. Listens to and enjoys simple short stories, poems, rhymes
    C. Listens when others speak in both group and individual situations
    D. Listens attentively to records, radio, and television appropriate to age level

E. Comprehends simple social language amenities (e.g., please, thank you, etc.)

Suggested Activities

Provide opportunities for children to listen to and follow verbal directions in all activities throughout the day. Use simple directions such as, "Take out your red crayon, draw a circle on the page." "Pick up the paper scraps and put them in the waste basket." "Please take this note across the hall to Miss Smith, and wait for her to write an answer to me." (2A)

Have children listen to and respond to action songs that the teacher or children sing, or from records. *Looby Loo, This is the Way We Brush Our Teeth, Here We Go Round the Mulberry Bush* are examples of songs that may be used. (2A)

Make a tape recording that gives children specific verbal instructions. Instructions may be given to individual children or to the whole class. Instructions may be whimsical or serious, as the teacher chooses. For example, the recording may tell Billy to get down on his knees and pretend that he is a cat, and then tell Susie to pretend she is feeding the cat, and tell Bobby to pet the cat. Instructions may also be given to the whole class. For example, children may be directed to put their heads down on their desks, clap their hands, sit on the floor, watch the second hand on the clock until it goes all the way around, etc. (2A)

Read or tell simple short stories to children. Talk about the story and ask questions about it to check the comprehension. (2B)

Show short films and filmstrip stories. Talk about them, and have children draw pictures about the story or pantomime parts of it to add to the enjoyment and check the children's comprehension of the story. (2B)

Use puppets and flannel board figures to illustrate short stories. Have children identify characters in the story, place pictures in proper sequence, manipulate the puppets, and answer questions about the story. (2B)

Write short, simple, high-interest experience chart stories. Use the children's suggestions in the stories. Read the stories to the children periodically, adding new parts to them as new experiences take place. (2B)

Use simple social expressions consistently at every opportunity throughout the day. (2C)

Role-play various social situations that provide learning and practice in the use of social expressions (e.g., meeting a classmate, the principal, or a relative; using table manners; apologizing; answering the door or telephone). (2C)

Provide opportunities for using social expressions and skills by having simple social functions such as Mother's Day teas, visitors to the classroom, parties, programs, etc. (2C)

GOAL 3. Attaches meaning to actions, nonverbal activities, and conversations

A. Understands simple gestures
B. Listens to and understands the interpersonal verbal communications and those of his primary group
C. Begins to attach meaning to the nonverbal events and situations such as people hurrying, a cloudy sky indicating rain, a siren, an accident

Suggested Activities

Have "secret" signals that require the children to respond in certain ways, e.g., the teacher holds up two fingers; children are required to take their seats; teacher places one finger on her mouth; children are expected to be quiet; teacher points to the door; children are to leave the room. (3A)

Show children pictures from magazines and books of people, animals, and things that show gestures and facial expressions. Have them guess what the gestures and expressions mean. (3A)

Have children pantomime parts of familiar stories, using gestures such as shaking hands, pointing, doubling the fist, etc. (3A)

Provide many opportunities for children to talk with each other. A particular time of day may be set aside for "talking time" during which children are allowed to move about the room and converse with friends. Teacher can encourage children to converse freely and to have things to talk about by noticing and remembering items of interest throughout the day, and reminding them at talking time. (3B)

Bring a variety of resource people to the classroom to talk to the children, to help them understand various speech patterns and mannerisms, e.g., bus driver, store clerk, policeman, other teachers, etc. Discuss the content, voices, and mannerisms of the speakers after they have left. (3B)

Make a series of transparencies, to be used on an overhead projector, that show nonverbal events and situations. Have the children look at the transparencies and tell what meaning they attach to them, e.g., two cars heading toward each other on a street, dark clouds and lightning, a dog digging a hole under a fence, etc. The teacher should ask questions such as, "What do you think is about to happen?" or "What do you suppose has happened?" (3C)

Look at pictures in magazines and books. Point out the nonverbal situations that the children can convert into meaningful speech, e.g., a picture of someone water skiing. Child could be expected to say that this was a person going fast, on water, being pulled by a boat, etc. (3C)

Take walks around the neighborhood and observe and talk about all the things that are seen, e.g., "That lady is in a hurry. She is probably late," or "That tree was chopped down," or "That bush is growing," etc. (3C)

Use a short, simple film. Turn the sound off during certain high-action sections. Have the children tell what they think is happening during this section, then rewind, and show section again with the sound, to see how nearly correct they were. (3C)

GOAL 4. Utilizes sound
   A. Locates the direction from which sounds come
   B. Judges distance between source and self (knows if sound is near or far, approaching or diminishing, etc.)

Suggested Activities

Use stereophonic demonstration records with recorded environmental noises approaching and departing, such as fire engine, airplane, train, etc. (4A)

   Have one child, with eyes closed, make noise while approaching or departing from group and have children try to identify whether the noise is coming toward the group or going away from the group. (4A)

   Using noise makers, make noises in different parts of room while children (with eyes closed) point in direction of sound. (4A)

   Hide the loud-ticking cheap clock or time bomb (toy) for children to locate from sound. (4A)

   Have children find source of sound made with walkie-talkie. (4A)

   Conduct listening walks with discussion of sounds near and far away. (4B)

Primary Level (6–9 Years)

Thinking

1. Begins to label, associate, and categorize familiar people, places, animals, and events
   A. Categorizes and labels at the level of utility (daddys work, people talk, crayons color)
   B. Begins to differentiate between opposites (big–little, up–down)
   C. Begins to understand that different words have the same meaning (synonyms such as cat–kitty, town–city)
   D. Begins to notice similarities and differences in size, shape, color, and form
2. Begins to associate words with feelings (happy, surprise, cry, hurt)
3. Begins to arrange experiences into sequential order
   A. Develops elementary time and space concepts
   B. Arranges events and pictures into sequence
4. Begins to develop problem-solving techniques
   A. Recognizes auditory and visual absurdities

B. Solves simple everyday problems by beginning to use elementary suppositions, evaluative, predictive, and inferential thinking (e.g., What would you
do if? What do you think will happen next? How did this happen?)

C. Recognizes missing parts in pictures and in simple sentences

D. Begins to ask simple questions

5. Begins to develop elementary grammatical forms and concepts

A. Attaches meaning to prepositions, endings, plurals

B. Usually recognizes the differences in tense and gender

6. Begins to memorize simple rote information

A. Recites finger plays and verses for enjoyment

B. Memorizes some vital information (e.g., name, address)

SUGGESTED LANGUAGE AND SPEECH PROGRAM FOR PRIMARY GROUP (6-9 YEARS)

Thinking

GOAL 1. Begins to label, associate, and categorize familiar people, places, animals, and events

A. Categorizes and labels at the level of utility (daddys work, people talk, crayons color)

B. Begins to differentiate between opposites (big–little, up–down)

C. Begins to understand that different words have the same meaning (synonyms such as cat–kitty, town–city)

D. Begins to notice similarities and differences in size, shape, color, and form

Suggested Activities

Select a category for questions. Ask categorical questions such as, "Who can name some things to drink?" or "What are cars, buses, taxis, and trains for?" (1A)

Play "Concentration" using picture cards consisting of similar, identical, or related parts that are arranged randomly in rows on the table. The child turns over any two cards, one at a time. If the cards match he keeps the set. If they do not match, he replaces the cards and the next child takes a turn. To be successful, the child must remember the positions of the cards. (1A)

Play "Picture Lotto." Have the child match the chosen picture with an identical picture on his game card. Game may be varied by asking the child to match his chosen picture on his game card, which is different but belongs in the same category, e.g., straight-backed chair—upholstered chair. (1A)

Present two to five stimulus pictures representing different categories to the child, e.g., something to eat, something to wear, something to ride. The child is given a group of cards that he must arrange or categorize under the proper stimulus picture categories. (1A)

Discuss the meaning of opposites. Give examples of extreme opposites such as night-day, black-white, fat-skinny. (1B)

Play a game of opposites. The teacher gives a word that has an opposite. The first child to raise his hand and give the correct opposite becomes "it"; he then gives a word and the rest of the class tries to guess the opposite of it. (1B)

Make pairs of flash cards that contain pictures of opposites. Use these for drills in identifying opposites or for a variety of matching games. (1B)

Read sentences to the children. Reread them, leaving out certain words. Ask the children to fill in the blanks with different words that have the same meaning, e.g., the little boy had a *large* red ball; children could change the words to: The little boy had a *big* red ball. (1C)

Have the children choose the one that does not belong in the groups of pictures, objects, designs, or lists of words, e.g., in a group of pictures of a cat, a dog, a horse, and a chair, the child would be required to choose the chair. (1D)

Have children sort and arrange objects or pictures according to size, color, or shape, e.g., all the black buttons together, all the small buttons together, all the nails or screws together, or all the dog pictures together. (1D)

Place a number of objects on the table and have the children look at them and then close their eyes. After the teacher takes one away the children must identify the missing object. As the children become more proficient, the number of objects may be increased. (1D)

GOAL 2. Begin to associate words with feelings (happy, surprise, cry, hurt)

Suggested Activities

Play a game that requires children to make faces that depict certain feelings. Give them each a word such as happy, surprised, sad, sleepy, and so on, and ask them to make a face that shows the feeling the word conveys. (2)

Show children pictures that show feeling and emotion; ask children to think of words that tell what the feelings are, e.g., children at a party (happy), two people fighting (mad), and so on. (2)

GOAL 3. Begins to arrange experiences into sequential order
  A.   Develops elementary time and space concepts
  B.   Arranges events and pictures into sequence

Suggested Activities

Make a bulletin board that illustrates special events for a month. Items such as Johnny's birthday, beginning swimming classes, holidays, and the like can be included. Talk about the events each day, using time concept words such as last week, next week, tomorrow, yesterday, and the like. (3A)

Use *Judy* "See-Quees" sequencing story boards. Require children to arrange pictures in proper order. (3B)

Draw simple sequence pictures. Cut them apart and have children arrange them in order. Use familiar sequences such as a picture of an orange, then a half-peeled orange, a fully peeled orange, and possibly a half-eaten orange. As children increase in skill, more pictures of increasing difficulty can be added. (3B)

GOAL 4. Begins to develop problem-solving techniques
   A. Recognizes auditory and visual absurdities
   B. Solves simple everyday problems by beginning to use elementary suppositional, evaluative, predictive, and inferential thinking (e.g., What would you do if? What do you think will happen next? How did this happen?)
   C. Recognizes missing parts in pictures and in simple sentences
   D. Begins to ask simple questions

Suggested Activities

Use *Continental Press* visual absurdities work sheets. Require children to look at the pictures, recognize the absurdity, and talk about what is wrong with the picture. (4A)

Give children sentences that have an incorrect or absurd word included in them. Require them to fill in a correct word, e.g., Father painted the *cat* yesterday. Children should replace the word "cat" with one that makes sense, such as "house," "barn," "table," etc. (4A)

Give the child a sentence with a word missing. The child must supply an appropriate word, e.g., "The cat ran up the —." Any appropriate word is considered correct. (4B)

Help pupils pair objects as to use or function, e.g., needles and thread, ball and bat, etc. (4B)

Help child to interpret pictures in familiar stories, e.g., teacher asks, "What has happened to the girl's hat?" Child may say, "Blown off." Then teacher asks, "What do you think blew her hat off?" (4B)

Ask questions, e.g., "Would you find a bed in the kitchen?" The child is to answer yes or no. The teacher helps the children think of reasons. (4B)

Use puzzles to emphasize individual problem solving. Using a large magazine picture cut into squares so that the child is required to use picture content instead of piece configuration for clues. (4B)

Help the child to complete human stick or geometric figures that have parts missing. (4C)

Draw simple pictures on an overhead projector. Leave obvious missing parts. Have children draw the missing parts into the picture. (4C)

Give children precise directions for obtaining certain information that will require them to ask simple questions, e.g., Billy must find out what Janice had for breakfast; Janie must find out what Betty's favorite color is; Judy must find out what TV show Joey saw last night, etc. Set a time limit on the questioning period, and have each child report the information back to the class and tell how he asked the questions. (4D)

GOAL 5. Begins to develop elementary grammatical forms and concepts
  A.   Attaches meaning to prepositions, endings, plurals
  B.   Usually recognizes the differences in tense and gender

Suggested Activities

Use the *Instructor* poster cards that illustrate commonly used prepositions such as up, down, in, and the like. Talk about the pictures and have children attempt to think of other ways the words could be illustrated. (5A)

Play a modified version of "Simon Says" that uses as many prepositions as possible.

Use a chalk board or overhead projector. Draw one stick figure, a boy. Ask children to change the picture so that it will be boys (plural). Point out the difference in the way plurals sound and in the meaning of plurals. Use pictures of apples, circles, trees, and so on to continue with this activity. (5A)

Read sentences to the children that have obvious errors in tense or gender. Require the children to correct them, e.g., Mary went to the store to buy *his* doll a dress. Children should replace "his" with "her." (5B)

Make flash cards illustrating familiar pronouns that include the word and a picture, e.g., girls and women or cards that have the words "she, her, hers," etc. (5A)

GOAL 6. Begins to memorize simple rote information
  A.   Recites finger plays and verses for enjoyment
  B.   Memorizes some vital personal information (e.g., name, address)

Suggested Activities

Teach children several finger plays and verses such as "Jack in the Box," "Ten Little Indians," "Fuzzy Orange Caterpillar," and so on. Provide opportunities for children to recite the finger plays; let them take turns leading the group. (6A)

Have the children play a memory game by taking turns adding appropriate words to chain of words, e.g., "We went to the zoo and saw a bear and an elephant," etc. (6A)

Whisper a word to a child. Have children "pass it on" from one to another. Child at the end of the row tells what word he heard. (6B)

Have the child repeat an increasing number of numbers, words, syllables, tapping or clapping activities that are presented at decreasing speeds to improve memory span. Start with two per second, one per second, one per half-second. (6B)

Teach children their names and addresses. Occasionally have a share time or roll-card period during which each child is required to stand and give her name, address, age, and as much information as she can. (6B)

Development of Expressing Skills
Primary Level (6–9 Years)

Expressing

1. Responds with correct verbal forms to immediate environment
    A. Uses appropriate labels for people, places, and things (choo-choo becomes train, bye-bye becomes goodbye)
    B. Gives simple description of familiar objects
    C. Describes function of familiar objects, places, and people (e.g., what do you do with a spoon?)
    D. Verbalizes personal experiences (show-and-tell)
    E. Responds appropriately to simple questions
2. Begins to use language to adapt to environment
    A. Verbalizes personal needs and feelings
    B. Uses simple social amenities
    C. Relates personal information (name, address, etc.)
3. Begins to use correct enunciation, grammatical form in self-expression
    A. Uses simple sentences correctly
    B. Asks simple questions correctly
    C. Attempts to say words clearly when corrected
4. Begins to use language for enjoyment
    A. Recites simple nursery rhymes and sings simple songs
    B. Converses with others

SUGGESTED LANGUAGE AND SPEECH PROGRAM FOR PRIMARY GROUP (6-9 YEARS)

Expressing

GOAL 1. Responds with correct verbal forms to immediate environment
        A. Uses appropriate labels for people, places, and things (choo-choo becomes train, bye-bye becomes goodbye)
        B. Gives simple description of familiar objects
        C. Describes function of familiar objects, places, and people (e.g., what do you do with a spoon?)
        D. Verbalizes personal experiences (show-and-tell)
        E. Responds appropriately to simple questions

Suggested Activities

Take short neighborhood field trips and utilize observations from the classroom windows to stimulate or develop ideas for discussion. (1A)

Bring toys, gadgets, bric-a-brac, and other articles for observation, manipulation, touch, smell, and discussion. Have students talk about these objects, i.e., their shape, size, color, and function. Occasionally include simple items such as a bar of soap, granules, a ball-point pen, and an ink pen in order to bring about discussions of similarities and differences. (1A)

Have the children dress full-size boy and girl toy dolls according to weather and situation. Ask questions such as "When do we use a rain coat?" "What would we wear to a party or to a picnic?" (1A)

Use a dollhouse. Have the children place the furniture in the proper room; as they do this they can discuss how each piece is used. (1A)

Name familiar objects and people through use of "treasure box," a large box with many play things in it. Each child may reach into the box and take out an object, such as a car, a truck, a ball, and so on, with which he would like to play. When the child correctly names the object, he may play with it for the play period. (1A)

Have children describe how objects change. "This is a circle" (draw a picture of a circle on the board with white chalk). "Now it is a red circle" (draw a circle approximately the same size on the board using red chalk). "Now it is a large red circle" (draw a noticeably larger red circle on the board). "Now it is a small red circle" (draw a noticeably smaller red circle on the board).

Use a peek box to elicit descriptions of common objects. "This is a shoe box with a cellophane or Saran Wrap window on one end." Have the children look through the window and describe the object they see. The objects in the box can be changed for each child. The class can guess what the object is. (1B)

Use a pocket chart with several pictures of various animals. Make up a riddle about a picture and see if the children can guess which one it is. A child may give the clues eventually, i.e., "I give milk. My baby is a calf. Who am I?" Child: "You are a cow." "Yes, I am a cow." (1C)

Use riddles to elicit names of common objects, i.e., "I use it to eat soup with. What is it?" (1C)

Play a guessing game with Peabody Kit people cards, e.g., Who cuts people's hair? Who fills our car with gasoline? etc. If the children are able to name the proper person, they will be permitted to hold the picture card for the rest of the lesson. (1A–C)

Have a show-and-tell period each day during which time the children are encouraged to share experiences. (1D)

Take several trips to neighborhood places such as the grocery store, the fire department, the police station, the park, the public library, the bakery shop, and the pet store. When the class gets back to the classroom, have the children discuss their experience. (1A–D)

Use a photograph of each child engaged in some activity. A Polaroid camera is particularly valuable since the results are seen immediately. Make a book of the pictures. Each child's name is placed under his picture. The class or a child "reads" the book and tells who is on each picture and what she is doing. (1D)

Use varied questioning techniques, i.e., "What is your name?," "What is your first name?" (1E)

GOAL 2. Begins to use language to adapt to environment
   A. Verbalizes personal needs and feelings
   B. Uses simple social amenities
   C. Relates personal information (name, address, etc.)

Suggested Activities

Role-play, having the children demonstrate to the class the type of emotions that they feel when they are hurt, angry, happy, sad, and so on. (2A)

Use riddles to discuss personal needs. I cut my finger, what do I need? My face is dirty, what do I need? I want to buy a dress, what do I need? I am thirsty, what do I need? (2A)

Introduce visitors and new children. Observe all courtesy during the class day, during such activities as snack time, lunch time, birthday parties, and the like. Greet the bus driver, attendants, and therapists. Try to talk to each child individually sometime during the class day. (2B)

Read Munroe Leaf's *Manners Can Be Fun.* Discuss good manners. Have each child make a poster illustrating one "good manner," which he shows to and tells the class about. Use pictures cut from magazines to illustrate poster. (2B)

Have children draw or make a "model" from a cardboard box of their homes. Have them include addresses on the picture or model. Have children talk about their home to the class, giving a description, general location (near the shopping center, etc.), and address. (2C)

Use role playing to elicit the name and address of the child, e.g., a policeman and a lost child, the school bus or a local bus where the child has to tell the driver where she wants to get off, a taxi ride to the child's house. (2C)

GOAL 3. Begins to use correct enunciation and grammatical form in self-expression
        A. Uses simple sentences correctly
        B. Asks simple questions correctly
        C. Attempts to say words clearly when corrected

Suggested Activities

Use a "Lotto" game to elicit answers to questions such as, "Who has a bird?" "I have the bird." "Who has the wagon with the missing wheel?" "I have the wagon with the missing wheel?" (3A)

Use a surprise box to encourage development of questioning techniques. Each child would be in charge of the box at one time or another as he guesses what is in the box. The class has to ask questions such as, Is it red? Is it big? The child in charge will answer the questions. (3B)

Have the children engage in role playing. One child is a policeman and another child is lost. The lost child and the policeman have to ask and answer questions such as, What is your name? Where do you live? Where is your mother? (3B)

Use a modified TV-type quiz show to stimulate verbal questioning, e.g., a show like "What's My Line?" (What community helper am I?) The panel attempts to guess the community helper by asking questions while the contestant answers the questions or uses pantomime to stimulate the panel. (3B)

GOAL 4. Begins to use language for enjoyment
        A. Recites simple nursery rhymes and sings simple songs
        B. Converses with others

Suggested Activities

Have some children pantomime the Mother Goose rhymes as the class recites them. (4A)

Use a tape recorder while children are singing or participating in a choral speaking activity. As they listen to the replay, they could act out the verse or song. (4A)

Sing songs that have some sort of action in them or in which each child could sing her own part herself, i.e., "The Muffin Man," "Five Little Ducks That I Once Knew," "Old McDonald." (4A)

Sing songs such as "Old McDonald" and show pictures of animals as songs are sung. (4A)

Use flannel board cues. Play a record several times so that the children are acquainted with a song. Place felt picture cues on the flannel board as they occur in the song and point to them as they are repeated. Encourage the children to sing along. A child may place the pieces on the flannel board for the others to follow or as an independent activity. (4A)

Have a class discussion, recalling the day's activities. Encourage children to talk freely with each other during the discussion. (4B)

Make a bulletin board or conversation center of "good things to talk about." Place items of high interest on the board or table, and provide specific times that the children may talk with each other about them. New toys, books, pictures of exciting school or community events, plants, etc., could be used for the conversation center. (4B)

THE INTERMEDIATE LEVEL

Development of Receiving Skills
Intermediate Level (10–12 Years)

Receiving

1. Develops fine discrimination of speech sounds
    A. Discriminates between most speech sounds (e.g., f from th, s from sh)
    B. Makes fine discrimination in pitch, quality, intensity, and rhythm of speech, music, and nature
2. Develops appropriate listening skills and behavior
    A. Understands two-to-three-step verbal directions
    B. Listens for specific information (e.g., information in a story, a weather forecast, an announcement)
    C. Maintains eye contact with speaker
    D. Listens attentively to members of peer group in conversation or formal class participation (e.g., student oral report, show-and-tell)
    E. Listens attentively in formal group situations (e.g., theater, church, school assembly)
    F. Begins to respond appropriately to social amenities

3. Attaches meanings to more complex actions, nonverbal activities, and conversation
   A. Understands complex gestures such as motions, pantomime, hand signals
   B. Attaches meaning to facial expressions
   C. Understands the verbal communication of those in primary group and some from secondary group
   D. Attaches meaning to a wide variety of events and situations encountered
4. Attaches meaning to a variety of environmental sounds. Knows that certain sounds mean danger, that certain sounds require specific action, such as school bells, fire bells, alarm clock, etc.

Receiving

GOAL 1. Develops fine discrimination of speech sounds
   A. Discriminates between most speech sounds (e.g., f from th, s from sh)
   B. Makes fine discrimination in pitch, quality, intensity, and rhythm of speech, music, and nature

Suggested Activities

Read a story or paragraph to the class making intentional sound errors. Ask the children to raise their hands when they hear a sound error and then give the correct sound. (1A)

Work on a new sound every 10 days (e.g., /b/). Label everything starting with /b/ in the room. Find pictures that begin with /b/ (baby, balloon). Set up a bulletin board of /b/ objects. Adapt games to responses starting with /b/. (1A)

Have a word written on cards. Child must use initial sound of word correctly before he can put the card down (version of "Pitty Pat" card game). (1A)

Introduce a story that uses a particular sound frequently. Do not name or stress the sound directly to the class, as the first day's activities are aimed at creating an interest in the story as well as impressing the children with the specific sound. (1A)

Relate particular sound drilled on to classroom activities. Find things in classroom that contain the /s/ sound. (1A)

Use choral speaking to help children hear correct articulation sounds in words. Have children listen and watch as the teacher makes the sound, then imitate it. This can be taped and children can listen for words said correctly. (1A)

Play rhyming game. Start a word like "bake." Each person must give a new word that rhymes with "bake." (1A)

Draw attention to and talk about differences and similarities in sounds, words, phrases, environmental sounds, street sounds, and classroom sounds that children hear each day. (1A)

"I'm thinking of a word beginning with —." Be sure to say a sound and not a letter. The children have three guesses. If a child guesses correctly, she can say a new sound. If no one guesses after three chances, the teacher chooses someone to continue the game. (1A)

"End and begin." First child says a word. The next child says a word, but it must begin with the sound that the first word ended with. It is fun to see how long this activity can continue without a mistake. (1A)

Tape-record various sounds in the home, school, playground, and so on. Have children identify them. Have children make up story using the sounds on the tape. (1B)

Play parts of popular music and ask children to identify songs. (1B)

Have children put heads down on desk and attempt to identify sounds (e.g., voice of another pupil, musical instruments). (1B)

Have children put heads down on desks. Toss pennies around the room. Have them see if they can locate where the pennies fall without looking up. (1B)

Collect records of songs that are high, low, fast, slow, loud, and soft. Play them and have children categorize them accordingly. (1B)

GOAL 2. Develops appropriate listening skills and behavior
    A. Understands two- to three-step verbal directions
    B. Listens for specific information (e.g., information in a story, a weather forecast, an announcement)
    C. Maintains eye contact with speaker
    D. Listens attentively to members of peer group in conversation or formal class participation (e.g., student oral report, show-and-tell)
    E. Listens attentively in formal group situations (e.g., theater, church, school assembly)
    F. Begins to respond appropriately to social amenities

Suggested Activities

Have children carry out simple directions individually. Tasks should be varied and interesting and amusing enough so that there is attentive listening (e.g., Comb your hair. Brush your teeth. Cross your legs.). (2A)

Have children see if they can carry out a set of directions in an art lesson (e.g., Take your black crayon, draw a circle and color it black and red.).

Play a following directions game. Boys are called red and girls are called green. When teacher says green, girls follow directions (e.g., Red: stand up and turn around. Green: clap hands and touch your head.). (2A)

Provide opportunities for children to follow directions throughout the day (e.g., Put a piece of chalk on the teacher's desk.).

Gradually, increase the difficulty of the oral instructions (e.g., Go to the cupboard. Go to the cupboard and get me a book. Go to the cupboard and get me the red book.). (2A)

Have children write words, short phrases, and sentences from dictation. (2B)

Read the complete weather report to children. Ask one child to listen for the temperature, another child the winds, another the clouds, and so on, so that they can repeat them back to the class. (2B)

Read simple problem (e.g., David has four balls. The balls cost 25 cents. The balls are red and blue.). Ask questions: (1) How many balls does David have? (2) What do the balls cost? (3) What color are the balls? (2B)

Explain to children that having eye contact with speakers helps them to listen better. Practice having children establish and maintain eye contact by speaking to them while holding a card or sheet of paper over the mouth. (2C)

Conduct a staring contest. Divide the children into pairs, and have the children stare at each other. The first child to laugh or break the stare loses. (2C)

Have child listen to and retell in his own words recorded short stories and anecdotes. (2D)

Assign simple oral reports on topics of interest. Have children prepare and give the reports before the class. These reports can be recorded on tape and listened to at later dates to check improvement, retention of content, and so on. (2D)

Take children to assemblies, concerts, possibly the theater. Discuss good listening habits and skills before attending the affairs. Make poster that illustrates good listening habits; post it in the room. Make a chart that checks how well each child conformed to the listening habits on the poster. Check the chart after attendance at the affairs. Ask questions about the content to check attentiveness and comprehension. (2E)

Show filmstrips "Manners at School," and "Manners in the Neighborhood" to show children appropriate responses to social amenities. (2F)

Make a tape of simple social comments that require children to make responses. Make the comment, then leave blank tape to allow time for child to make response; next record statement that will tell child whether her response was correct or not. For example, teacher says, on tape, "Hello, Mary. My, you look nice today." (Child responds orally during blank tape lasting from 30 seconds to 1 minute.) Teacher then says, "If you said something like 'hello,' or 'hi,' and also said 'thank you,' then you said the right thing." A variety of common social comments may be used. (2F)

GOAL 3. Attaches meanings to more complex actions, nonverbal activities, and conversation
   A. Understands complex gestures such as motions, pantomime, hand signals
   B. Attaches meaning to facial expressions
   C. Understands the verbal communication of those in primary group and some from secondary group

D. Attaches meaning to a wide variety of events and situations encountered

Suggested Activities

Have children play simple charades. Devise a set of gestures and signals that mean certain things, which they must use in the charades. (3A)

Discuss common motions and signals that are used in football, baseball, traffic, etc. Role-play situations that will require the use of these signals. (3A)

Draw cartoon faces on an overhead projector. Have children talk about the facial expressions and the meaning that is conveyed by them. (3B)

Make a scrapbook of pictures of faces that show feeling. Discuss the differences in feelings, and how one can discern different feelings through facial expressions. (3B)

Play a "making faces" game. Assign each child to make a face that shows anger, fear, happiness, etc. Have the other children guess what feeling is being conveyed by the face. (3B)

Form a class club. Have children formulate plans for social affairs, solving problems, and planning projects, giving them opportunity for constructive discussion together. (3C)

Role play situations that require children to listen carefully and listen to the communications of others, e.g., situations involving parents, school authorities, check-out clerks in stores, etc. (3C)

Watch designated television shows together. Discuss the words and content of the shows. Weather and newscasts, special events, and educational programs may be used.

GOAL 4. Attaches meaning to a variety of environmental sounds. Knows that certain sounds mean danger, that certain sounds require specific action such as school bells, fire bells, alarm clocks, etc.

Suggested Activities

Record a variety of environmental sounds on a tape, leaving 1 or 2 minutes between sounds. Provide children with a dittoed sheet that has pictures of the way people respond to the sounds. Have children mark the appropriate picture as they hear the sound. Instructions may be given on tape to mark the picture that shows what people do when they hear this sound with a red crayon; or circle the picture that goes with this sound, etc. Sounds such as alarm clocks, telephones, dogs barking fiercely, and the like may be used. (4)

Development of Thinking Skills
Intermediate Level (10–12 Years)

Thinking

1. Categorizes, labels, and associates names and symbols of people, places, and events
   A. Categorizes familiar symbols into classes (bananas, oranges, and apples are fruit; baseball and football are games, etc.)
   B. Differentiates between opposites
   C. Recognizes synonyms
   D. Notices similarities and differences
   E. Knows that there are words that sound the same but have different meanings (blue–blew, red–read, etc.)
2. Associates a wider variety of words with feelings (sorry, worry, angry)
3. Continues to develop the ability to arrange experiences into sequential order
   A. Extends understanding of time and space relationship (e.g., past, present, future, days, weeks, months, seasons, far, near)
   B. Finishes incomplete sentences, events, and stories logically
4. Increases in the development of problem-solving techniques
   A. Asks questions to gain information to solve problems
   B. Begins to discriminate between relevant and irrelevant
   C. Information, fact from fantasy
5. Understands some of the basic grammatical forms that govern language usage
   A. Correctly formulates statements comparing two objects
   B. Correctly formulates negative statements
6. Increases ability to memorize simple rote information
   A. Recites six- to eight-line poems and songs for enjoyment
   B. Knows important and vital information (such as bus schedules, birthdate, etc.)

SUGGESTED LANGUAGE AND SPEECH
PROGRAM FOR INTERMEDIATE
GROUP (10–12 YEARS)

Thinking

GOAL 1. Categorizes, labels, and associates names and symbols of people, places, and events
      A. Categorizes familiar symbols into classes (bananas, oranges, and apples are fruit; baseball and football are games, etc.)

    B.   Differentiates between opposites

    C.   Recognizes synonyms

    D.   Notices similarities and differences

    E.   Knows that there are words that sound the same but have different meanings (blue–blew, red–read, etc.)

Suggested Activities

Divide class into two groups as in a spelling bee. Give each team a category, such as animal, fruit, vegetable, etc. Have team members take turns giving names of items in the proper category, as in a spelling bee. When a member misses, it counts only as a point against the team but does not eliminate the member from the game. (1A)

    Take a trip to the grocery store. Go to the vegetable, cereal, fruit, frozen foods, and other departments. After the trip, have children name as many things as possible that they saw in each department. (1A)

    Place boxes or sacks on a table in the room. Have the boxes labeled with category words, such as animals, people, fruit, dishes, birds, clothes, and the like. Have children select pictures or small toys from an assortment into the correct boxes or sacks. (1A)

    Ask children to name as many items as they can that would be found in a school gym, a filling station, a restaurant, an art room, an auditorium, and so on. (1A)

    Each child has a 6-inch by 6-inch light cardboard card in front of him. On each side of the square is written an answer to one or more of the teacher's questions. Each child responds by holding the correct edge of the card up. This way all children must react to the question. The teacher, at a glance, can find those with the wrong answer.

Example for
categories (1A)

    d. Flowers   a. Cars   c. Clothes

    b. Furniture

Compile a group of pictures illustrating various emotions such as anger, happiness, sadness. Assign a word conveying a feeling to each child. Have each child find a picture showing this feeling. As children display their pictures have them tell why they made that choice. (1C)

    Have a contest for finding synonyms. Divide the class into groups, assigning each group a word for which they are to find as many synonyms as possible. The group that finds the most synonyms wins the contest. (1C)

    Read short stories to children. Stop frequently and discuss the words. Ask children to think of words they could change in the sentences without changing the meaning, e.g., "The building was very tall" might be changed to, "The building was very high." (1C)

Use real objects to help children develop meanings and concepts of tactile words, e.g., rough (sandpaper, bark, etc.), smooth (piece of lumber, glass, etc.). (1D)

Read pairs of words that sound similar but differ slightly. Encourage children to listen for and identify the differences and similarities in the words, e.g., dream–drink begin the same but end differently; boy and joy rhyme, end the same, but begin differently; store and stare begin the same, etc. (1D)

Make a list of homonyms on the board. Have the child choose a set of homonyms and use each one in a sentence. (1E)

GOAL 2. Associates a wider variety of words with feelings (sorry, worry, angry)

Suggested Activities

Have children role-play meaningful situations that will provide opportunities for them to demonstrate how actions and words elicit feelings, e.g., children might be picking flowers as they wait for the bus. The lady who planted the flowers discovered them. The lady is angry and scolds them; the children are frightened, and finally remorseful and apologetic. They should be helped to use appropriate words that convey feelings the situations demand. (2)

Have words that depict various moods written on strips of paper. Pass the strips of paper to the children and have them act out the mood. Have the other children guess what mood is being portrayed. Use words such as worried, sad, mad, tired, etc. (2)

Write questions on separate slips of paper. Place questions in a box. Have children draw slips and respond to the questions by making appropriate sounds. Use questions such as, "What sound would you make if you were unhappy?" "What sound would you make if you had a cold?" "What sound would you make if you heard a funny story?" (2)

GOAL 3. Continues to develop the ability to arrange experiences into sequential order
  A. Extends understanding of time and space relationship, e.g., past, present, future, days, weeks, months, far, near
  B. Finishes incomplete sentences, events, and stories logically

Suggested Activities

Play games in which one child acts out teacher's directions (or directions given on phonograph or tape recorder) which involve these concepts relating to space:

```
up      — down      high  — low
in      — out       top   — bottom
inside  — outside   front — back
on      — off
```
(3A)

Put slips of paper in a box on which the days of the week are written. Have a child draw one and use it in a sentence, e.g., "Sunday, I went to church." (3A)

Name the days of the week in sequence. Then have pupils associate each day with events of personal significance. (3A)

Play hiding games in which participants must give or respond to hints regarding the location of hidden objects. Emphasize words relating to space, e.g., under, over, higher, lower, left, right, above, beneath, below, near, far, forward, back, behind, in front of, beginning, end. (3A)

Read the following sentences to be completed by children:

In the morning we eat _____ .

At night we go to _____ .

We go home to eat _____ .

Yesterday we came to _____ .

Tomorrow we will come to _____ .

It gets dark at _____ .

In the afternoon after school we _____ . (3A)

Discuss all the things children do in: morning, afternoon, evening. (3A)

Put three paper bags in front of the room. They should be of three different sizes, and numbered 1, 2, and 3. Show children items of different sizes and have children identify items and decide which bag would hold them. (3A)

Have children sit in a circle. The teacher or a child starts off with a word such as "Stanley." The next child adds a new word repeating the first, as "Stanley was." Each child adds a new word until a sentence is given. The game can be continued until a complete story about the initial word is completed. (3B)

Read three or four lines of an unknown story or verse to the children, who then supply endings. These may be original or existing stories. (3B)

Have children complete sentences, e.g.,

Mrs. Brown is your _____ .

Your teacher is _____ .

You come to school for five _____ .

For 5 days you come to _____ .

You live in a _____ .

A house is where you _____ . (3B)

Have one child begin telling a story. Stop the first child suddenly and point to someone else in the group who is to continue. Have second player add a few lines to the story and stop him. Second player points to someone else to continue the story. (3B)

Use filmstrips without dialogue and have class formulate dialogue as filmstrip is being shown, e.g., Row Peterson's *Tell Another Story.* (3B)

GOAL 4.   Increases in the development of problem-solving techniques
        A.   Asks questions to gain information to solve problems
        B.   Begins to discriminate between relevant and irrelevant information, fact and fantasy

Suggested Activities

Have a problem-solving discussion centered around difficulties that can be prevented by learning and knowing rules, e.g., playground field trip, cooking experience. (4A)

Have a child make three statements to describe something she sees. Other children guess what is being described by asking questions such as: Do you see a boy? (4A)

Have children give short "newscasts" over a play or real microphone about personal or news items that they can share with classmates. Have the listeners answer pertinent questions about what they have heard. Teacher or the "newscaster" may ask the questions. (4A)

Have children listen while one child tells a spontaneous story. If a listener believes this is a true story, he puts the caption "true tale" on his desk. If a listener recognizes it as a tall tale, he displays a "tall-tale" caption. If the speaker rambles from one type of story to another, listeners are to place a hand over caption. (4A)

Have one child relate a real or imaginary event. Ask the other members of the class to guess whether it is fact or fantasy. (4B)

Play a game similar to the TV show "To Tell the Truth" in which the children are quizzed by each other and may answer with true or false answers. Have a panel who decide whether the content of what they hear is true or untrue. (4B)

Write a short description of some familiar object or person on the chalkboard. Ask the pupils to read the description silently, then to name what or who has been described, e.g., "This object is made of wood; it has a square, flat top and four legs." (table) "He is a boy; he has blue eyes, dark hair, and writes right-handed." (Bill) (4B)

Put a set of words or pictures on board (e.g., cow–horse, car–truck) and have children list what these sets have in common (leg–ears, wheel–engine). (4B)

Have class name all the things they think of when you say a familiar word, e.g., green, round, bumpy, wet, etc. (4B)

GOAL 5. Understands some of the basic grammatical forms that govern language usage
   A.   Correctly formulates statements comparing two objects
   B.   Correctly formulates negative statements

Suggested Activities

Demonstrate the meaning of a preposition for class by placing an object such as a pencil, a handkerchief, or a book in various places *emphasizing the preposition with the action,* e.g., place the pencil *in* the drawer, *on* the table, *under* the table, *on* your head, and so on. (5)

Write groups of words on the blackboard. Have children rearrange in proper order, e.g.,
   (a)   window man the opens the
   (b)   man paper the reads the old
   (c)   wooden on green desk plant the put the (5)

Use a language or speech box. Place various objects inside the box. Have a youngster choose an object from the box and say a short sentence about it, e.g., if object is a bird, the sentence might be, "A bird can fly." (5)

Make a word dice game, putting words on four sides of dice. Have children see if they can make sentences out of the dice words that appear after they have rolled the dice. Points may be given for each sentence made. (5)

Place two objects on a table. Help children compare and describe them in relation to each other, e.g., "This is the small book, this one is larger." By adding additional objects, the context may be changed requiring youngsters to make more complex comparisons. Adding another book of the same size as one already on the table, but of different color, for example, would require an additional variable. (5A)

Play a game involving a variety of familiar objects that requires children to answer questions with statements such as, "No, this is not a bicycle." "These are not people." "I'm not a girl." (5B)

GOAL 6. Increases ability to memorize simple rote information
   A.   Recites six- to eight-line poems and songs for enjoyment

B. Knows important and vital information (such as bus schedules, birthdate, etc.)

Suggested Activities

Use clichés and familiar sayings to facilitate recall, e.g., teacher writes sayings on board leaving a blank space. Children are to supply the word from rote recall.

1. Light as a _____ (feather)

2. Blind as a _____ (bat)

3. Wise as an _____ (owl)

4. Cool as a _____ (cucumber)

5. Bright as a _____ (penny)

6. Hot as a _____ (firecracker)

7. Green as _____ (grass)

8. Old as _____ (Methuselah)

9. Dumb as an _____ (ox)

10. Heavy as _____ (lead)

11. Green as _____ (Jolly Green Giant)

12. Young as _____ (Pepsi generation) (6A)

Teach children popular songs, favorite camp, Scout, and seasonal songs. Provide opportunities for them to sing them before the class, other classes, or parents. (6A)

Tell jokes that require complete recall. (6A)

Use TV commercials to test recall. (6A)

Place a series of drawings of coins on the board. Have children look at them, then cover and have them see if they can name the coins written on board. (6B)

Write a short sentence on the board that the class can read aloud, such as, "I answered the front doorbell." Have class read it a few times aloud, then have them say the sentence looking away from the board. (6B)

Have class listen to a series of numbers or words said by teacher. See if pupils can repeat them. Begin with three numbers or words. Gradually increase the length of the series. (6B)

Have class look up a telephone number of a particular store; have them look at number, then close book quickly, and call on someone to repeat the telephone number. (6B)

Intermediate Level (10–12 Years)

Expressing

1. Responds verbally to meet the demands of an expanding environment
   A. Increases vocabulary
   B. Describes experiences more accurately and completely
   C. Begins to use elaboration in his conversation, i.e., uses more detail in relating events and ideas
   D. Begins to gain and give information through questioning and discussion
2. Uses language to meet social needs
   A. Gives vital information accurately (name, address, birthdate, parents' names, etc.)
   B. Responds appropriately to questions
   C. Begins to use the telephone for communication
   D. Verbalizes feelings and emotions
   E. Delivers simple messages
   F. Extends use of social amenities (handles simple introductions, excuse me, I am sorry)
3. Begins to use acceptable language patterns
   A. Uses correct elementary grammatical constructions
   B. Speaks comfortably and intelligibly in interpersonal and small group situations
   C. Gives oral reports using four to ten sentences
4. Uses language for enjoyment
   A. Participates in role playing and simple skits
   B. Recites poems and songs of several verses
   C. Converses with friends freely on topics of mutual interest

SUGGESTED LANGUAGE AND SPEECH PROGRAM FOR INTERMEDIATE GROUP (10–12 YEARS)

Expressing

GOAL 1. Responds verbally to meet the demands of an expanding environment
   A. Increases vocabulary
   B. Describes experiences more accurately and completely
   C. Begins to use elaboration in conversation, i.e., uses more detail in relating events and ideas

D. Begins to gain and give information through questioning and discussion

Suggested Activities

Use a modified TV-type quiz show to stimulate children's use of spoken vocabulary, e.g., "What's My Line" or "To Tell the Truth," in which panel participates and attempts to guess the particular community worker pantomimed or portrayed by the contestant. (1A)

Expose class to a new situation, e.g., a smorgasbord or beach facility or gadgets brought in by teacher. Teacher introduces the new vocabulary and provides an opportunity for the class to use this new vocabulary. (1A)

Write experience chart story with class participation on new experiences, e.g., field trip. Have child circle new words as teacher says them. Reward children with candy treat for correct response. (1A)

Use riddles to increase vocabulary, such as

She helps sick people. (She is a *doctor.*)

He puts out fires. (He is a *fireman.*)

Use pictures of animals, cars, trains, and planes. Ask questions such as

Which is the fastest? (slowest, largest)

Which are animals?

Put various objects in a box and have children close their eyes as they take turns pulling an object out of box. With eyes closed, have the children describe the object from the sense of touch. (1B)

Have children tell routine of each day, recall jobs they have done, experiences they have shared. (1B)

Ask child to look at a colorful magazine picture. Then ask him to tell a story to the class from the picture. Ask the child to keep in mind what happened before, during, and after the picture. When story is completed, ask the class if they agree, or would they change the story in any way. (1B)

GOAL 2. Uses language to meet social needs

    A. Gives vital information accurately (name, address, birthdate, parents' names, etc.)

    B. Responds appropriately to questions

    C. Begins to use the telephone for communication

    D. Verbalizes feelings and emotions

    E. Delivers simple messages

    F. Extends use of social amenities (handles simple introductions, excuse me, I am sorry)

Suggested Activities

Scramble the seven digits of child's phone number. Have her unscramble it. (2A)

Put house numbers on one side of chalkboard and street names on the other. Have children match their addresses with their street names. (2A)

Write the names of the streets that the children live on and ask each one to come to the board and circle his or her street. (2A)

Develop a list of questions (e.g., What time is it? Where do you live?) Use these questions to play a game. Children must answer in full sentences. (2B)

Give verbal absurdities in sentences in order to get appropriate responses, e.g., Can meatballs fly? Do boys run? (2B)

Obtain Tele Trainer set up from the Bell Telephone Company. Practice phone courtesy and telephone conversation. (2C)

Use Bell Telephone booklet, "How to Get Help" and Tele Trainer set-up. Discuss how to dial and whom to call in each type of emergency. Then give each child an opportunity to make a call for an emergency situation. (2C)

Have class make a list of sounds boys and girls can make (e.g., laugh, cry, talk, whistle, sneeze, cough, mumble, moan, scream, hiccup, snore, whine, hum, and giggle). Ask a child to make one of the sounds. Another child must come to the board and point to the word imitated. (2D)

Use role playing. Have two children act out a certain emotion (e.g., fighting, anger). Have class discuss a better way of handling the situation. (2D)

Use pictures showing people in various situations (e.g., crying). Class discusses the situation, why the person feels the way she does, and what they would do in this situation. (2D)

Whisper simple directions to the first person in a circle and have him whisper it to the next person and so on. The last person must stand up and follow the direction. You can use such directions as

1. Go to the blackboard. 2. Spin around. 3. Touch your nose. (2E)

Send child to another teacher with a verbal message requiring an answer. (2E)

Role-play. Members of class assume roles of different people (e.g., mother, teacher). Practice introducing the character to various class members. (2F)

Teacher tells brief story with a nonsense ending (e.g., While walking down the street I bumped into a lady. I said, "Thank You." What did I do wrong? Have children retell story correctly. (2F)

Develop bulletin board to stress use of social amenities calling good manner words, "magic" words. Have cards with please, thank you, excuse me, on the bulletin board. Explain to children that these words are like magic because they can suddenly change the way that others feel. (2F)

GOAL 3. Begins to use acceptable language patterns

      A. Uses correct elementary grammatical construction

B. Speaks comfortably and intelligibly in interpersonal and small group situations

C. Gives oral reports using four to ten sentences.

Suggested Activities

Use puppets to stimulate group into oral discussion (e.g., have puppets introduce new words using them correctly in sentences). (3A)

Place nouns on board (house, ball, dog, boy, etc.). Ask children to tell about the nouns: size, color, pretty, ugly, mean, nice, etc. Develop adjective use. (3A)

Make word cards of nouns (places-things) and make action cards (run-running, walk-walking, play, eat, sing). If child is nonreader, then use pictures of nouns and actions. Have child take word card from each pile and make a sentence from the two words. (3A)

Say sentence using incorrect grammar. Have class try to pick out errors and repeat the sentence correctly. (3A)

Give students a topic (e.g., talk about trees) after a spontaneous talk; members of the class discuss and criticize the talk. (3B)

Have children take turns teaching a familiar concept to the class, such as pasting, cutting, throwing a ball. Have the child describe verbally how the activity is to be performed using any visual aids he needs. (3B)

Put up different pictures that show people at various activities or moods. Have the pupils make their own story orally about the people that they choose. (3C)

Assign different TV programs such as news, sports, weather, or a favorite show for children to watch. Have individual children tell about the show the following day. (3C)

Set up corner in the room with a new picture every day focusing on a high interest item. Give each child a chance to give an oral report about the picture. (3C)

GOAL 4. Uses language for enjoyment
   A. Participates in role playing and simple skits
   B. Recites poems and songs of several verses
   C. Converses with friends freely on topics of mutual interest

Suggested Activities

Use role play to increase general vocal ability. Have children do role playing to such situations as

1. Learning to meet new people, responding to and making introductions

2. Answering the telephone correctly

3. Answering the door bell and responding to strangers, i.e., salespersons, postman, cleaners, etc.

4. Being a radio or TV announcer, i.e., disc jockey

5. Asking directions to get to specific places (4A)

Allow children to appear in school assembly program. With another special class, prepare a small program for regular grades. (4B)

Make puppets of socks or paper maché. Learn poem or song and allow puppets to recite poem or song. Give children a chance to handle puppets and recite. (4B)

Have an exhibit of art and craft work. Have children show work and tell about it to visitors to the exhibit. (4C)

Set up a hobby corner. Allow two children at a time to use the corner to inspect the materials. This can be done after work is completed. This encourages conversation in an area of mutual interest. (4C)

THE SECONDARY LEVEL

Development of Receiving Skills
Secondary Level (13–18 Years)

Receiving

1. Uses fine-sound discrimination functionally
   A. Hears and evaluates own speech performance
   B. Hears and evaluates speech performance of others
   C. Recognizes feelings conveyed by voice, intonation, and the subtleties of speech, e.g., Look out! (danger); Look out. (watch)
   D. Attaches appropriate meaning to environmental sounds
2. Uses good adult listening skills, habits, and courtesies
   A. Listens attentively when others are speaking
   B. Listens for the purpose of remembering
   C. Understands four- to six-step verbal direction
   D. Remembers verbally described people, places, pictures, events, and objects in a sequential order
   E. Responds appropriately to common social amenities
   F. Demonstrates appropriate listening behavior and skill as a part of an audience
3. Understands a wide variety of verbal and nonverbal cues that enable him to meet situations adequately

A. Appraises the intent of strangers through their facial expressions, gestures, and voice intonations
B. Understands a technical vocabulary to satisfy vocational and social needs
C. Understands the verbal communication of those in his secondary group in a wide variety of situations

SUGGESTED LANGUAGE AND SPEECH PROGRAM FOR SECONDARY GROUP (13–18 YEARS)

Receiving

GOAL 1. Uses fine sound discrimination functionally
A. Hears and evaluates own speech performance
B. Hears and evaluates speech performance of others
C. Recognizes feelings conveyed by voice, intonation, and the subtleties of speech, e.g., Look out! (danger); Look out. (watch)

Suggested Activities

Use tape recorder, Language Master, or other machine that will allow recording and play-back of pupils' voices. Have pupils listen for errors, improvements, and voice quality. (1A)

Divide class into pairs. Assign each pair of youngsters a topic. Have them plan short "minute" talks about their topic. Have them practice together, evaluating and criticizing each other's speech. Finally, have each pair present their talks to the whole class. (1B)

Have speakers come in and talk to the students about a variety of topics, such as teenage fashion, driving skills, sports, etc. Have students discuss the speeches and make some appraisal of them. (1B)

Have drama or speech students come to the classroom. Have them give readings and skits that show emotions and subtleties of expression. Have students listen particularly for subtle sounds that add to the emotional impact of the readings, e.g., shaking, quivering, or cracking voice, loud or soft sounds, stammering, etc. (1C)

Use recording of three people saying same sentences showing different emotions, e.g., "hello" said showing surprise, anger, anxiety, etc. Have student answer question related to the way the speaker seemed to feel. (1C)

Have students discriminate among three sounds, one of which will answer a question. Which would a waitress hear at work? (umpire yelling, customer placing an order, buzzing saw). (1D)

GOAL 2. Uses good adult listening skills, habits, and courtesies
A. Listens attentively when others are speaking
B. Listens for the purpose of remembering
C. Remembers verbally described people, places, pictures, events, and objects in a sequential order
D. Understands four- to six-step verbal directions
E. Responds appropriately to common social amenities
F. Demonstrates appropriate listening behavior and skill as a part of an audience

Suggested Activities

Read stories or other material; give true–false or multiple choice tests after the youngsters have heard the material. Youngsters may be informed in advance of certain information for which they must listen in order to take the test. (2A)

Assign report topics that will require students to listen attentively, remember what they have heard, and report back to the class, e.g., listening to a news broadcast, interviewing the principal or a new student in school, listening to a recorded story or a book review. (2A)

Discuss the importance of listening while others speak, on the job, in social situations, etc. Make a list of good listening skills and have students use this as a check sheet for references as they attempt to develop and improve their listening skills. (2A)

Play "the whisper game." Have youngsters pass verbal messages from one to another by whispering. The last youngster to receive the message repeats it aloud. (2B)

Use toy or real telephones. Have students practice giving and taking telephone messages through role play situations. (2B)

Play games that require following directions, e.g., finding hidden objects in the room. (2B)

Discuss the importance of following directions in jobs, social situations, fire drills, etc. (2B)

Have children listen to and carry out instructions for student-directed activities such as arranging chairs, putting up a ladder, and so on. (2B)

Have pupils complete worksheets that require the ability to follow verbal directions. (2B)

Prepare tape-recorded lessons, which require the youngsters to listen to and follow four- to six-step verbal directions. (2C)

Assign weekly jobs in the school and classroom with four- to six-step directions. (2C)

Cut comic strips, printed sentences, and illustrations from books into parts. Have students practice placing them in sequential order. (2D)

Read paragraphs of a simple story or directions for performing a skill in mixed-up order. Have students retell in sequential order. (2D)

Dramatize and role-play social situations that stress the use of social amenities, e.g., telephone conversations, job interviews, opening doors, bumping into someone, etc. (2E)

Provide opportunities for children to attend assemblies, programs, and other situations requiring them to be a part of an audience. (2F)

Make a chart showing illustrations of how to behave in audience situations. Illustrate such things as sitting quietly, listening to and watching the speaker or stage, and so on. (2F)

Require children to give brief reports on the things they saw and heard as a part of an audience. (2F)

GOAL 3.   Understands a wide variety of verbal and nonverbal cues that enable him to meet situations adequately
A.   Appraises the intent of strangers through their facial expressions, gestures, and voice intonation
B.   Understands a technical vocabulary to satisfy vocational and social needs
C.   Understands the verbal communication of those in his secondary group in a wide variety of situations

Suggested Activities

Listen to a tape recording of an interview and check off the important items covered. (3B)

Make a list of terminology applicable to specific jobs. Discuss the meanings of the terms, how they are used, and provide practice in using them. Include the names of tools and equipment, mannerisms and technical terms, e.g., dock, dolly, cart, "Step to the rear of the car, please," bill of lading, shopping order. (3B)

Discuss and examine application blanks, social security forms, banking material, tax forms, etc. (3B)

Discuss the meaning of work mottos that employees may see or hear on the job, e.g., "Time is money," "A job worth doing is worth doing well," "The customer is always right," "We aim to please," "Plan ahead." (3C)

Development of Thinking Skills
Secondary Level (13–18 Years)

Thinking

1. Expands ability to categorize and classify meaning-symbols
   A. Categorizes symbols into larger more abstract categories (e.g., milk, water, tea, coke, and coffee are all liquid; or policeman, sheriff, governor, principal, and bosses are all authorities)
   B. Uses language to make assumptions
   C. Formulates generalizations
   D. Draws conclusions
2. Associates subtle language expressions with feelings and emotions (reacts to voice tone and inflection, facial expression, choice of words, gestures)
3. Develops systematic methods for organizing and retaining information
   A. Evaluates information to select relevant data
   B. Develops methods for learning new words (prefix, suffix, compound words, rhyming words)
   C. Retains several ideas simultaneously
      1. Formulates and gives directions
      2. Sees cause and effect relationships; understands sequence of events
      3. Sees interrelationships of ideas, events, and feelings
4. Uses language to solve problems effectively
   A. Knows how and where to ask questions when help is needed for clarification and information
   B. Interprets and analyzes unfamiliar situations, makes correct responses (meeting new people, emergency situations)
5. Continues to understand and use more of the basic grammatical forms important to standard language and speech
   A. Uses more verbs, adjectives, and adverbs than nouns in daily conversation
   B. Rewords ideas when not understood
   C. Can elaborate on ideas
6. Memorizes and automatically recalls pertinent information
   A. Knows important dates such as school graduation, birthdate, dates of employment
   B. Knows telephone numbers of family, friends, place of employment
   C. Knows social security number, zip code, address
7. Is aware that one's behavior may be influenced by persuasive language
   A. Recognizes some of the ways that advertising may influence him, e.g., "Be a He-Man"; "Only 2 left—Hurry!"; "Join the 'in' group."
   B. Becomes aware that people do not always mean what they say when there

is personal gain involved, e.g., "I'll do this only for you"; "I love you"; "I won't tell anybody."

C. Is aware that slogans are used to communicate ideas; e.g., "Equal Opportunity"; "Uncle Sam Needs You"; "Safety First."

SUGGESTED LANGUAGE AND SPEECH PROGRAM FOR SECONDARY GROUP (13-18 YEARS)

Thinking

GOAL 1. Expands ability to categorize and classify meaningful symbols
    A. Categorizes symbols into larger more abstract categories (e.g., milk, water, tea, coke, and coffee are all liquid; or policeman, sheriff, governor, principal, and bosses are all authorities)
    B. Uses language to make assumptions
    C. Formulates generalizations
    D. Draws conclusions

Suggested Activities

Make a bulletin board or chart illustrating how small categories and classifications fit into large categories; e.g., a policeman, sheriff, governor (men); a teacher, mother, cafeteria manager (women); a nurse and a doctor (medical; could be shown to all fit into the category of authority figures). (1A)

Discuss objects in the classroom or school, pointing out more abstract categories, suggesting that many different things are alike in one way, e.g., the vase, the window, the glasses that the teacher wears, the cover on the face of the clock, etc., are all different but could be grouped into one category, since they are all made from glass. Encourage pupils to look for common qualities in objects they see and to think of possible categories for them. (1A)

Play concept concentration game with concept cards of related words placed in two rows face down. Student turns over one card from one row (waitress) and another card from the other row (tray). She can keep cards if she can verbalize a way they relate to each other ("A waitress uses a tray on her job"). (1A)

Prepare seat work that has rows of pictures of objects that are alike in at least one way and one object that has no relationship to others. Require students to find the one that does not belong and to be able to tell how the others are alike. (1A)

Prepare short paragraphs for the pupils to read. Prepare written questions that will require the pupils to make assumptions and formulate generalizations, e.g., "John was running down the street, as fast as he could go. He ran so fast that he didn't even notice his friend Joe standing on the corner at the bus stop. He ran straight into Miller's Market, through the store, into the back room, and hung up his coat on the hook. Then he quickly put on an apron, as he looked at the clock on the wall."

Questions:

1. John was (a) being chased by someone, (b) late for work, or (c) mad at his friend Joe.
2. Joe was probably (a) waiting for a bus, (b) taking a walk, or (c) late for work.
3. John was (a) a little boy, (b) a big fat man, or (c) probably a teen-ager.

Questions may be true-false, multiple choice, or completion, and may be written or oral. Discussion that explores reasons for basing answers on certain assumptions or generalizations should follow. (1B-C)

Show thought-provoking or action-filled pictures on an opaque projector. Have pupils take a pointer, go to the projected image, and tell what they think is happening in the picture, why it is happening, and who it involves. Discuss. Ask pupils why they believe certain things about the picture. (1B-C)

Structure problem situations in which students must generalize about the realistic life goals of handicapped people. "John is very good at putting things together but doesn't read well. A good job for John would be_____. Why? A job not suited for John would be _____. Why?" (1C-D)

Read stories to youngsters that concern problem situations they might be confronted with, e.g., being lost at the state fair, losing a wallet, having a fight with a best friend, etc. Have youngsters try to think of different solutions to the problems that were presented in the stories; ask them what they would have done and why they would have taken certain action. (1D)

Have the pupils read unfinished stories. Let them finish the stories, orally or in written form. (1D)

GOAL 2. Associates subtle language expressions with feelings and emotions (reacts to voice tone and inflection, facial expression, choice of words, gestures)

Suggested Activities

Play a game with words or phrases that will illustrate how expression and inflection can add or change the meaning of words. Pupils are given one word or phrase, and asked to say it in a variety of ways. For example, a pupil might be asked to say the word "mother" as he would if (a) he was calling her to the telephone, (b) he was mad because she wouldn't let him go to a show, (c) he was sad because she was very ill, (d) he was teasing her, or (e) he was awakened suddenly in the night, was afraid, and was calling for her. Names, salutations, and commonly used phrases are especially good for this game. (2)

Record brief excerpts of dialogue from television shows. Have pupils listen to the excerpts and attempt to identify the emotion of the person who is talking. (2)

GOAL 3. Develops systematic methods for organizing and retaining information
  A. Evaluates information to select relevant data
  B. Develops methods for learning new words (prefix, suffix, compound words, rhyming words)
  C. Retains several ideas simultaneously
    1. Formulates and gives directions
    2. Sees cause and effect relationships—understands sequence of events
    3. Sees interrelationships of ideas, events, and feelings

Suggested Activities

Give students sets of directions for completing tasks. Include some superfluous information, some absurdities. Have pupils listen carefully to the directions once. Give directions a second time, and have pupils raise their hands when they hear unnecessary or absurd directions. As pupils develop ability to evaluate information, increase the difficulty by making the superfluous information more subtle. Initially directions might be similar to the following. Italicized portions should be identified by students as superfluous: "Deliver this message to Mrs. White in the room across the hall. *The room number is 180. Mrs. White has blue eyes.* Ask Mrs. White to read the message and write an answer to it. Wait for her answer. *Mrs. White will write an answer.* Return the message to me. My room number is 182." (3A)

Pose problems to the students that require them to determine information needed for solution, e.g., Betty and Mary have moved to a new neighborhood. They know that they will be taking a bus to school, but do not know where to catch it, what time it leaves, nor what number the bus is. They are going to call the school office to find out about the bus. What information will they need to do this? (the school telephone number, their address, time they need to be at school); or Mary is going to make herself a new dress. She is going to the store to buy the material for it. What information will she need? (her measurements, a pattern, the yardage required). (3A)

Discuss compound words. Illustrate how words can be changed into new words by adding to or combining words. Together, formulate a list of compound words that can be added to as they are discovered by the students in their reading or other work. (3B)

Have students make a word circle with one prefix or suffix on a tab extending beyond the circumference of the circle. The root words are written on the circle. By turning the dial, new words can be formed. (3B)

Play "fix-a-word," a card game that uses prefixes and suffixes. Make word cards, each card containing a familiar word that can be changed by the use of a prefix or suffix. Make cards with suffixes or prefixes on them. Each player is given three word cards; the other word cards are placed face down in the center of the table. All the suffix and prefix cards are placed face down on a separate stack in the center of the table. Each player draws from the suffix-prefix stack for the first turn (known as the "fix" stack). If the card he draws can be combined with one of his word cards to make a word, he places them together face up on the table; if not he may hold it or discard it. If he chooses to hold it, he may discard one of the words instead. At each turn, the players draw a card from either the word or the fix stack, and discard a card. Object of the game is to match words with prefixes or suffixes until all the cards in the players' hands are played. (3B)

Assign each student a topic for formulating and giving directions. Student must formulate and give directions orally to the class. He should be encouraged to practice following the directions himself before giving them to the class. Directions for going to a pupil's home, for making a cake-mix cake, or for doing a simple art project could be used for this activity. (3C1)

Spell a word from the class vocabulary list having a student pronounce the word and give (1) a synonym, (2) an antonym: "work; employment; leisure." (3C)

Show pupils high-interest, provocative pictures. Ask them to make up and tell short stories about events leading up to the situation shown in the pictures, and suggest what might happen next, e.g., a little boy crying, with torn clothing and a black eye; a teen-age girl offering her boyfriend a plate of homemade cookies; a Boy Scout being presented with a merit badge; or a group of boys swimming in a lake with an overturned boat beside them might be good pictures to elicit responses from the students. (3C2)

Give pupils examples of relationships, such as an orange is to a tree as a grape is to a vine, a baby is to cry as a man is to shout. After the pupils begin to see the relationships, give them the opportunity to fill in words. Say, for example, "Shoe is to foot as glove is to _____," or "Boy is to man as girl is to _____." (3C3)

GOAL 4. Uses language to solve problems effectively
   A. Knows how and where to ask questions when help is needed for clarification and information
   B. Interprets and analyzes unfamiliar situations, makes correct reponses (meeting people, emergency situation)

Suggested Activities

Give students problems to solve, but give them less information than they need for the solving. As student realizes that she does not have adequate information to solve the problem, help her formulate clear logical questions for finding the additional information. (4A)

Make use of job advertisements in newspapers. Have students (small groups of them) seek out an application for the job advertised. Students must utilize various informative sources such as phone directory. (4A)

Discuss the sources from which students can seek information they need, e.g., librarians, custodians, bosses, telephone operators, teachers, parents, store clerks, and the like. Take trips around the school to visit some of these people. Provide opportunities for students to ask for certain assigned information they need during these trips. Discuss the results of the information seeking afterward. (4A)

Prepare seat work comprised of completion questions, e.g. (1) If I wanted to find a good book about horses I would go to _____. (2) If I needed to know how much it costs to call long distance to Syracuse, I would _____ . (3) If I needed to know how much it costs to buy a driver's license I would call_____ ____ . (4A)

Role-play various emergency situations. (4B)

Make posters revolving around certain emergency situations. List dos and don'ts for such situations. Red Cross safety manuals, National Safety Council, Boy and Girl Scout handbooks, and so on can provide rules that can be adapted for use on the posters. (4B)

Practice using the telephone for unfamiliar or emergency situations. Use real telephone provided by the telephone company, or go outside the school and use pay telephones. (4B)

Plan simple social affairs or invite visitors into the classroom. Have students be hosts or hostesses, meeting guests and introducing each other. (4B)

GOAL 5. Continues to understand and use more of the basic grammatical forms important to standard language and speech
   A. Uses more verbs, adjectives, and adverbs than nouns in daily conversation
   B. Rewords ideas when not understood
   C. Can elaborate on ideas

Suggested Activities

Prepare worksheets that require students to select correct grammatical forms, e.g. (1) You (was, were) going to town (wasn't, weren't) you? (2) I (did, done) a good job on that paper. (3) I (saw, seen) a (real, very) good TV show last night. (5)

Discuss good grammatical forms. Have students write simple compositions. Check and correct the grammar, and have students rewrite the compositions. Finally, have them read them to the class. Provide them the opportunity to compare the first attempt with the corrected composition. (5)

GOAL 6. Memorizes and automatically recalls pertinent information
A. Knows important dates such as school graduation, birthdate, dates of employment
B. Knows telephone numbers of family, friends, place of employment
C. Knows social security number, zip code, address

Suggested Activities

Have students compile lists of important dates and other pertinent information. Have them memorize certain parts in a designated period of time; learn the first four items by Friday and be able to give that much in class without looking at your list, etc. Provide repeated practice periods for pupils to give the information they have learned. (6ABC)

Make individual personal telephone directories. Small personal directories can be obtained from the telephone company. Follow the same procedure as above, learning the number by sections, until all the important numbers are learned. (6ABC)

Have a test that requires students to give pertinent information from memory. Test can be oral or written. (6ABC)

Role-play interview situations, such as interviewing for a job, driver's license, opening a charge account, registering for the draft, etc., which will provide practice in recalling pertinent information. (6ABC)

GOAL 7. Is aware that one's behavior may be influenced by persuasive language
A. Recognizes some of the ways that advertising may influence, e.g., "Be a He-man."; "Only 2 left—Hurry!"; "Join the 'in' group!"
B. Becomes aware that people do not always mean what they say when there is personal gain involved, e.g., "I'll do this only for you." "I love you." "I won't tell anybody."
C. Is aware that slogans are used to communicate ideas, e.g., "Equal Opportunity"; "Uncle Sam Needs You"; "Safety First."

Suggested Activities

Clip phrases or entire ads, and project them on a screen. Have students select convincing words that are intended to influence buyers. Analyze words to discover the reasons for their use. (7A)

Take field trips into plants to observe whether the slogans advertised by the employers are being followed. Use current slogans such as: "More jobs for minority groups and women." "Equal opportunity." "Hire the handicapped for good business." (7B)

Clip parallel stories from various newspapers. Compare the treatment of the subject by selecting the specific words that are intended to "slant" meaning. (7C)

Role-play situations involving such social persuasions as: "For Adults Only," "Be one of the crowd," "Join the 'in' group," "Don't flake out," "I love you." Encourage different reactions to the same situations. (7D)

Development of Expression Skills
Secondary Level (13–18 Years)

Expressing

1. Uses appropriate speech and language to meet social and occupational demands
   A. Increases vocabulary to include many work-related terms such as foreman, check, time-clock, double time, and so on.
   B. Uses socially acceptable speech and language forms in a variety of situations, e.g., doesn't swear in mixed company, chooses acceptable topics for conversation, doesn't dominate conversations, etc.
   C. Regulates pitch, rate, and volume appropriately to the demands of specific situations
2. Uses language as an adaptive manipulative and modifying tool of his environment
   A. Gives personal information effectively in interviews
   B. Responds verbally without tension or undue hesitation
   C. Asks questions to obtain information or assistance
   D. Responds appropriately to unfamiliar or stress situations (police, fire, accident)
   E. Expresses respect, admiration, friendship, and apologies through appropriate language goals
   F. Expresses disagreement in an acceptable fashion
3. Speaks intelligibly, fluently, and comfortably with strangers and in large-group situations.
4. Uses language for enjoyment
   A. Uses telephone effectively for social and business needs
   B. Exchanges ideas, information, and interests freely with others
   C. Participates in choral speaking, dramatic skits, role playing, and the like
   D. Meets and relates well with others

SUGGESTED LANGUAGE AND SPEECH PROGRAM FOR SECONDARY GROUP (13-18 YEARS)

EXPRESSING

GOAL 1. Uses appropriate speech and language to meet social and occupational demands

    A. Increases vocabulary to include many work-related terms such as foreman, check, time clock, double-time, etc.

    B. Uses socially acceptable speech and language forms in a variety of situations, e.g., doesn't swear in mixed company, chooses acceptable topics for conversation, doesn't dominate conversations, etc.

    C. Regulates pitch, rate, and volume appropriately to the demands of specific situations

Suggested Activities

Discuss, study, and list teen-age vernacular. Talk about when it is all right to use slang and when it is not (1A)

Make a series of bulletin boards that illustrate specific vocabulary for various vocational situations. Place pictures or objects on the board, along with word cards. Have pupils learn to spell, read, and correctly use the vocabulary words. (1A)

Use word cards taken from bulletin boards (above). Mix up the vocabulary cards from several vocations. Have pupils separate the cards, placing them in the correct vocational category. (1A)

Have students role-play a job interview two times. During the first, the applicant uses slang; in the second, the applicant tries to use correct English. Have the class compare the effect of the two approaches on a possible employer. (1A)

Make tape recordings of pupils' voices, relating familiar experiences or talking about a topic of interest. Play tape. Have pupils listen for grammatical errors and problems in pitch, rate, and volume. Stop tape periodically and give pupils an opportunity to criticize, suggest ways of improving, and comment about the speech they hear. Make subsequent tapes of similar recordings and compare with earlier attempts, particularly emphasizing improvements. (1B)

Take pupils in and around the school to show that volume of speaking is different in different areas. Go to the gym, auditorium, cafeteria, grounds, etc. Have pupils practice speaking and listening in these areas, varying the volume and pitch. (1B)

GOAL 2. Uses language as an adaptive manipulative and modifying tool of environment

    A. Gives personal information effectively in interviews

    B. Responds verbally without tension or undue hesitation

    C. Asks questions to obtain information or assistance

    D. Responds appropriately to unfamiliar or stress situations (police, fire, accident)

    E. Expresses respect, admiration, friendship, and apologies through appropriate language forms

    F. Expresses disagreement in an acceptable fashion

Suggested Activities

Have prospective employers, social security workers, traffic bureau people come in to the classroom and talk with pupils about interviews. Have them explain the information that pupils should have at hand, how they should act, and so on. Let pupils visit and talk with the people, helping to reduce tension and apprehension of interview situations they might be facing. (2A)

Show the film strip, "The Job Interview" (Eyegate). Discuss the film strip and have pupils practice similar situations. (2A)

Play games such as "College Bowl," quizzing students on their full name, address, birthdate, etc., and give points for an accurate and quick response. (2B)

Provide opportunities for students to speak in front of their classmates and, later, in front of larger groups. Short talks about safety, grooming, good citizenship, or book reports can be used for this. As the students gain proficiency, they might give their lecture talks to other classes or groups. (2B)

Provide situations in which students must make phone calls or visits to obtain information concerning such subjects as bus schedules, weather report, assistance in the library, material in the supply room, etc. (2C)

Plan "fake" accidents that happen without warning during the school day. Keep students unaware of the planned accident in order to check their responses in emergency situations. One or two students can be selected to be a part of the accident each time. (2D)

Have periodic fire drills, air raid warnings, etc. Be sure students have been informed of the proper procedures to follow during these drills. (2D)

Collect various kinds of greeting cards, e.g., sympathy cards, friendship cards, congratulatory cards, etc. Have pupils read them to discover appropriate language forms for use at particular times. Build vocabulary lists from the cards, giving each list in the vocabulary a category such as "words to use when we are sorry" or "good words to use for good friends" or "happy words." (2E)

Write an experience chart story together about the meaning of respect. Emphasize points such as what respect is, who and what deserves respect, and how respect is shown. (2E)

Give the class a hypothetical situation that might lead to opportunities to show respect or friendship. Let the class develop the story in a round-robin fashion, e.g., "John and Bill were walking down the beach when they met John's friend Susan. . . ."

GOAL 3. Speaks intelligibly, fluently, and comfortably with strangers and in large-group situations

Suggested Activities

Play games such as "Who am I?" "What am I?" or "Where am I?" Teacher and/or student describes people, places, pictures, events, or objects and students respond to the clue. (3)

Ask students questions. Require them to answer with several sentences. Provide seat work papers that ask similar questions requiring students to write several sentences in answer. Questions such as, "Why do you like to play baseball?" or "Why don't you like arithmetic?" or "What is bad about having a little brother?" should elicit a response of several sentences. (3)

Provide opportunities for pupils to talk in a variety of situations; free conversation, greeting guests, giving directions, asking questions, etc. Correct them when they commit gross errors, and remind them to watch for and correct their own mistakes. (3)

GOAL 4. Uses language for enjoyment
    A. Uses telephone effectively for social and business needs
    B. Exchanges ideas, information, and interests freely with others
    C. Participates in choral speaking, dramatic skits, role playing, and the like
    D. Meets and relates well with others

Suggested Activities

Assign pupils telephone assignments that they can do at home or at school. Such telephone tasks as calling a friend for a certain piece of information, issuing an invitation, making an apology, inquiring about services from businesses, and so on can be used. After the pupil has completed the telephone call, have him report back to the class what the results were and any difficulties he might have encountered. (4A)

Have a weekly contest for the "most interesting news item of the week." Have pupils listen to newscasts, read papers, and watch for interesting happenings. During a class session, pupils give the items they have collected during the week. A panel composed of students decides which item was most interesting; the winner is awarded a certificate. (4B)

Have "buzz" groups about controversial topics of high interest to the pupils, e.g., miniskirts, LSD, segregation, rules of the school, parental authority, etc. Have buzz groups report back to the class the main ideas that were discussed and the areas of general agreement or disagreement. (4B)

Plan short programs for the class or for use in school assemblies or special functions. Use simple or two-act plays, skits, singing, or choral speaking. Holidays, PTA meetings, and the like provide many opportunities for such programs. (4C)

Take pupils on trips to homes for the aged, hospital wards, children's homes, recreation centers, etc. Discuss how they are to act and what they are to do before going on the trips. Each trip should have a purpose, e.g., taking gifts they have made, performing skits or singing, watching a ball game, or participating in recreational activities. Encourage pupils to talk and visit with the people they meet in a relaxed, friendly manner. (4D)

chapter eight
supplemental materials
for programming

The suggested classroom program provides a basis for the teacher of the retarded in structuring lessons for developmental language. The teacher can add original ideas to supplement those that are included or can incorporate suggestions and materials from commercially available products or from books and articles from the literature. To assist in this regard a listing of these sources follows, with the recommendation that the teacher use these as a library of available resources to add to the program that is suggested here.

In addition, some specific exercises that may be used to add to aspects of this program or to use in meeting specific deficits that may be discovered in a particular group of children, are described by sections labeled receiving, thinking, and expressing. By now, the teacher recognizes that these categories are not as discrete as the divisions seem to suggest. Language is too complex for that. However, an attempt has been made to divide the exercises on the basis of what appears to be their dominant thrust. Their only possible disadvantage appears to be that the children may receive practice in some areas in which they do not need assistance. The thesis that success experiences are desirable for them and that we need not continually be on the alert to discover programming at which they will fail is repeated here as a defense. Those persons who disagree may express their disagreement by the judicious selection of what they consider to be appropriate for their classes.

COMMERCIAL LANGUAGE PROGRAMS

Ausberger, C., *Syntax One,* Communication Skill Builders, Inc., 817 East Broadway/Box 6081-K, Tucson, Arizona, 85733. Can be used individually or in groups with children over 5 years (mental age). Children should be able to attend to one task for a period of time.

Dunn, L., Horton, K., and Smith, J., *Peabody Language Development Kit, Level P.,* Mental Ages 3-5, American Guidance Service, Incorporated, Circle Pines, Minnesota, 1968. Presents a daily program through a teacher's manual and a number of pictures, puppets, records, and tapes.

Dunn, L., and Smith, J., *Peabody Language Development Kit, Level 1,* Mental Ages 4½ to 6½, American Guidance Service, Incorporated, Circle Pines, Minnesota, 1965. Same as above.

Dunn, L., and Smith, J., *Peabody Language Development Kit, Level 2,* Mental Ages 6 to 8, American Guidance Service, Incorporated, Circle Pines, Minnesota, 1966. Same as above.

Dunn, L., and Smith, J., *Peabody Language Development Kit, Level 3,* Mental Ages 7½ to 9½, American Guidance Service, Incorporated, Circle Pines, Minnesota, 1967. Same as above.

Engelmann, S., Osborn, J., and Engelmann, T., *Distar Language—An Instructional System, Level 1,* Science Research Associates, 259 East Erie Street, Chicago, Illinois, 60611, 1970. Intended to teach basic language concepts to children who have not learned them. Includes a number of concepts developed through stories and activities.

Engelmann, S., and Osborn, J., *Distar Language—An Instructional System,* Science Research Associates, 259 East Erie Street, Chicago, Illinois, 60611, 1970. Designed to teach children how to describe relationships and qualities observed in the world.

Karnes, M., *Goal Language Development,* Milton Bradley, Education Department, Springfield, Massachusetts, 01101, 1974. Designed to help children acquire information processing skills at the preschool level.

Minskoff, J., Wiseman, D., and Minskoff, E., *The MWM Program for Developing Language Abilities,* Educational Performance Associates, 563 Westview Avenue, Ridgefield, New Jersey, 07657. Includes a teacher's guide in three sections, an Inventory of Language Abilities or comprehensive screening device, six Teaching Manuals that provide step-by-step directions, and five workbooks.

Bright, H., *Remediation of Some Basic Concepts of Language,* Redwood Publishing Company, 3860 South Higuers Space 105, San Luis Obispo, California, 93401, 1975. Work sheets and teaching text to aid in the remediation of 50 language concepts.

Bush, W., and Giles, M., *Aids to Psycholinguistic Teaching,* Charles E. Merrill Publishing Company, 1300 Alum Creek Drive, Columbus, Ohio, 43216, 1969.

Duchan, J., *A Curriculum Guide for Language Therapy,* The Madison Public Schools, Madison, Wisconsin, 1968. A guide to teaching language structure and content.

SOURCES OF PROGRAMMING IN BOOKS AND ARTICLES

A Sequentially Compiled List of Instructional Materials for Remediational Use with the ITPA, Rocky Mountain Special Instructional Materials Center, Greeley, Colorado, published by Office of Education, Washington, D.C., Division of Handicapped Children and Youth, order number ED 036 041. Title explains content.

Bereiter, C., and Englemann, S., *Teaching Disadvantaged Children in the Preschool,* Prentice Hall, Inc., Englewood Cliffs, New Jersey, 1966. Materials for use in syntax development.

Blumberg, H., *A Program of Sequential Language Development,* Charles C. Thomas Publisher, 301-327 East Laurence Avenue, Springfield, Illinois, 62717, 1975. Planned to assist the teacher in everyday instructional activities as well as in specific oral language development classes.

Fokes, Joanne, *Fokes Sentence Building Program,* Teaching Resources Corporation, 100 Boylston Street, Boston, Massachusetts, 02116. Uses a Fitzgerald key approach in a syntax training program.

Guralnick, M., "Language Development Program for Severely Handicapped Children," *Exceptional Children,* 399, 1972, pages 45–49. Nonprofessionals are used to promote language development.

Gray, B., and Ryan, B., *A Language Program for the Nonlanguage Child,* Research Press, 2612 North Mattis, Champaign, Illinois, 61820, 1974. The purpose of this program is to teach nonlanguage children how to talk through programmed conditioning.

Handbook of Remedial Techniques for Children and Young Adolescents, West Texas State Universtiy, Canyon, Texas, 1967. Activities by grade are presented for the subtests of the Illinois Test of Psycholinguistic Abilities.

ITPA Lessons-Activities-Programs, Marylou Noone, Francis E. Plumeau, Director, Educational Services Center, Title I ESEA, 485 Glen Street, Glens Falls, New York, 12801 ($2.00). Aimed at remediating ITPA discovered deficits.

Karnes, M., *Helping Young Children Develop Language Skills,* The Council for Exceptional Children, Reston, Virginia, 1968. Activities based on the Illinois Test of Psycholinguistic Abilities and aimed at strengthening language skills in preschool children.

Kent, L., *Language Acquisition Program for Severely Retarded,* Research Press, 2612 North Mattis Avenue, Champaign, Illinois, 61820, 1974. The Language Acquisition Program (LAP) is for severely retarded children and is designed to teach a language system.

Language and Cognitive Development Activities, Curriculum Bulletin #360, Department of Special Education, St. Paul Public Schools, District #625, St. Paul, Minnesota, 55102. Activities to assist teachers in language and cognition programming.

Novakovich, Harriet, and Zoslow, Sylvia, *Target on Language*, Christ Church Child Center, 8011 Old Georgetown Road, Bethesda, Md., 20014, 1973. Programs classified by curriculum and psycholinguistic areas.

Simmars, V., and Williams, I., *Steps Up to Language in the Learning Impaired: Attending,* Communication Skill Builders, Inc., 817 East Broadway/Box 6081-K, Tucson, Arizona, 85733.

Smith, M., *Language Development for Special Classes,* Knoxville City Schools, Knoxville, Tennessee. The second half of the guide is made up of three indices to assist the teacher in making the Peabody Language Development Kits more flexible. The first index lists the different types of activities, the second classifies the activities according to content and concept, and the third is a cross reference for the other two.

Stremel, Kathleen, "Language Training: A Program for Retarded Children," *Mental Retardation,* 2, 47-49, 1972. An early language program for teaching basic grammatical relations to moderately and severely retarded children.

Wilson, S., *Wilson Initial Syntax Program*, Educator Publishing Service, 75 Moulton Street, Cambridge, Massachusetts, 02138, 1972.

Wiseman, D., "A Classroom Procedure for Identifying and Remediating Language Problems," *Mental Retardation,* 3, 21-24, 1965. Uses ITPA model to serve as a basis for systematically identifying and remediating areas of language disabilities.

VISUAL AND AUDITORY MATERIALS

Frostig, M., and Horne, D., *The Frostig Program for the Development of Visual Perception,* Follett Educational Corporation, Chicago, Illinois, 1964. Aimed at improving visual perceptual skills when deficient in children. Based on the Frostig Test.

Herr, S., *Perceptual Communication Skills: Developing Auditory Awareness and Insight,* Instructional Materials and Equipment Distributors, 1415 Westwood Boulevard, Los Angeles, California, 90024, 1969. Aimed at developing auditory awareness, vocabulary, and concepts. Includes eighty-eight lessons for preschool to third grade, for fourth to sixth grade, and for junior high to adulthood.

Lindamood, C., and Lindamood, P., *Auditory Discrimination in Depth (A.D.D.),* Teaching Resources Corporation, 100 Boylston Street, Boston, Massachusetts, 02116, 1969. The phonological system of the language, emphasizing auditory discrimination, is taught from preschool to adult levels.

OTHER APPLICABLE MATERIALS

Chalfant, J., Kirk, G., and Jensen, K., "Systematic Language Instruction: An Approach for Teaching Receptive Language to Young Trainable Children," *Teaching Exceptional Children,* Vol. 1, No. 1, November. 1968. pp. 1-13. A specific program presented for use by classroom teachers of young trainables.

Quick, A., Little, T., and Campell, A., *Project Memphis Lesson Plans: Guides to Teaching Preacademic Skills,* Department of Special Education and Rehabilitation, College of Education, Memphis State University, Memphis, Tennessee, 38152, 1972. Lesson plans designed to teach skills in five areas of development.

Sayre, J., and Mack, J., *Think, Listen and Say,* Eye Gate House, Jamaica, New York, 11435, 1967. Records and filmstrips prepared to improve listening abilities, auditory discrimination, and comprehension from preschool to primary levels.

Montessori, M., *The Montessori Method,* Schocken Books (paperback), New York, 1964.

Scott, R., *The Learning Readiness System: Classification and Seriation Kit,* Harper and Row, New York, 1968.

Step-by-Step Language Skills—Kits A and B, The Continental Press, Incorporated, Elizabethtown, Pennsylvania, 17022. Liquid duplicating materials in kit form. Includes a testing program for diagnosing problem areas and evaluating progress.

Stewart, F., "A Vocal-Motor Program for Teaching Nonverbal Children," *Education and Training of the Mentally Retarded*, Vol. 7, No. 4, 1972, pp. 176–182. Objective ways to develop echoic vocal or motor responses in nonverbal children.

System Fore—An approach to individualized instruction. Produced by the staff of the Project Assessment Services Center for the Handicapped, Los Angeles Unified School District, Los Angeles, California, 1972. Individualizes instruction in language, reading, and math.

Systematic Instruction for Retarded Children: The Illinois Program, The Interstate Printers and Publishers, Incorporated, Danville, Illinois, 61832, 1972. A four-part curriculum guide for the trainable mentally retarded. It is described as a systematic, integrated approach for instruction.

Talkington, L., and Hall, S. "Matrix Language Program with Mongoloids," *American Journal of Mental Deficiency,* Vol. 75, 1970, pp. 88–91. Used Matrix Games to discover that language training with mongoloids is feasible and effective.

ADDITIONAL PROGRAM MATERIALS

The following suggestions for exercises may be added to previous materials to stress certain areas, or can be used to assist children with specific deficits.

PREDOMINATELY RECEIVING

1. Divide the children into two teams. Have Team A imitate one animal each, while their team tries to guess what it is. You whisper the name of an animal to

a child who imitates it and tell team B what it is. Keep track of the time: limit of three minutes. Use animals such as dog, cat, cow, sheep, lion, monkey, bear, bird, bee, etc. Allow the children to supplement with gestural activity.

2. Ask the children to close their eyes and identify what you are doing. Have them put their heads down on their desks and then: clap your hands, write on the board, shuffle your feet, open the door, close the door, run the pencil sharpener, snap your fingers, tap on the window, knock on your desk, cut with a scissors, etc.

3. Have one child start by saying, "Who am I?" while the entire class has their heads on their desks and their eyes closed. The first child says "Who am I, Mary?" and Mary guesses. You then tap another child and that child asks the question and adds the name he or she wants. After playing this way for awhile, have the children try to disguise their voices and repeat the game in the same way.

4. Tape record sounds from television. Use sound effects, theme songs, voices of familiar characters, commercials, etc. Ask children to identify these.

5. Play "Can You Tell Me What I Said?" Put a pencil between your teeth and read a sentence to the children. See if they can repeat it. Do the same while chewing gum, filling your mouth with jelly beans, stuffing a handkerchief in it, or covering your mouth with your hand.

6. Play, "Put Words Together." Fractionate words of three sounds into parts and see if the children can identify the words. Begin with short gaps and gradually lengthen the gaps to increase the difficulty.

   (a) h-e-n
   (b) s-oa-p
   (c) h-ea-d
   (d) p-o-p
   (e) b-i-ke
   (f) s-ou-p
   (g) r-e-d
   (h) cl-i-mb
   (i) pl-a-ne
   (j) j-u-mp

7. Announce to the children, "I am going to read a story. I will then read it again. The second time I will leave some words out and ask you what they are. Listen carefully so you will be able to answer. 'Brian had a *dog* named *Luke. Luke* was a *big bulldog.* Bulldogs look very *fierce.* Luke was not fierce. Luke would not *hurt* anyone. Luke liked to *chase cats* and *bark at cars.* One day Brian took Luke with him when he walked *to the store* for his *mother.* His mother had given him some *money* to buy some *food.* As Brian was walking to the store *two older boys* came up to Brian and said, *"Hey, kid, ya got any money?"* Brian didn't know what to say. His mother had taught him always to *tell the truth.* If he told the truth the older and bigger boys would *take the money* from

him. The boys said, "C'mon, kid, quit stalling." Just then *Luke growled.* He didn't like the *way they were talking to Brian.* The boys took one look at Luke and *ran.* After Brian went to the store he went home and told his mother what had happened. She *patted* Luke *on the head* and said, "Good dog, Luke. You helped Brian stay *honest!*'" (Italicized words are those to be questioned.) Discuss the story in regard to word meanings. What does a bulldog look like? What does "the truth" mean? Can you growl like a dog? Make believe you are patting a dog on the head. What does honest mean?

8. Ask the children to listen carefully while you say something because you are going to ask them to repeat what you said in their own way. Then use sentences such as the following:
    (a) My sister and I went to the store to get milk and bread.
    (b) At the zoo we saw big animals like elephants and little animals like rabbits.
    (c) We went to the lake to go fishing, but it was raining too hard.
    (d) The cowboy rode his horse to the river so the horse could get a drink.
    (Accept different wording but guide toward complete sentences.)

9. Read short paragraphs from various books. Ask the children to tell what a paragraph was about. Read a paragraph with one sentence left out. Ask the children where the sentence was left out. Ask the children to tell what is going to follow what you have read.

PREDOMINATELY THINKING

1. Play the game, "I'm thinking of something that's —"
    (a) Play it with colors.
    (b) Play it with shape.
    (c) Play it with size.
    (d) Play it with texture or the way something feels.
    (e) Play it with taste.
    (f) Play it with hardness or composition.
    Let children take turns being the person who "thinks."

2. Pass out dittoed sheets on which a circle, square, and a cross are drawn. Say to the children, "Put an X on the circle and draw a circle in the square. Draw a circle around the X. Draw a line from the circle to the X. Draw a line from the square to the circle. Draw a line from the square to the triangle." After about 15 seconds say, "That's silly of me. There isn't any triangle. What should you do when someone tells you to do something you can't do?" Discuss.

3. Practice "following directions" at their initial level of competence:
    (a) Shake your head, blink your eyes, bend your elbow, etc.
    (b) Stand up and then pat your head. Look up and then clap your hands. Tap your toes on the floor and then touch your knees. Rub your cheeks and then put your arms out straight.

(c) Go touch Bobby on the shoulder, then softly pat on Tommy's head. Go shake hands with Mary and then put your hand on top of Jimmy's. Say hello to Beth and then ask Sue how old she is.

(d) Open the door, touch my chair and then go touch the window. Put a mark on the chalkboard, go touch Steve's arm and then go to your desk and turn around when you get there.

(e) Continue to increase number of items and the need for memory of each item.

4. Play "Simon says" with the entire class.

5. Play the game, "I'm thinking of something —," but relate it to specific locations.

(a) I'm thinking of something on a farm that goes "moo."
Give as many or as few clues as are necessary for success.

(b) I'm thinking of something at the zoo.

(c) I'm thinking of something in your kitchen at home.

(d) I'm thinking of something by a lake.

6. Play the game, "I'm thinking of someone who —"

(a) With children in the room.

(b) With sports figures.

(c) With persons on television.

(d) With famous people (depending on the children's abilities).

7. Ask children to imitate activities such as brushing teeth, combing hair, putting on shoes, making toast, buttering bread, drying dishes, dusting the table, sweeping the floor. Tell only the child assigned the task what it is and have the other children guess.

8. Whisper an action verb to one child to imitate (jump, salute, run, skip, frown, etc.). Have the other children guess what the child is acting out.

9. Have a child sort the different cards from a regular deck of playing cards into like groups (kings, threes, etc.) and then into suits (diamonds, spades, etc.).

10. Draw geometric designs such as circles, squares, triangles, octagons, or parallelograms on 3" X 5" cards. Have several of each. Have the children sort these into the appropriate piles.

11. Ask a question and then say to the children, "I am going to tell you three answers but only one will be correct. As soon as you hear the correct one, raise your hand."

12. Tap out a rhythmic series and have a child imitate. Vary loudness, rhythm, and timing. For example: Tap, Tap—Tap Tap; Tap—Tap Tap; Tap—Tap—Tap.

13. Play a game in which all the children look out the window. You start the game by saying, "I'm looking out the window, and the thing that I can see, looks like it's a —, that's how it looks to me. What do you see, Shari?" The next child uses the same carrier phrase and names something seen and then the name of the next player.

14. Print the letters of the alphabet on 3″ X 5″ cards and have the children sort a few of them that have been mixed together. Start with two, then three, etc. Do not identify by letter name, merely ask them to sort the forms.

15. Play a game in which you look out the window and guess what someone is seeing. Start by saying, "I'm looking out the window and you will have to guess. What I am seeing is (green and big, or black with wheels, etc.)." Provide at least two clues and then ask someone to guess.

16. Play "charades," in two teams, on subjects that you select, and are not difficult to act out and can be identified. You might wish to ditto-off possible activities so that the children will know what to look for. Time the two teams. Activities such as washing the dishes, lighting and blowing out a candle, and pumping up a flat tire might be used.

17. Cut pictures out of magazines. Ask a child to mark,
    (a) "Everything that is red." (using colors)
    (b) "Everything that is round." (using shape)
    (c) "Everything that is fast." (using other features)
    Exhaust the possibilities of the picture.

18. Mix two decks of cards. There are a number of different types of "Old Maid" cards. Have the children sort the cards into the correct piles without looking at the backs. Have a child sort out the different characters in an Old Maid deck.

19. Take pictures of various items that have been cut from a book, and have the children sort them by color. See if they can sort shades of a color into the correct piles.

20. Cut out several pictures of a number of things such as dogs, cats, airplanes, silverware, dishes, cars, trucks, houses, boats, dresses, hats, chairs, trees, flowers, and birds.
    (a) Mix a few of each of two types together. Ask child or children to sort them as to type.
    (b) Mix three types together, then four, and then five.
    (c) Mix all pictures together. Have teams, and time them as they sort these into piles of like items.
    (d) Sort in more difficult ways: "Put all the dogs you think are big in this pile, and all the dogs you think are small in this pile."
    (e) Have the teams do the same thing and have the other children serve as judges as to the correct decisions. Be prepared for differences of opinion and guide in a manner dictated by the differences.

21. Find pictures that represent pairs of opposites. Show a child one of a pair and have him or her find its opposite. Use concepts such as high-low, in-out, up-down, wet-dry, tall-short, happy-sad, early-late, hot-cold, on-off, dark-light, and strong-weak.

22. Place a number of items in a paper bag. First have the children guess what is in

the bag. Write their guesses on the board. Then have a child, after placing his or her hand in the bag, describe one item. After each new clue, have the other children guess. At the end see how many items were guessed.

23. Act out various gestures that we see in our daily lives, and ask the children to guess what you are doing. Act out: shading your eyes from the sun, looking through binoculars, a traffic policeman directing traffic, an old man walking with a cane, someone waving goodbye, someone responding: "I don't know," beckon with your index finger, say "no-no" by waving your index finger, lift something heavy, beckon someone to follow you, bounce a ball, kick, throw, or catch one, hit a ball with a bat, tell someone to be quiet, tell someone you can't hear by cupping your hand over your ear, shake your finger angrily at someone, menace with your fist, or applaud something you like.

24. Ask the children how you are feeling and then look: sad, happy, puzzled, surprised, confused, afraid, or fierce. Have the children act out these "faces" and see if you can guess.

25. Ask the children to name various things in a category, in a rhythmic manner. Go around the room in a planned sequence. You announce the category and the first child claps three times and then says her or his answer. For example, you say, "birds." The first child claps three times and says "robin." The next child claps three times and says "sparrow." If children can't succeed in this manner merely have them name birds or items from whatever the category. The children who do not succeed can be stopped from continuing, but this creates in them a feeling of failure that isn't desirable. It's better to have them remain in and try again. Try categories such as: birds, cars, animals, trees, flowers, stores, streets, teachers, children in class, things in the school, things in the kitchen at home, things in the living room at home, television programs, songs, bands, singers, or sports teams.

26. Play, "Tell me this —."
    (a) We walk on the sidewalk; we ride in —.
    (b) We need a boat to ride on the water; we need a — to ride in the sky.
    (c) We use a broom to sweep the floor; we need a — to sweep leaves.
    (d) We walk when we have time; when we are in a hurry we —.
    (e) We laugh when we're happy; we — when we're sad.
    (f) We put the light on when we're awake; we turn it — when we sleep.
    (g) We put water in the tub when we take a bath; we let the water — when we're through.
    (h) We drink our milk; we — our bread.
    (i) We sit when we eat; we — when we dry dishes.
    (j) We're warm when the weather is warm; we're — when the weather is not warm.

27. Play, "Rhyme my riddle." The teacher gives easy riddles and a child rhymes them.

(a) I'm thinking of something I wear on my head that rhymes with fat.

(b) I'm thinking of something that I wear on my hand and rhymes with love.

(c) I'm thinking of something that I ride in, and it rhymes with tar.

(d) I'm thinking of something that I ride on, and it rhymes with Mike.

(e) I'm thinking of a girl or boy's nickname, and it rhymes with handy.

(f) I'm thinking of something that a girl wears, and it rhymes with chess.

(g) I'm thinking of something that girls and boys wear, and it rhymes with cleans.

(h) I'm thinking of something that's up in the sky, and it rhymes with June.

(i) I'm thinking of something that you use to buy things, and it rhymes with honey.

(j) I'm thinking of something that a boy wears, and it rhymes with skirt.

28. Play, "Add a word." Say, "I went to the store and I bought bread." The first child then says, "I went to the store and I bought bread, and soup." The next child says, "I went to the store and I bought bread, soup, and cheese." Continue like this. Change the topic. For example, "On the farm I saw —."

29. Ask a child to repeat words after you, in order. Start with two words such as big-cold, stop-plant, car-rug. If the children can succeed go to three words, jump-build-doll, toy-run-farm, record-tired-job, blue-far-chair, soup-stove-cat. Increase the number of words if some of them can succeed.

30. Use four soundmakers of the same kind. A front desk type of bell is best, so it rings when the child strikes it. Play a question game with four panelists. The first one who rings the soundmaker may attempt the answer.

31. Play, "What did I leave out." Tell the children you will name two things the first time, and the second time you will leave something out, and they will have to try and remember it. Then say such things as "table-floor (pause) floor. What did I leave out?" Mention three things such as: "tooth-child-today (pause) tooth-today. What did I leave out?" Try four or five items if the children can succeed.

32. Explain to the children that you will ask them a question. They are not to answer the question until you signal them. Raise your index finger and arm to your shoulder. Ask a question, then silently count to five to yourself and then point at a child for an answer. During the silent period the children are to think of the answer; but, more important, they are to think of how they are going to give the answer using a complete sentence.

33. Practice lip reading. Tell the children to watch your lips and say words silently. See how many can tell what you are saying. Use words that have p's, b's, and m's that are formed on the lips, and then advance to some that are not. If children have difficulty, assist them by whispering some part of the word. If they can succeed at words, try short phrases.

34. Find sequences in comic strips that portray action. Cut them out, mount them on 3" X 5" or 4" X 6" cards and have the children put them in sequence.

These may also be used to have them describe the sequence of events. A third step might be to have them make up a story on "what happened after that." Sometimes the logical order can be changed to create still a different story.

PREDOMINANTLY EXPRESSING

1. Follow the comic strips and magazines to find illustrations of basic verbs such as: sit, eat, jump, stand, smile, laugh, frown, bend, carry, come, go, run, cut, give, help, hold, keep, let, like, love, make, read, say, show, sleep, take, walk, watch, bite, and go. Start by having a child "Point to the one that is a reminder of the word ____." At first, exhibit only two choices, but with success, gradually increase these. Later, say, "Show me the one in which someone is ____ ing." Still later, say, "Today I see a person____. Yesterday, that person did the same thing, he (or she)____ ed. Show me that."

2. Use the verb cards and ask the child, "What do we say the person is doing?" Try to elicit an ____ ing ending.

3. Tell the children to listen carefully because after you read a story to them, you are going to ask them to tell it in their words. "When Mike ran down the road he didn't know all the things that were about to happen to him. He was running so fast that he didn't see the lady who was taking her dog for a walk. The dog barked and jumped at Mike, knocking him down. Mike cut his head a little, and it began to bleed a few drops. The lady scolded her dog and wiped the few drops of blood from Mike's forehead. Then she took him into the drug store and bought some band aids. She put one on Mike's forehead and the rest in his coat pocket. She also bought him an ice cream soda and told him she would like to take him to a movie sometime if it was all right with his mother. Mike went home and told his parents. His Dad laughed when Mike said, 'Some accidents aren't so bad!' "

4. Practice choral reading. Find a section of the reading material that is not too difficult for most class members. Have them read aloud together in a steady, relatively slow, tempo.

5. Play a game, "How many things can you do with —?" Use words such as: screwdriver, string, pillow, ruler, marking pen, ice cube, fire, water, grass, roses, onions, horses, rabbits, envelopes, or paper clips. Give hints and encourage children to use their imaginations—even to develop fairly unrealistic responses. The aim is to encourage divergent thinking, not to produce practical solutions.

6. Give the children some relatively easy spelling words. Have them write the words as they say each letter aloud and in unison. Say, "Let's spell the word dog as we write (or print) it. Here we go, d—o—g."

7. In somewhat sing-song fashion, say a phrase and have them respond appropriately. Initially, use short words that end in vowel sounds.

A word to rhyme with_____for me.
Tell me a rhyming word, 1, 2, 3_____."
see, may, dough, my, do, play, blow, etc.

8. Follow the comic strips and magazines to find pictures of basic nouns such as: arm, baby, back, ball, bed, book, can, car, child, cup, daddy, dog, fire, fish, girl, hat, home, horse, knife, letter, men, money, mother, people, plate, rain, room, school, shoe, spoon, summer, table, teacher, truck, water. Put out two cards at first, and say to the child, "Show me the (or a, an)_____." Increase the number of cards that are laid out. Later, put out two pictures and say, "What are these?" Try to elicit a "These are a shoe and a spoon," response.

9. Ask the children to complete the following sentences:
    (a) At night I put on my pajamas and go to_____.
    (b) When I go fishing I use_____.
    (c) My father takes the car to the gas station_____.
    (d) You have to be careful when you ride a bicycle_____.
    (e) When people tell you a secret_____.
    (f) Rain is very good_____.
    (g) It's fun to grow plants in the house_____.

10. Discuss the silly aspects of the following statements:
    (a) Mr. Johnson filled up his boots with water and put them on.
    (b) Geraldine put jam in her hair to make it look better.
    (c) Sue emptied the bathtub and then got in to take her bath.
    (d) The car started my father and went to work.
    (e) We put clean dishes in the dishwasher and dirty ones on the table.
    (f) Our basement is on the second floor.

11. Have the children describe ways in which things are the same and not the same. Use such things as a broom and a lake, a tire and a plant, a factory and a house, a coat and a dress.

12. Ask the children what they would do if:
    (a) They found an envelope on the sidewalk with a stamp on it.
    (b) Found a little lost girl about three years old.
    (c) Lost the money their mother gave them to buy a loaf of bread.
    (d) Forgot where they left their raincoat.
    (e) Got lost on the way home from school.
    (f) Saw someone steal something in a drugstore.
    (g) Found a sick dog.
    (h) Accidently broke someone's window with a ball.
    Discuss the answers after trying to secure several responses from class members.

13. Ask children to tell you the consequences of actions:
    (a) What would happen if we didn't wear rubbers when it rains?
    (b) —we walked out in a busy street?
    (c) —we ate too much ice cream?

(d) —we ate the wrong kinds of food?

(e) —we didn't sleep at all?

(f) —we never took baths?

(g) —we didn't have television?

(h) —we didn't go to school?

(i) —we didn't have the sun?

(j) —we used rocks for money?

14. Read the children a story about three-quarters of the way through. Ask a child to finish it. Ask another child if that's the way he or she thinks the story ended. Have them change it, or parts of it, if they wish. After the discussion, finish the story and see how it comes out. Ask the children which ending they liked the best.

15. Have one child begin a story. Have each child, in turn, add something to it.

16. Have the children describe:

(a) How they shovel the walk.

(b) Put on a sweater.

(c) Pour a glass of milk.

(d) Get to school.

(e) Ride in a car.

(f) Answer the telephone.

(g) Decide what to watch on television.

(h) Color a picture.

(i) Clean up their room.

(j) Eat breakfast.

17. Discuss: "What would you need if —"

(a) You were going fishing.

(b) You wanted to make a picnic lunch.

(c) You wanted to build a bird house.

(d) You wanted to keep a record of all the different birds you saw.

(e) You were going to buy your friend a birthday present.

(f) You wanted to collect match box covers.

(g) You wanted to grow a tomato plant.

(h) You wanted to paint a dog house.

(i) You wanted to feed wild birds.

(j) You wanted to go to a football game on a cold day.

Try not to stifle the quantity of the responses by commenting on, or allowing class members to comment on, the quality of responses.

18. Play, "If you have a_____ you need a_____ ."

(a) If you have a lock, you need a_____ .

(b) If you have a dog, you need a_____ .

(c) If you have a boat, you need_____ .

(d) If you have a car, you need_____ .

(e) If you have a glove, you need_____ .

     (f)   If you have a bird, you need_____.

     (g)   If you have a truck, you need_____.

     (h)   If you have a hat, you need_____.

     (i)   If you have a cup, you need_____.

     (j)   If you have a baseball, you need_____.

     (k)   If you have a chair, you need_____.

19. Ask the children to describe what happened to them on the way to school. Ask them to describe what they like the best and the least. Ask them to describe their favorite holiday. Ask them to describe their favorite animal. Ask them to discuss their favorite television program.

20. Discuss the meaning of common expressions and why people use them.

     (a)   You're nuts

     (b)   Shut up

     (c)   Sharp as a tack

     (d)   Dummy

     (e)   Creep

     (f)   What's up

     (g)   Cool it

     (h)   Forget it

    Since such expressions are often regional and change rapidly, the teacher will have to use appropriate material here.

21. Play, "Guess who I am?"

     (a)   I paint houses. I'm a_____.

     (b)   I drive buses. I'm a_____.

     (c)   I try to catch robbers. I'm a_____.

     (d)   I sell you food, soap, and things like that. I'm a_____.

     (e)   I fly an airplane. I'm a_____.

     (f)   I teach you in school. I'm a_____.

     (g)   I earn my living by playing football. I'm a_____.

     (h)   I help you get well when you're sick. I'm a_____.

     (i)   I bring you your mail. I'm a_____.

     (j)   I put gas in your car. I'm a_____.

    Preface each sentence by, "Guess who I am? I —"

22. Play "When there's one it's —, when there's two it's —" Find a number of pictures and have the children take turns drawing a picture without looking and saying, "When there's one it's — and when there's two (or three) it's —." Use such pictures as girl, boy, man, woman, box, baby, car, airplane, truck, dog, cat, mouse, coat, jacket, spoon, deer, fish, bear, gun, knife, leaf, star, or circle.

23. Play, "How many in thirty seconds?" Ask a child to name as many responses to a specific category in thirty seconds. Use colors, animals, flowers, teams, words beginning with a certain letter, words ending with a certain letter, words with a certain letter in it, words that rhyme with a given word, words that you

would find in a grocery store, words that you would find in a drugstore, words that you would find in a department store, words that you would find in a school, words that you would find when walking down the street, words that you would find on a farm, words that you would find in the zoo.

24. Select a time, such as immediately after a rest period or a break of some other kind, in the daily schedule. Inform the children that for the next five minutes, or until you tell them it's over, it will be "Good Talking Time." During that time everyone (including you) will talk slowly, distinctly, and in complete sentences. Enforce this to the point of stilted conversation.

25. Play "What do we mean by —?"
    Begin with easy words and progress to more difficult ones.
    (a) car, bike, house, doll
    (b) truck, orange, plant, piano
    (c) water, tire, apron, sink
    (d) air, warm, balloon, handkerchief
    (e) happy, tired, lazy, think
    (f) free, cheat, sick, dive
    (g) love, smart, mistake, question

26. Have children tell all they can about objects in the room. Prompt them so they will include: color, shape, use, position, location, age, etc.

27. Have children tell stories.
    (a) Something they did the day before.
    (b) Their favorite story.
    (c) A repeat of a story previously heard in class.
    (d) A topic assigned by the teacher the day in advance.
    (e) Topics written on slips of paper drawn from a cup.
    (f) A story made up about a picture the teacher gives the child.
    (g) A story about another child in the class.
    (h) A story that includes three words assigned by the teacher.

28. Ask a child to explain:
    (a) How to get to his house from school.
    (b) How to get to the grocery store from his house.
    (c) How to get to the drugstore from his house.
    (d) How to get to the movies from his house.
    (e) How to (do something the child knows how to do).
    (f) How to read the TV schedule (if the child can).
    (g) How to find out what's showing at the movie.

29. Have the children role play. Assign a role to each of two children and set the scene. Act as director and prompt the children as needed.
    (a) The father and the child who have come home late.
    (b) The child trying to buy a birthday present for a friend.
    (c) The bus driver and the passenger.
    (d) The principal and the child who came to school late.

(e) The teacher and the child who didn't finish his work.

(f) The doctor and the patient who has a sore throat.

(g) The hungry child and the mother who doesn't have dinner ready.

(h) The father who wants the driveway shoveled and the child who doesn't want to do it.

You may wish to taperecord the ''acting'' and play it back for the actors.

30. Assign the children a television program to watch (one that they say their families watch regularly). Ask them to describe what happened in one episode.

31. Ask a child to make a sentence of a word you assign. Use such words as in, on, under, up, between, outside of, instead of, before, after, behind, in front of, over, near to, away from, through, but, because, or then.

32. Play "I'll give the answer; you give the question." Use answers such as school, football, hide and seek, cowboy, butter, pop, or candy. For school, the child might ask, "Where do we go every day?" Accept inaccuracy such as this but insist on complete questions.

33. Play "rhyme a name." Give the idea by illustrating, for example, "Sam, Sam, doesn't like ham." "Mary, Mary, she don't carry." Then start with a child's name from the class and pick a child who will have to finish. "John, John —" Help those children who have difficulty. Don't insist on exact rhyming.

34. Ask the children to complete the phrase or sentence.

(a) We use _____ to make pop cold.

(b) To stir up things when she cooks, Mother uses a _____ .

(c) We heat water on the _____.

(d) We put _____ on bread.

(e) We light fires with a _____.

(f) When it's cold outside we wear a warm _____ .

(g) When we go swimming we wear a _____.

(h) When we want to keep something cold overnight we use a _____.

(i) We wash dishes in the _____.

(j) We clean the rugs with a _____.

35. Play, "Say it better."

Mention a sentence with one word pronounced incorrectly or indistinctly. Have a child correct it with careful articulation.

(a) I *saw* the boat.

(b) She *ran* very fast.

(c) He likes to *play* in the *sand.*

(d) *She* caught a big *fish.*

(e) *Roger* bought a dozen *roses.*

(f) Al doesn't like to *brush* his *teeth.*

(g) Joyce *walked* all the way to *work.*

(h) Steve *sank* the log.

(i) Jessie *washed* the *dishes.*

(j) Joe *hurt* his toe on the *stone.*

36. Select a panel of four children. Have them sit in the front of the room. Have the children ask questions appropriate to current classroom activities. Each child in turn receives a question. Work toward proper framing of the question and complete sentence response.

37. Have the children join you in making each of them a "Communications Workbook." As usual, they can design the cover, etc. Include weekly goals and some exercises the children can take home to show their parents and continue to work on at home. The exercises may include speech activities, listening activities, or other language activities.

38. Play, "Say it the way I say it." Say something using either correct speech and language or including errors. Have a child imitate accurately. Use lisps, other misarticulations, poor syntax, or wrong words. After saying it correctly, say it the correct way.

39. Ask the children "why" questions.
    (a) Why do babies cry?
    (b) —fish swim?
    (c) —trucks have big tires?
    (d) —streets have sidewalks?
    (e) —yards have grass?
    (f) —people plant flowers?
    (g) —birds have wings?
    (h) —cars have steering wheels?
    (i) —cities have firemen?
    (j) —policemen have whistles?

40. Play, "why?" Ask questions beginning with "why" and guide the children to respond in complete and appropriate form.
    (a) Why does it rain?
    (b) Why do we keep animals on a farm?
    (c) Why do people live in cities?
    (d) Why do we drive cars?
    (e) Why do we eat three times a day?
    (f) Why should we make certain that we eat good, healthy food?
    (g) Why should we obey all the traffic laws while riding on our bikes?
    (h) Why does a bird build a nest?
    (i) Why do we have policemen and firemen?
    (j) Why do we have calendars?
    The single sentence answer can also lead to class discussion.

41. Play, "What is he or she doing?" Have one child perform a motor act (go over this with the actor first) and have another child describe the activity. Activities might be planting a seed in the garden, eating lunch, or getting dressed.

42. Have a child pantomime an activity and describe what he or she is doing while doing it.

43. Play, "You say it wrong, I'll say it correctly." Tell the children that you will

ask them a question. They should answer it with the correct information but in some way that is wrong. You will then attempt to figure out the correct way to say it. For example, the question might be, "Where do we use shingles?" The child might say, "On the up roof" or "Down in the roof," and you would correct it to "Up on the roof." If the children can succeed in developing an understanding of the process, see if they can act as "correctors."

44. Play, "Follow my words." Have a child follow your words orally, as closely as possible. Tell a short story and have the child repeat your words as closely behind your saying them as possible.

CHApTER NiNE
lANGUAGE ANd spEECH:
MATERiAls ANd EQUipMENT

This chapter contains a listing of materials and equipment that may be useful to the teacher and the speech-language pathologist in implementing the speech and language program.

The chapter is divided into sections consisting of a list of multimedia equipment and a list of speech and language materials. The materials lists are subdivided for easy use into categories including references, books and workbooks, teaching devices, records, games, films, and filmstrips. Sections of the materials lists have been coded according to suggested usage levels: P, Primary; I, Intermediate; and S, Secondary Levels of the school program for the mentally retarded. This coding is more appropriate for the higher retarded. The assignments are arbitrary. The specialist should investigate materials of interest to determine suitability. Prices listed are those available at the time of publication. They may vary with time.

A vendor's list follows the listings of the items appearing in this chapter. Most vendors have catalogues that more completely describe their products.

MULTIMEDIA INSTRUCTIONAL DEVICES

Ar-Tik' Speech and Hearing Recorder ($937.50), Arion.

Bell & Howell Language Master ($99.95 and up), Bell & Howell.

DuKane Filmstrip Viewer Model 576-48 A ($74.50), Film Mart.

Echorder (Echordettes $398 and up. Echorders $498 and up), RIL Electronics.

Filmstrips and Records
The combination of filmstrip and record has been highly successful in motivating children to verbalize. They learn to look carefully, listen attentively, remember sequential events, and enjoy retelling the story.

Flannel Boards

Flat Pictures. Should be attractively mounted.

Listening Center—4' X 4' ($99.50), Beckley Cardy. The entire laboratory is contained in a carrying case. Eight head sets can be connected to a tape recorder, record player, or movie projector.

Manipulative Profile Charts. Especially useful for the primary group.

Opaque Projector. Material can be shown from books, magazines.

Pocket Charts

Puppets

Radio

Record Player. In addition to an extensive list of stories and songs, there are many instructional records in the field of phonics and speech improvement.

Rexographed Materials

Slide Sets. Available commercially or can be locally produced.

Talking Books. Package of tape plus six copies of a book. The children are instructed on tape, and as a result of this auditory plus experience, there is an improvement in listening, speaking, and other related skills.

Tape Recorder. A minimum-frequency response to 8000Hz is recommended.

Tapes. Teacher and/or speech-language pathologist can develop lessons on speech improvement. Also, language patterns can be reinforced with the teacher or SLP serving as the model on the tape. Lessons can be used in conjunction with earphones, which reduce distraction. "Repeat after me" activities can also be useful.

Television. Both open- and closed-circuit TV programs can be extremely helpful. Children are accustomed to attending to TV and have positive feelings regarding its interest level.

Teletrainer Unit. Local telephone business offices can explain available services.

Transparencies. Use with the overhead projector. Proper use permits the teacher to develop and present subject matter with increased motivation for the children.

Typewriter. Useful in secondary classes. An adding machine and cash register can also be interest-producing.

The vendors' names of the following materials are abbreviated. (See vendor list for complete name and address.)

REFERENCES	VENDOR
1. *A Child Learns to Speak: A Guide for Parents and Teachers of Preschool Children* (Leitch)	Charles C. Thomas
2. *A Curriculum Guide for Teachers of the*	Interstate

     Educable Mentally Handicapped (Goldstein
     and Siegle) $4.95

3. *AID* (Accepting Individual Differences)   DLM
    $25.00

4. *A Language Program for the Non-Language*   Special Learning
    Child (Gray and Ryan) $7.95

5. *A Manual for Parents and Teachers of*   IMRID
    Severely and Moderately Retarded Children
    (Larsen and Bricker)

6. *American Association for the Education*   ERIC
    of the Severely Profoundly Handicapped
    Annotated Bibliography

7. *An Education Curriculum for the*   Charles C. Thomas
    Moderately, Severely and Profoundly
    Mentally Handicapped Pupil (Adams) $5.95

8. *An Educational Program for Multihandi-*   ERIC Clearinghouse
    capped Children $12.52

9. *An Instructional Guide for Parents*   ERIC
    (Carambio)

10. *A Program for Teaching the Under-*   DLM
    standing of Functional Words and Phrases
    $4.00

11. *A Selected Bibliography Related to the*   ERIC
    Vocational Training of Severely Handi-
    capped Persons

12. *A Speech Therapy Program for Mentally*   Interstate
    Handicapped Children (Jensen) $8.25

13. *A Step-by-Step Learning Guide for*   Childcraft
    Retarded Infants and Children
    (Johnson and Werner) $5.95

14. *Art Experiences for Young Children*   Teacher's Publishing
    (Pile) $7.95

15. *Beginning Language Arts Instruction with*   Charles Merrill
    Children (Shane, Howard, Reddin, Mary E.,
    and Gillespie, Margaret C.) $9.95

16. *Better Speech and Better Reading*   Expression Company
    (Schoolfield, L. D.) $5.50

17. *Books for Young People* (Bobbs-Merrill)   Charles E. Merrill
    $3.60

18. *Children's Spatial Development*   Charles C. Thomas
    (Eliot and Salkind)

19. *Classroom-Tested Bulletin Boards*   Fearon

(Examples and Suggestions for making
them.) $1.75

20. *Communication Assessment and Interven-*   Mafex
    tion Strategies (Lloyd) $16.50
21. *Correction of Defective Consonant Sounds*   Expression Company
    (Nemoy and Davis) $8.00
22. *Creative Activities* (Augustine) $6.50   Stanwix
23. *Creative Dramatization* (Van Tassel and   Teacher's Publishing
    Greimann) $7.95
24. *Developmental Language Lessons*   Teaching Resources
    (Mowery and Replagle) $39.95
25. *Developmental Skills for Early Childhood*   T. S. Denison
    $7.95
26. *Early Childhood Continuum*   Taylor Publishing
27. *Educating Exceptional Children*   Houghton Mifflin
    (Kirk, Samuel A.) $14.50
28. *Educating the Retarded Child*   Houghton Mifflin
    (Kirk and Johnson) $11.95
29. *Educational Games and Activities*   Teacher's Publishing
    (Wagner, Hosier, Blackman, and Gillogly)
    A sourcebook for parents and teachers.
30. *Educational Technology for the Severely*   ERIC
    Handicapped: A Comprehensive
    Bibliography
31. *Educators Guide to Free Film*   Educators Progress Service
    $13.70
32. *English Syntax: An Outline for Clinicians*   Charles C. Thomas
    and Teachers of Language Handicapped
    Children (Hargis)
33. *Evaluating the Audiogram* (Omer) $1.00   Interstate
34. *Expressive Language Remediation for the*   Interstate
    Older Elementary Child (Beveridge) $1.95
35. *Finding and Helping Handicapped Children*   Special Learning
    (Cross and Gon) $9.95
36. *Free & Inexpensive Learning Materials* $3.50   George Peabody
37. *Helpful Books to Use with Retarded*   *Elementary School Jour-*
    Children (Smith)   *nal* March, 1952, p. 390
38. *Language Acquisition Program for the*   Research Press
    Retarded or Multiply Impaired (Kent) $6.95
39. *Language Acquisition* (Quigley) $3.50   *The Volta Review*
         January, 1968
40. *Language and Communication in the*   Mafex
    Mentally Handicapped (Berry) $16.50

41. *Language and Mental Retardation* (Schiefelbusch, Copeland, Smith)	Holt, Rinehart & Winston
42. *Language Arts in the Elementary School* (Strickland, Ruth)	D. C. Heath
43. *Language Development Experiences for Young Children* $10.95	Univ. of Southern California
44. *Language Development for the Young Child* (Rainey) $6.90	Special Learning
45. *Language Development of Exceptional Children* (Love, Mainord, and Naylor)	Charles C. Thomas
46. *Language Development Through Perceptual-Motor Activities* (Flowers) $8.25	Interstate
47. *Language of the Mentally Retarded* (Schiefelbusch) $14.50	Mafex
48. *Language Motivating Experiences* (Engel, Rose C.) $3.45	D. F. A. Publications
49. *Language Perspectives-Acquisition, Retardation and Intervention* (Schiefelbusch and Lloyd) $14.50	Mafex
50. *Language, Reading and Learning Disabilities* (Bannatyne) $14.95	Charles C. Thomas
51. *Language Rehabilitation Program* (Hainard Lanier) $31.95	Teaching Resources
52. *Language Skills and Social Concepts* $6.95	Bardeen
53. *Mainstreaming Series* (Fairchild) $29.70	Learning Concepts
54. *Manual for Effective Use of "The Best Speech Series" with Special Pupils* (Matthew, Birch, and Burgi) $16.50	Stanwix
55. *Measurement Procedures in Speech, Hearing, and Language* (Singh) $18.50	Mafex
56. *Music Therapy: An Introduction to Therapy and Special Education Through Music* (Michel) $9.75	Charles C. Thomas
57. *Phonovisual Textbook for Teachers* (Smith) $5.50	Phonovisual Products
58. *Play Acting with Mentally Retarded Children* (Filegler)	Exceptional Children, Volume 15, November 1952, pp. 52–60
59. *Play Activities for the Retarded Child* (Carlson, Bernice Wells and Ginglend, David R.) $6.95	Abingdon Press
60. *Prescriptive Teaching* (Banas and Wills)	Charles C. Thomas
61. *Procedure Guides for Evaluation of Speech*	Interstate

and Language Disorders in Children
(Sanders) $3.95

62. *Programmed Lessons for Young Language-*   Charles C. Thomas
    Disabled Children: A Handbook for
    Therapists, Educators and Parents
    (Heasley) $8.50

63. *Puppets & Puppetry*—Curriculum Guide for   Board of Education,
    using puppets (Grades 2–6) $1.00   New York City

64. *Remediating Auditory Learning and*   Interstate
    Language Disabilities—Ideas and Activities
    (Medlen and Quatrochi) $8.25

65. *Special Education: Speech Therapy*   T. S. Denison
    (handbook) $7.95

66. *Speech and Hearing: A Guide for Determin-*   Special Learning
    ing Needs and Setting Priorities $24.50

67. *Speech and Hearing Therapy* (Irwin) #0820   Stanwix
    $9.50

68. *Speech and Language Delay: A Home*   Charles C. Thomas
    Training Program (Battin) $5.50

69. *Speech and Language Development of the*   Charles C. Thomas
    Preschool Child: A Survey $11.75

70. *Speech and Language Development Manuals*   Communication Skill
    $7.50   Builders

71. *Speech Correction in the Schools*   Macmillan
    (Eisenson, Jon) $12.95

72. *Speech Handicapped School Children*   Harper & Row
    (Johnson) $16.95

73. *Speech of the Retarded Child* (Curriculum   New York City Board of
    Bulletin, Bd. of Ed. N.Y.C. 1958–59,   Education
    Series #7, 1960) $2.50

74. *Steps Up to Language for the Learning-*   Mafex
    Impaired: Attending $10.00

75. *Structured Language for Children with*   Alexander Graham Bell
    Special Language Learning Problems
    (Monsees) $9.75

76. *Symbol Communication for the Mentally*   ERIC
    Handicapped (Vanderheiden)

77. *Syntax, Speech and Hearing: Applied*   Alexander Graham Bell
    Linguistics for Teachers of Children with
    Language and Hearing Disabilities
    (Streng) $17.50

78. *Systematic Instruction for Retarded*   Interstate

Children: The Illinois Program (Chalfard &
Silikovitz) $10.40

79. *Talk! Talk! Talk!* (A Language Curriculum)   Mafex
    $17.50

80. *Teacher's Handbook of Diagnostic Screening:*   Mafex
    Auditory, Visual, Motor, and Language
    (Mann and Suiter) $21.95

81. *Teacher's Handbook of Diagnostic Inven-*   Mafex
    tories: Spelling, Handwriting, Reading and
    Arithmetic (Mann and Suiter) $21.95

82. *Teaching Language Arts to Mentally*   T. S. Denison
    Retarded Children $7.95

83. *Teaching of Reading to Slow Learning*   Houghton Mifflin
    Children (Kirk), January, 1978

84. *Teaching Reading Readiness to the Mentally*   T. S. Denison
    Retarded (Handbook) $7.95

85. *Teaching the Pre-Academic Child*   Charles C. Thomas
    (Mott) $9.75

86. *Teaching the Retarded Child to Talk*   John Day

87. *The Design and Implementation of an*   ERIC
    Empirically Based Instructional Program for
    Young Severely Handicapped Students:
    Toward Rejection of the Exclusion Principle
    (Brown) $20.41

88. *The Language of Classifications* (Rush) $4.95   Alexander Graham Bell

89. *The Non-Verbal Child: An Introduction to*   Charles C. Thomas
    Pediatric Language Pathology (Adler) $13.50

90. *The Right to Education Child:* A Curriculum   Charles C. Thomas
    for the Severely and Profoundly Mentally
    Retarded. $9.75

91. *The Teaching Research Curriculum For*   Charles C. Thomas
    Moderately and Severely Handicapped
    (Bud) $18.50

92. *Threshold Language Skills and Social*   Teacher's Publishing
    Concepts (Orast, Eloy, Kaup, and Lader)
    $7.95

93. *Training Children to Listen* Monograph #80   Row Peterson
    (Pratt, L.)

94. *Training the Developmentally Young*
    (Stephens)

95. *Understanding and Teaching the Dependent*   Teacher's Publishing
    Retarded Child (Rosenzweig and Long)

96. *Valuable Language Programs* (Kent)   Special Learning Corp.
A Language Acquisition Program for the
Retarded or Multiply Impaired. $7.95

BOOKS AND WORKBOOKS FOR CHILDREN

	Vendor	Level		
		P	I	S
1. *Alike Because Book* $7.50	Teaching Resources	X		
2. *All About the Eggs* $4.95	Childcraft	X		
3. *At Home* (Hanna & Hoyt)	Scott, Foresman	X		
4. *Awareness Books* $4.50	Special Learning	X		
5. *Beginning Dictionary*	Scott, Foresman	X		
Junior Dictionary			X	X
6. *Best Speech Series* x/Manual	Stanwix House		X	
(Series of Books and manuals)				
My Sound Books (For s.r.th.l.				
k.g.sh. sounds.) $2.00 ea.				
7. *Better Speech Can Be Fun*	Expression	X	X	
(Goldberg & Brasslow) $1.50				
f-Booklet				
l-Booklet				
r-Booklet				
s-Booklet				
th-Booklet				
8. *Big Book of Sounds* $5.00	King	X	X	
9. *Book of Riddles,* Beginner Books	Random House		X	
(Cerf, Bennett) $3.69				
10. *Categories: Clothing and*	Teaching Resources	X		
Household Items $6.40				
11. *Categories: Food and Animals*	Teaching Resources	X		
$6.40				
12. *Categories: Varied* $5.35	Teaching Resources	X		
13. *Clap, Snap, and Tap Band*	T. S. Denison	X		
(Carl W. Vandre) Book of				
rhythms utilizing body parts,				
hands, knees, mouth-as instruments.				
$5.95				
14. *Comparisons* (Ellison) $11.50	Teaching Resources	X		

15.	*Cowboy Sam Books* *Jerry Books* *Farm Life Readers*	Beckley-Cardy	X	
16.	*Easy Skits for Youngsters* Collection of skits requiring no scenery, costumes, minimum preparation. $3.00	T. S. Denison	X	
17.	*Enrichment Books for Children*	Experimental Development Program	X	
18.	*Famous Stories* (Beals)	L. W. Singer		X
19.	*Fingerplay Approach Through* *Dramatization* (Mary Jackson Ellis) Finger plays are stories with rhymes used to provide a basis for creative dramatics. $3.50	T. S. Denison	X	
20.	*First Picture Books* $3.95 ea.	Lakeshore	X	
21.	*Fitzhugh Plus Program* (five workbooks) Number (three workbooks) Spatial (three workbooks) Language Complete set $25.00	Allied Education Council	X X	
22.	*Five in the Family*	Scott, Foresman	X	
23.	*Five Minutes Play for Children* (Haney Germaine) Plays youthful actors that portray real people in childlike activities. $1.95	T. S. Denison	X	
24.	*Follett BIR Picture Dictionary* (McIntire) $2.97	Follett	X X	
25.	*Galloping Sounds* (Ainsworth) $3.00	Expression	X	
26.	*Getting a Job* (Florence Randall) $2.80	Fearon		X
27.	*Hank* (Broderick, Dorothy M.) $6.79	Harper & Row		X
28.	*Happiness Hill Merry-Go-Round* (Jacobs, Tumer) $3.84	Charles Merrill	X	
29.	*Help Yourself to Read, Write and* *Spell* (Loesel) (Vol. I & II) $5.50 ea. vol.	Ginn		X
30.	*I Can Do It* (Clore and Rumsey) A Series of Manipulative Books.	Bowmar	X	

Two series: $44.10 and $43.20 respectively.				
31. *Language Experience Programs*	Encyclopedia Britannica	X	X	
32. *Let's Find Out* (three pupil parts, two teaching guides, two related classroom guides) $1.35 per year per pupil.	Scholastic Magazine	X	X	X
33. *Let's Imagine Sounds* (Wolff, Janet, and Owett, Bernard)	E. P. Dutton	X		
34. *Listen–Hear Books* (Slepian, Jan, and Seidler, Ann) $30.00 *Jr. Listen–Hear Books* (Slepian and Seidler) $30.00	Follett		X	
35. *Listening Aids Through the Grades* (Russell, David and Elizabeth) $3.25	Teacher's College Press		X	
36. *Listening for Speech Sounds* (Zedler) $12.95	Harper		X	
37. *Listening Games* $2.95 *Language Games* $2.95 (Wagner, Guy, May, Hosier and Blackman) Two books	Teacher's Publishing		X	
38. *Mine, Yours, Ours* (Albert) $4.00	Albert Whitman	X		
39. *Mott Basic Language Skill Program* (Thirty-five books, semi-programmed) $89.95 complete program	Allied Education Council		X	X
40. *Once There Was a Rabbit* *Once There Was a Bear* *Once There Was a Dog* *Once There Was an Elephant* *I Like Cats* $2.88 each	Garrard	X		
41. *Peek-thru Overlays* $1.69 per set	Zaner-Bloser	X		
42. *Picture Story Books* $62.20 kit *Did You Ever See* $ .85 *1-2-3 Going to See* $ .75 *Where Is Everybody* $ .95	Scholastic Book Service	X		
43. *Reading Series* (Turner-Livingston) The Television You Watch Phone Calls You Make	Follett			X

Newspapers You Read
Movies You See
The Language You Speak
(six titles) $1.38 ea.

#	Title	Publisher			
44.	*Sounds for Little Folks* (Stoddard) $4.50	Expression	X		
45.	*Sounds Like Fun* (Parker, Jayne, and Hall) Aid in development of listening skills, contains rhymes stressing consonant sounds. $3.25	Interstate		X	
46.	*Speech Drills for Children in the Form of Play* (Barrows and Case) $2.00	Expression	X	X	
47.	*Speech Improvement Work and Practice Book* (McCullough) $3.00	Expression		X	X
48.	*Speech Through Pictures* (McCausland) $2.50	Expression	X	X	X
49.	*Talking Time* (Scott, Louise, and Thompson, J. J.) For speech and speech improvement with drill materials. $8.74	Webster/McGraw-Hill	X	X	X
50.	*The Big Book of Language Through Sounds* $5.95	Interstate	X	X	X
51.	*The Child's Book of Speech Sounds* (Chipman) $1.50	Expression	X		
52.	*The Clown Family Speech Book* (Pollack and Pollack) $6.50	Charles C. Thomas	X		
53.	*The Job Ahead* (Goldberg, Herman, and Brumber, Winifred) Levels I, II, III　$4.25 ea. Resource Books　$4.25 ea. Instructor's Guide　$3.95	Science Research Associates			X
54.	*The Noise Books* (Brown, Margaret Wise) The City Noisy Book The Indoor Noisy Book The Quiet Noisy Book The Seashore Noisy Book The Summer Noisy Book The Winter Noisy Book $5.79 ea.	Harper	X		
55.	*Useful Language*	Continental	X		

56. *Well, Why Didn't You Say So?* Story to help children become aware of the importance of talking. $4.00	Albert Whitman	X		
57. *Words to Read, Write and Spell* A picture dictionary containing over 1,000 entries. $4.80	Harper			X
58. *You and Your Family*–Four books (Body parts, Members of family) *You and Your Friends* (Classroom, School) $1.80 ea.	Benefic	X		
59. *"Your World" Books* (Pope and Emmons) Designed to involve children in realistic experiences in the familiar world around them. $20.00 set	Taylor	X		

MATERIALS

1. *Alike and Not Alike* $3.00 ea.	Mafex	X		
2. *Art Experiences for Young Children* (Pile) $7.95	Teacher's Publishing	X		
3. *Auditory Closure Cards* $4.35	Mafex	X		
4. *Bank Street College Inter-Act Materials*	Constructive Playthings	X		
5. *Basic Materials Resource Kit* $41.00	Teaching Resources	X		
6. *Bowmar Artworlds Develops Verbal and Visual Fluency* (Mandlin) $195.00	Bowmar	X		
7. *Bowmar Language Stimulus Program* (Allinson, Allinson, and McInnes) $25.00	Bowmar	X	X	X
8. *Classification Play Tray Card Sets* (Prices variable)	Interstate	X		
9. *Colors Everywhere* $189.95	Special Learning	X		
10. *Community Worker Puppets* (Set of 4 puppets) Available in white or black. $12.00/set	J. L. Hammett	X		

11. *Developmental Skills for Early Childhood* $7.95	T. S. Denison	X		
12. *Developmental Syntax Program* (Coughman and Liles) $29.95	Learning Concepts	X	X	
13. *Early Childhood Series* (Curry, Jaynes, Crume, and Radlauer) $390.00	Bowmar	X		
14. *Early Language Activities* (Karnes) $49.95	Childcraft	X		
15. *Emerging Language 2* (Halton, Gomen, and Lent) $5.95	Communication Skill Builders	X		
16. *Everyday Language Skill Charts* Twenty colorful charts display essential oral and written language skills. $2.75	Beckley Cardy	X		
17. *Flannel Board Aids* Opposites $5.00 Story Kits $4.00 Build a Story $4.00	Milton Bradley	X	X	
18. *Fokes Sentence Builder* (Fokes) Comprehensive oral-language program.	Teaching Resources	X	X	X
19. *Goal: Level 1 Language Development* $130.00	Milton Bradley	X		
20. *Goal: Level 2 Language Development* $130.00	Milton Bradley	X	X	
21. *Handwriting Programs* (Prices Variable)	Zaner-Blosner		X	X
22. *Ideal Rhyming Puzzles* $2.35	Ideal School Supply	X	X	
23. *Informal Dramatics: A Language Arts Activity for the Special Pupil* $2.75	Stanwix	X		
24. *Instructo Activity Kits* (Summer, Spring, Winter, Fall) Sequence opposites: beginning sounds, farm animals, zoo community helpers, creating stories.	Beckley Cardy	X		
25. *Instructo Flannel Board* Aides: safety, family, party. Halloween: original story set. (five sets, $8.00)	Beckley Cardy	X		
26. *Instructo Language Arts* (twelve sets, each set $2.95)	Beckley Cardy	X		

27. *Laidlaw Linguistic Laboratory* Each laboratory contains thirty laboratories, teacher's guide, a class progress chart, and thirty answer guide cards. Complete lab. $142.56 ea.	Laidlaw Bros.			X
28. *Language Association Boards* Prepositions $5.50 Verbs $5.50 Adjectives $5.50	Modern Education Corp.	X	X	
29. *Language Big Box* $90.00	DLM	X		
30. *Language Building Cards* (Flowers) Matching and Serial Speech $9.75 ea.	Interstate	X		
31. *Language Development:*	Lakeshore	X	X	X
"See How You Feel Card Set" $9.50		X	X	X
"Prepositions" $4.95		X	X	X
"Spatial Relationship Concept Cards" $4.95		X	X	X
"Why-Because Card Set" $4.95		X	X	X
"Opposites-Concept Cards" $7.25		X	X	X
"Action Cards"		X	X	X
32. *Language Development Overhead Transparencies* Seven different sets available. Prices variable.	GAF	X		
33. *Language Development Phonics Transparencies* $264.00	Noble and Noble	X	X	X
34. *Language Structure Simplified* (Millstein) Sentence formulation and syntax development. $48.00 (Adult or older student version, $48.00.)	Educational Activities	X		X
35. *Language Through Play Acting* (Betty Mintz) $5.95	Mafex	X		
36. *Large Picture Rubber Stamps* Classification and expressive language skills.	Childcraft	X		
37. *Letter Sounds All Around*	Bowmar	X		
38. *Learning Staircase* (Coughran and Goff) $199.95	Learning Concepts	X	X	X

39. *Learning Through Factual Units* $5.95	T. S. Denison	X		
40. *Learning Through Songs* General knowledge, classification, and language development. $23.00	Teaching Resources	X		
41. *Learning to Develop Language Skills*-Unit II $60.00	Milton Bradley	X		
42. *Language: Verb Action Pictures and Plural Action Pictures* (Parker) $12.25 ea.	Whitehaven	X	X	
43. *Learning to Listen Lessons* $6.95	T. S. Denison	X		
44. *Leaves Alike and Not Alike* $7.00	Mafex	X		
45. *On Stage: Wally, Bertha, and You* Multimedia Kit focusing on self-confidence, personal awareness, and oral expression. $69.95	Encyclopedia Britannica		X	X
46. *Parts of Speech* (Brown) (Language development cards.)	Teaching Resources	X	X	X
47. *Peabody Language Development Kits* Level P (3–5) $192.00 Level 1 (4½–6½) $74.00 Level 2 (6–8) $88.00 Level 3 (M.A. 7½–9½) $66.00 (Self-contained kit designed to stimulate oral language—materials, plus lesson plans.)	American Guidance	X	X	X
48. *People, Places, and Things* $5.75	Teaching Resources	X		
49. *Perceive and Respond* Auditory Discrimination Program: Volume I: Environmental Sounds $70.00 Volume II: Auditory Discrimination $90.00 Volume III: Auditory Sequential Memory $50.00	Modern Education	X	X	
		X	X	
		X	X	
50. *Phonovisual Method Charts* $5.00 *Phonovisual Book of Games* $3.00 *Phonovisual Consonant Film-strips* $3.00 *Vowel Phonovisual Picture Pak* $3.00 (vowel and consonants)	Phono Visual Products	X	X	

Phonovisual Work Book $1.10
Road to Power & Confidence Workbook $1.25
Phonovisual Diagnostic Test $3.00
Phonovisual Magnetic Boards
(consonant, $24.00)
(vowels, $20.00)

51.	*Phonetic Drill Cards* $2.75	Milton Bradley		X	X
52.	*Photo Sequence Cards* Occupations, recreation, and daily living activities. $16.00 ea.	Modern Education	X	X	X
53.	*Picture Sequence Cards* Indoor and outdoor activities. $14.00 ea.	Modern Education	X	X	
54.	*Picture Sequence Cards* $2.00	Milton Bradley	X	X	
55.	*Puppet Enrichment Program* $49.50	Constructive Playthings	X		
56.	*Puzzles—Various Concepts* Prices Variable	Constructive Playthings	X		
57.	*Rexograph Materials* Dittoes on developmental language concepts.	Continental Press	X	X	
58.	*Rhythm Band for 16 Players* Instruction book with musical numbers plus sticks, clogs, bells, triangle, tom tom, baton, cymbals. $9.95	Beckley Cardy	X		
59.	*Rhymitts* Two terry cloth mitts with bells attached, marked left and right. $2.50	Creative Playthings	X		
60.	*Scenes Around Us Story Posters* $8.50	Milton Bradley	X	X	
61.	*SEARCH:* Structured Environmental Activities for the Rehabilitation of the Communicatively Handicapped. (Wilmot, Bober, A'skew) $225.00	Learning Concepts	X		
62.	*See Quee Sequence Boards* four piece $2.35 ea. six piece $2.65 ea. twelve piece $3.90 ea.	Judy Co.	X	X	
63.	*Sequence Pictures for Storytelling* (Parker) $10.95	Whitehaven	X	X	

64.	*Shape and Size Perception Materials* (Prices Variable)	Constructive Playthings	X	
65.	*Size Sequencing Cards* $2.50	DLM	X X	
66.	*Sound Out: Listening Skills Program* $21.75	Mafex		
67.	*Storytelling with the Flannel Board* $21.75	Constructive Playthings	X	
68.	*TAD Kit:* Toward Affective Development. Program of lessons, activities, and materials designed to stimulate psychological and affective development.	AGS	X	
69.	*Talking with Mike* Designed to help the child who speaks one of the nonstandard American dialects acquire the standard American English dialect. $49.95	Special Learning	X X X	
70.	*The Learning Well* (Inseland Edson) $95.00	Educational Activities	X	
71.	*The MWM Program for Developing Language Abilities* (Minskoff, Wiseman, and Minskoff) $195.00	Childcraft	X X X	
72.	*Think, Tell, and See* $9.50	Mafex	X	
73.	*Touch and Tell* Identifying and Describing Textures. $8.75	Ideal School Supply	X	
74.	*Traffic Signs* (set of four) $12.00 set	J. L. Hammett	X	
75.	*TRY: Experiences for Young Children* $46.00	Noble and Noble	X X	
76.	*Verb Puzzles* $4.75	DLM	X X	
77.	*Vinel Family Hand Puppets* Set of five puppets—white or black. $15.00 set	J. L. Hammett	X	
78.	*Visual Motor Teaching Materials Kit* Complete kit including puzzles, geometric forms, size shapes (games—not available). Various visual motor kits are available, each includes some of the above materials.	Teaching Resources	X X X	

79.	*Visual Perception Big Box* $77.00	DLM	X	X
80.	*What's Cooking* (Cook) $40.00	Bowmar	X	
81.	*What's Next* $5.50	Mafex	X	
82.	*Word Prefixes/Suffixes* Sets of cards with words and meaning. $.59 per set	Bardeen		X

RECORDS

1.	*Basic Awareness Through Music* (1-12" 33 1/3 R.P.M.) $6.95	Educational Record	X		
2.	*Basic Concepts Thru Dance* Set 601 with three records $13.50 *Body Image* AR 601 $6.95 *Positioning Space* AR 603 $6.95	Educational Activities	X		
3.	*Basic Songs for the Exceptional Child*, Vols. I and II.	Concept Records	X	X	
4.	*Best in Children's Literature* Holidays, five senses, nature transportation, values, universe. Records or Cassettes	Bowmar	X	X	X
5.	*Bozo the Clown—Tubby Tuba* Talking story books.	Golden Press	X		
6.	*Downtown Story* (two parts) Department store and super- market. $6.98	Scholastic		X	
7.	*First Talking Alphabet* Twenty records, duplicating masters. $36.00	Scott Foresman	X		
8.	*First Talking Story Book Box* (21 books, 21 records) $57.00	Scott Foresman	X	X	
9.	*Fun with Speech* (Series of three records) $19.45	Encyclopedia Britannica	X	X	
10.	*I'm No Fool with Safety* Set $120.00 *Safety Study Prints* $19.00	Walt Disney			
11.	*Invitations to Story Time* (Set includes two records, four posters, two cutout sets, two puzzles, mobiles) $42.00	Scott Foresman	X		
12.	*Learning As We Play*	Records Plus.	X		

(Stiles and Ginglend) "A Must for All Classes of Mentally Retarded Children." $6.98

13. *Learning Basic Skills to Music* *Vocabulary* $6.95	Educational Record	X		
14. *Listening Story Lessons Set* (Eight record-lessons) $59.00	Walt Disney	X		
15. *Listening with Mr. Bunny Big* *Ears* Encourages listening through sound discrimination activities— speaking through active partici- pation in dramatic play. Each lesson emphasizes a sound. (Six records) $36.95	Stanwix		X	
16. *Music Listening Game* Big and Little—Here Are Your Eyes	Young People Record	X		
17. *Sing and Do* Vocal songs of action with manual of detailed suggestions.	Sing & Do		X	
18. *Songs About Me* Three 12" 33 1/3 R.P.M. records. $15.95	Educational Record	X		
19. *Songs for Children with Special* *Needs* Three 12" 33 1/3 R.P.M. records. $6.95 ea. Accompanying book. (Cole) $3.85	Bowmar	X	X	
20. *Smile* Coordinates music behavior and good speech habits.	Jeri Products	X	X	X
21. *Sounds I Can Hear* (Set of four albums plus charts, records, repro- ductions of sounds made by peo- ple, animals and objects in the world around us.) $20.00	Scott Foresman	X		
22. *Sounds of My City* Documentary of children, con- struction, subways, etc. of New York. $5.98	Scholastic			X
23. *The Art of Learning Through* *Movement* (Barlin) Two 7" records. $14.20	Bowmar	X	X	
24. *The Laundry & Bakery Story* A "live experience" record. $6.98	Scholastic			X

GAMES

	Item	Supplier			
1.	*ABC Lotto* $1.40	Childcraft	X		
2.	*Auditory Discrimination Game* $18.00	Modern Education	X	X	
3.	*Candy Land* $4.50	Childcraft	X		
4.	*Cartoon Board* $9.00	Modern Education		X	X
5.	*Checker Game* Book #1 $3.75 Book #2 $4.25	Whitehaven	X	X	
6.	*Farm Lotto* Code #82713 $2.00	J. L. Hammett	X		
7.	*Gameboards for Speech and Language Development* (Blockcolsky, Frazer, Kurn, and Metz) $39.00	Mafex	X	X	
8.	*Games and Activities for Early Childhood Education* (Wagner, Gilloley, Roth, and Cesinger) $2.95	Teacher's Publishing	X		
9.	*Language Games* $2.95	Teacher's Publishing	X	X	X
10.	*Language Lotto* (Gotkin, Lassar G.) $43.50	Appleton-Century-Crofts	X	X	X
.	*Listening Games* $2.95	Teacher's Publishing	X	X	X
12.	*Match and Check* Ten games— match colors, shapes, objects, beginning sounds, rhyming sounds, words. $4.00	Scott Foresman	X		
13.	*Object Lotto—Go-Mo Game Cards—Auto Race Games* (Prices varied)	Go-Mo	X		
14.	*Phonics We Use Games Kit* Ten separate games. $35.00 Replaced by: Phonics We Use Learning Game Kit 1 $87.00 Kit 2 $87.00	Rand McNally		X	X
15.	*Phono Junior and Phono Senior* Games $6.95 ea.	T. S. Denison	X	X	X
16.	*Phonovisual Games*	Phonovisual	X		
17.	*Read and Say Verb Game* $2.18	Garrard		X	X
18.	*Shapes and Rainbow* (Walker) $4.75	Stanwix	X		

19. *Sound Ladder Game* (Arnold) $3.00	Expression		X	X
20. *Speech-O, A Phonetic Game* (Arnold) $4.25	Expression		X	X
21. *Sports Assortment* (Folder Game) $6.00	Go-Mo			X
22. *Stimulation Cards* ID Cards, Speech Lingo, Spin It. $6.00 ea.	Modern Education	X	X	X
23. *What's Missing?* Story cards (Milton-Bradley) Cards with pictures from which a child must select a missing part to complete the picture. A vocabulary builder. $2.00	Beckley Cardy		X	
24. *What the Letters Say* Dolch Sounding Program. Every letter not only has a name but also "says a sound." $3.28	Garrard			
25. *Word Power Games* (Wagner, Hosier, and Cesinger) $4.95	Teacher's Publishing	X	X	

FILMS AND FILMSTRIPS

1. *Can You Describe It?* Series of four: What You Hear? What Can You See? What Can You Touch and Feel? What Can You Taste and Smell? $32.90	Encyclopedia Britannica	X	X	
2. *Filmstrip Series* (Listed according to academic levels.)	Educational Reading Service	X	X	X
3. *Filmstrips from Encyclopedia Britannica* Drug abuse. (Series of 4)	Encyclopedia Britannica			X
4. *Films for Developing Skills in Young Learners* (Set of seven.) $49.00	Stanley Bowman	X	X	
5. *Projecto-Aid-Overhead Transparencies* (On Jobs, Health, Communication, Sex)	GAF			

6. *Talking Time Series* (Includes talking helpers-consonant sounds.) $61.00	McGraw-Hill	X	X
7. *The Calendar* (Film—includes year, spring, summer, week, month, autumn, and winter.) $92.00	McGraw-Hill	X	X

VENDORS LIST

1. Abingdon Press
   201 8th Avenue, South
   Nashville, Tennessee 37202

2. Albert Whitman and Company
   560 West Lake Street
   Chicago, Illinois 60606

3. Alexander Graham Bell Association for the Deaf
   1537-35 Street, North West
   Washington, D.C. 20007

4. Allied Education Council
   P.O. Box 78
   Galien, Michigan 49113

5. American Annals of the Deaf
   Gallaudet College
   Seventh Street and Florida Avenue
   Washington, D.C. 20002

6. American Book Company (SWRL)
   Education Research & Development
   4665 Lampson Avenue
   Los Alamitos, California 90720

7. American Book Company
   Litton Educational Publishing, Inc.
   450 West 33rd Street
   New York, New York 10001

8. American Guidance Service, Incorporated
   Publishers Building
   Circle Pines, Minnesota 55014

9. American Records
   Freeport
   Long Island, New York

10. American Speech & Hearing Association
    10801 Rockville Pike
    Rockville, Maryland 20852

**Cross reference

11. Appleton-Century-Crofts
    Meridith Publishing Company
    440 Park Avenue South
    New York, New York 10016
12. Arion Products
    1022 Nicollet Avenue
    Minneapolis, Minnesota 55043
13. Associated Education Materials
    Glenwood at Hillsboro Street
    Raleigh, North Carolina
14. Bardeen, Incorporated
    Fisher Road
    East Syracuse, New York 13057
15. Beacon Press
    25 Beacon Street
    Boston, Massachusetts 02108
16. Beckley Cardy Corporation
    c/o Benefic Press
    1900 North Narragansette Avenue
    Chicago, Illinois 60639
17. Bell & Howell
    7100 North McCormick
    Chicago, Illinois 69645
    **Bowman—see Stanley Bowman listing
18. Bowmar Publishing Corporation
    4563 Colorado Boulevard
    Los Angeles, California 90039
    **Bradley—see Milton Bradley listing
19. Burgess Publishing Company
    426 South Sixth Street
    Minneapolis, Minnesota
20. Charles C. Thomas Publishers
    301-327 East Lawrence Avenue
    Springfield, Illinois 62717
21. Charles E. Merrill
    1300 Alum Creek Drive
    Columbus, Ohio 43216
22. Childcraft Educational Corporation
    20 Kilmer Road
    Edison, New Jersey 08817
23. Childrens Press
    1224 West Van Buren Street
    Chicago, Illinois 60607

24. Columbia University
    School of Library Services
    516 Butler Library
    New York, New York 10027
25. Columbia Record Company
    51 West 42nd Street
    New York, New York 10019
26. Council for Exceptional Children
    1920 Association Drive
    Reston, Virginia 22091
27. Communication Skill Builders, Incorporated
    817 East Broadway
    Post Office Box 6081-C
    Tucson, Arizona 85733
28. Constructive Playthings
    1040 East 85th Street
    Kansas City, Missouri
29. Concept Records
    Box 524
    N. Bellmore
    Long Island, New York
30. Continental Press
    Elizabeth, Pennsylvania 17022
31. Coronet Films
    65 East South Water Street
    Chicago, Illinois 60601
32. Creative Playthings
    Post Office Box 11
    Princeton, New Jersey 08540
33. Day Company
    275 Park Avenue South
    New York, New York 10010
34. D. C. Heath Company
    125 Spring Street
    Lexington, Massachusetts 02173
35. Decca Records
    Division of MCA Incorporated
    445 Park Avenue
    New York, New York 10022
36. Demco Educational Corporation
    Box 1488
    Madison, Wisconsin 53701

37. Developmental Learning Materials (DLM)
    7440 Natchez Avenue
    Niles, Illinois 60648

38. Di-Bur
    Box 1184
    Pueblo, Colorado

    **Dutton—see E. P. Dutton listing

39. Dolch, Garrard Publishing Company
    1607 Market Street
    Champaign, Illinois 61820

40. Eckstein Brothers
    48-7 West 118th Place
    Hawthorne, California 90251

41. Educational Activities, Incorporated
    Box 392
    Freeport, New York 11520

42. Educational Media
    Box 2067
    Van Nuys, California 01404

43. Educational Reading Services, Inc.
    320 Route 17
    Mahwah, New Jersey 07430

44. Educational Record Sales
    157 Chambers Street
    New York, New York 10007

45. Education Industry Service
    1225 East 60th Street
    Chicago 37, Illinois

46. Education Media Corporation
    555 Knollwood Road
    White Plains, New York 10603

47. Educators Progress Service, Incorporated
    214 Center Street
    Randolph, Wisconsin 53956

48. Educators Publishing Service
    301 Vassar Street
    Cambridge, Massachusetts 02139

49. Eldridge Publishing Company
    Franklin, Ohio 45005

50. Encyclopedia Britannica Educational Corporation
    425 North Michigan Avenue, Department 10A
    Chicago, Illinois 60611

51. E. P. Dutton Company
    201 Park Avenue, South
    New York, New York 10003
52. ERIC Document Reproduction Service
    Post Office Box 190
    Arlington, Virginia 22210
53. Eye-Gate House Incorporated
    146-01 Archer Avenue
    Jamaica, New York
54. Expression Company Publishers
    155 Columbus Avenue
    Boston, Massachusetts 02116
55. Fearon Publishers, Incorporated
    Pitman Publishing Corporation
    6 Davis Drive
    Belmont, California 94002
56. Folkways Scholastic Records
    906 Sylvan Avenue
    Englewood Cliffs, New Jersey 07632
57. Follett Publishing Company
    1010 West Washington Boulevard
    Chicago, Illinois 60607
58. GAF Corporation
    Audio/Visual Order Department
    Binghamton, New York 13902
59. Garrard Publishing Company
    1607 North Market Street
    Champaign, Illinois 61820
60. George Peabody College for Teachers
    Office of Educational Services
    Box 164
    Nashville, Tennessee 37203
61. Ginn and Company
    191 Spring Street
    Lexington, Massachusetts 02173
    Gilanor—See Harriet Gilanor listing
62. Golden Gate Junior Books
    Box 398
    San Carlos, California
63. Golden Press
    850 Third Avenue
    New York, New York 10022
64. Go-Mo Products

Post Office Box 143
Waterloo, Iowa 50704

65. Grossett & Dunlap, Incorporated
    51 Madison Avenue
    New York, New York 10010

66. Grune and Stratton, Incorporated
    111 Fifth Avenue
    New York, New York 10003

  **Hammett—See J. L. Hammett listing

67. Harper & Row Publisher
    10 East 53rd Street
    New York, New York 10022

68. Harriet Gilanor
    Rockaway, New York

  **Heath—See D. C. Heath listing

  **Hood—See Jack Hood listing

69. Houghton Mifflin Company
    110 Tremont Street
    Boston, Massachusetts 02107

70. Ideal School Supply Company
    11000 South Lavergne Avenue
    Oak Lawn, Illinois 60453

71. Industrial Relations Center
    University of Chicago
    Chicago, Illinois

72. Institute for Research on Exceptional Children
    University of Illinois
    Urbana, Illinois

73. Instructo Playthings
    Paoli, Pennsylvania 19301

74. Interstate Printers & Publishers Incorporated
    19-27 North Jackson Street
    Danville, Illinois 61832

75. Jack Hood School Supplies Company
    91-99 Erie Street
    Stratford, Ontario

76. J. B. Lippincott Company
    East Washington Square
    Philadelphia, Pennsylvania 19105

77. Jeri Productions
    Suite #209
    1213 North Highland Avenue
    Hollywood, California 90038

78. J. L. Hammett Company
    165 Water Street
    Lyons, New York 14489

79. Kenworthy Educational Service
    Post Office Box 3031
    Buffalo, New York 14205

80. Laidlaw Brothers
    A Division of Doubleday
    Thatcher & Madison
    River Forest, Illinois 60305

81. Lakeshore Curriculum Materials
    Los Angeles Teacher's Store
    8888 Venice Boulevard
    Los Angeles, California 90034

82. Language Research Associates
    175 East Delaware Place
    Chicago, Illinois 60611

83. Lansford Publishing Company
    Post Office Box 8711
    San Jose, California 95155

84. Lathrop, Lee & Shepard Company
    Division of William Morrow & Company
    105 Madison Avenue
    New York, New York 10016

85. Learning Concepts
    2501 North Lamar
    Austin, Texas 78705

86. Learning Resource Center Incorporated
    10655 West Greenburg Road
    Portland, Oregon 97223
    Lippincott—See J. B. Lippincott listing

87. Love Publishing Company
    6635 East Villanova Place
    Denver, Colorado 80222

88. Lyons and Carahan Incorporated Educational Publishers
    (Rand McNally)
    467 East 25th Street
    Chicago, Illinois 60610

89. Macmillan Publishing Company, Incorporated
    Front & Brown Streets
    Riverside, New Jersey 08075

90. Mafex Associates

90 Cherry Street
Johnstown, Pennsylvania 15902

91. McGraw-Hill Company
1221 Avenue of the Americas
New York, New York 10020

**Merrill—See Charles E. Merrill listing

92. Milton Bradley Company
Educational Division
Springfield, Massachusetts 01101

93. Modern Education Corporation
Post Office Box 721
Tulsa, Oklahoma 74101

94. National Society for Crippled Children and Adults
2023 West Ogden Avenue
Chicago, Illinois 60612

95. New England School Supply
Post Office Box 1581
Springfield, Massachusetts 01101

96. New York City Board of Education
Superintendent of Schools
Office of Publications
Room 136
110 Livingston Street
Brooklyn, New York 11201

97. Noble and Noble Publishers, Incorporated
1 Dag Hammarskjold Plaza
245 East 47th Street
New York, New York 10017

98. Parents Magazine Press
52 Vanderbilt Avenue
New York, New York 10017

99. Phonovisual Products, Incorporated
12216 Parklawn Drive
Rockville, Maryland 20852

100. Peter Pan Records
Division of Ambassador Records
145 Komoro Street
Newark, New Jersey 07105

101. Prentice-Hall, Incorporated
Educational Book Division
Englewood Cliffs, New Jersey 07632

102. Rand McNally & Company

Box 7600
Chicago, Illinois 60680

103. Random House School and Library Service, Incorporated
400 Hahn Road
Westminster, Maryland 21157

104. R. C. A. Victor Records
Division Education Department
155 East 24th Street
New York, New York 10010

105. Records Plus
906 Sylvan Avenue
Englewood Cliffs, New Jersey 07632

106. Remedial Education Press
Kingsbury Center
2138 Bancroft Place, North West
Washington, D.C. 20008

107. Research Press
2612 North Mattis Avenue
Champaign, Illinois 61820

108. RIL Electronics Corporation
Street Road & 2nd Street Pike
Southampton, Pennsylvania 18966

109. Ronald Press
15 East 26th Street
New York, New York 10010

110. Scholastic Magazine and Book Services
902-906 Sylvan Avenue
Englewood Cliffs, New Jersey 07632

111. Science Research Associates, Incorporated
Customer Correspondence
259 East Erie Street
Chicago, Illinois 60611

112. Scott Foresman and Company
99 Bauer Drive
Oakland, New Jersey 07436

113. Scott Foresman and Company
Glenview, Illinois 60025

114. Society for Visual Education
1345 Diversey Parkway
Chicago, Illinois 60614

115. Special Learning Corporation
42 Boston Post Road
Guilford, Connecticut 06437

116. Spes Record Company
     20 North Waker Drive
     Chicago, Illinois

117. Stanley Bowman Company, Incorporated
     12 Cleveland Street
     Valhalla, New York 10595

118. Stanwix House
     3020 Chartiers Avenue
     Pittsburgh, Pennsylvania 15024

119. Taylor Publishing Company
     Box 1392
     San Angelo, Texas 76901

120. Teacher's Publishing Corporation
     Division of Macmillan Publishing Company, Incorporated
     100F Brown Street
     Riverside, New Jersey 08075

121. Teachers College Press
     Teachers College Columbia University
     1234 Amsterdam Avenue
     New York, New York 10027

122. Teaching Resources Corporation
     100 Boylston Street
     Boston, Massachusetts 02116

123. The Judy Company
     250 James Street
     Morristown, New Jersey 07960

124. The King Company
     2414 West Lawrence Avenue
     Chicago, Illinois 60625
     **Thomas—See Charles C. Thomas listing

125. T. S. Denison & Company
     5100 West 82nd Street
     Minneapolis, Minnesota 55437

126. University of Chicago Press
     Journals Department
     11030 South Lanley Avenue
     Chicago, Illinois 60628

127. University of Southern California
     USC Bookstore
     Mail Order
     University Park
     Los Angeles, California 90007

128. Walt Disney

Educational Media Company (WDEMCO)
500 South Buena Vista Street
Burbank, California 91521

129. Whitehaven Publishing Company
Box 2
New Richmond, Wisconsin 54017

**Whitman—See Albert Whitman listing

130. Word Making Products, Incorporated
Post Office Box 1858
Salt Lake City, Utah 84110

131. Zaner-Bloser
612 North Park Street
Columbus, Ohio 43215

Catalogues

A few stamps and a limited expenditure of time and effort can result in the acquisition of catalogues from which to select additional materials. In addition, the catalogues often stimulate ideas for activities and teacher-made materials. Most catalogues are without cost. However, in some instances manufacturers may charge for their catalogues.

The listing of these sources implies no endorsement by the authors of the products, manufacturers, or distributors. It is intended solely to assist teachers and speech-language pathologists to become aware of a greater number of resources for the acquisition of materials and supplies. The listing of vendors is based on available materials. Omission of any vendor in no way reflects on the vendor or the associated products.

Glossary of Language, Speech, and Retardation TERMS

Following is a partial listing of terms pertaining to speech and hearing, language, mental retardation, and psychology.

a-, an- —a prefix for "without," "lacking," or "deprived of."

AAMD —the American Association for Mental Deficiency: an organization composed of professionals from various fields and laymen devoted to the study, habilitation, and interests of the mentally retarded.

aberrant —that which deviates from the normal in behavior.

abstract —refers to behavior, ideas, intelligence, or learning, in which symbolic activity rather than objects (concrete) are the focus.

academic achievement —the level of skill attained in educational activity.

acataphasia —a form of aphasia in which the manner words are arranged sequentially is affected.

acoustic phonetics —the analysis of the physical properties of speech sounds.

active voice —denotes that the subject of a sentence is performing or causing the action expressed by the verb.

actor-agent construction —the subject-predicate ordering of words typical of English syntax.

acuity —level or ability of stimuli, as in "hearing acuity."

AD —refers to the right ear (auris dextralis).

adjective —a part of speech used to modify a noun or other substantive by limiting, qualifying, or specifying.

adventitious —originating after birth.

adverb —a part of speech comprising a class of words that modify a verb, adjective, or another adverb.

afferent —nerve impulses going toward the brain or spinal cord.

affix —a word element that is attached to a base, stem, or root.

affricate   —a consonantal sound beginning as a stop (plosive) but expelled as a fricative. The *ch* and the *j* sounds in the words "chain" and "jump" are affricates.

age, mental   —see "mental age."

agenesis   —defective maturation as a result of heredity or adventitious factors.

agnosia   —loss of ability, due to brain injury, to interpret the meanings of sensory stimuli. May be visual, auditory, or tactual.

agraphia   —inability to call forth and write appropriate symbols or combinations of symbols that represent a word the individual wishes to express.

air conduction   —the transmission of sound through the ear canal, ear drum, and ossicles to the inner ear.

alexia   —difficulty in reading due to brain damage. More recently the term has been applied regardless of cause.

allaphones   —any of the various forms of a phoneme. For example, the *p* as in "pit" and the *p* in "spit" are allaphones of the phoneme *p.*

alveolor   —sounds produced with the tip of the tongue on the ridge (alveolor ridge), just behind the upper front teeth.

ament   —a term used to describe one who is classified mentally retarded.

amentia   —mental deficiency.

amnesia   —loss of memory.

anamnesis   —the information obtained from the individual with regard to the history or the complaint.

anaphony   —the simplest form of communication between animals; the simplest manner by which they convey messages.

animate subject   —nouns referring to humans.

anomia   —loss of ability to name objects.

anomaly   —anything contrary to the general rule.

anomaly   —arbitrary nature of language—suggests that words have no necessary relationship to the object they represent; word symbols exist by cultural agreement.

anorexia   —lack of appetite.

anoxemia   —deficiency in the oxygen content of the blood, with accompanying symptoms of disturbance in mental function.

antonymy   —two words having opposite meanings; though the words are related, they refer to the extremes of one aspect.

aphasia   —impairment, due to brain injury, in the use of meaningful symbols.

apraxia   —inability to use tools or mechanisms in purposive and intended ways.

article   —indefinite morphemes such as "a," "an," "the."

articulation   —the process of uttering the various speech sounds.

articulators   —the body parts used for production of speech; principally the tongue, lips, jaws, dental parts, and palatal structures.

AS   —refers to the left ear (auris sinistralis).

ASHA (the American Speech and Hearing Association)   —the scientific and professional organization that represents individuals in speech and language pathology, language related learning disabilities, audiology, and the hearing impaired.

aspiration   —the act of breathing or drawing in air.

asymptomatic   —the individual presents no evidence of a disease.

attention span   —the length of time an individual can relate to various tasks or stimuli.

atypical   —deviating from the norm.

audiogram   —a chart that graphically presents an individual's hearing thresholds.

audiology   —the science of hearing. Includes the study, diagnosis, prescription for, and treatment of, hearing loss. The determination of normal hearing and its study is a branch of this science as well.

auditory acuity   —sensitivity of the human ear to auditory stimuli.

auditory channel   —the hearing route information follows in the linguistic system.

auditory feedback   —the hearing of one's own speech in a monitoring manner.

auditory memory span   —the memory process relating to the ability to remember in sequence heard linguistic symbols.

auditory perception   —meaningful awareness and evaluation of stimulus through hearing.

auditory training   —the educational process of increasing use of an individual's auditory acuity through improvement of auditory discrimination, which includes development of the awareness of sounds, the differences between and among them, particularly those of speech.

aural   —pertaining to the ear.

autism   —a disorder in which the individual withdraws from, or has not established contact with, the environment.

autonomic nervous system   —the functional division of the nervous system that supplies the glands, heart, and smooth muscles with their afferent and efferent innervation.

auxiliary verb   —a verb that accompanies certain verb forms to express tense, mood, voice, or object.

babbling   —the vocal activity engaged in by infants during which random speech sounds are produced.

base structure   —see "deep structure."

behavior   —any activity whatsoever that is engaged in or performed by a human organism.

behavioral disorders   —performance that is characterized as hyperactive, explosive, erratic, or uninhibited.

behavioral theory   —a theory of meaning postulating that the meaning of a word or expression is the set of responses produced in a listener.

behaviorism   —a psychological frame of reference that stresses observations of overt behavior, emphasizes the theory of a machine-like quality in animal (including human) activity, and disavows introspection and consciousness.

binaural   —pertaining to both ears.

biological hypothesis   —holds that mental retardation is due to genetic, biochemical, or other defects.

bone conduction   —the transmission of sound through the bony structures of the head to the inner ear.

bone conduction testing   —administering measurement tests by setting the bony structures of the skull in vibration, usually in the area of the mastoid.

bound form   —parts of speech that cannot stand alone.

bound morph   —the parts of morphological units that cannot stand alone, for example, "-s," "-est."

brain damage or brain injury   —trauma to the brain identifiable by medical evaluation.

brain dysfunction   —lack of adequate function that appears to be related to an abnormality of brain function. May or may not be substantiated by medical evaluation.

CEC   —Council for Exceptional Children; an organization composed of professionals in all areas of exceptionality.

cerebral palsy   —group of conditions characterized by impairment and disorganization of motor functions due to damage to the motor control centers of the brain.

channels   —the sensory motor pathways along which symbol messages are received and responded to.

Chronological Age (C.A.)   —the age of an individual determined by subtracting the date of birth from the current date and expressing in years and months. (For example, 6-7 represents an age of six years, seven months.)

chunking —combining groups of words or concepts for greater efficiency in understanding or processing.

classical conditioning —S leads to R, S_1 leads to R. Habituating a response to a stimulus that accompanies an appropriate stimulus.

clusters —subunits of sentences in which some words are grouped together.

C.N.S. —the central nervous system, the brain, and spinal cord.

cochlea —the shell-shaped structure in the inner ear where physical vibration is transferred into nerve impulses.

code —any system of symbols agreed upon and used by a sender and receiver to communicate.

cognate —pairs of sounds, one voiced and the other unvoiced, that are produced, motorically, in the same way.

cognition —the process of knowing; knowledge or the capacity for it.

cognitive —relating to the faculty of knowing, perceiving, or being aware.

comprehension —the act of understanding.

conceptual disorders —difficulty in organizing materials and thoughts.

conducive hearing loss —a loss that originates in the outer or middle ear; interference with the conduction of sound to the middle ear.

congenital —existing from birth.

conjunction —a word connecting other words, phrases, clauses, or sentences

consonant —a speech sound, voiced or voiceless, in which the speech articulators interrupt the air stream to form distinctive sounds other than vowels.

continuant —a speech sound that can be prolonged without distortion.

convulsion —a violent, involuntary series of muscular contractions.

copula —a linking verb such as the verb "be" that has no meaning of its own.

corpus —in regard to speech, a set of utterances, some grammatical, some not.

cretinism —a type of mental deficiency associated with hyperfunctioning of the thyroid gland. Cretins are small, have short arms and legs, dry skin, protruding abdomens, and relatively large faces.

cultural —familial retardation or retardation occurring in the absence of cerebral pathology and with the expectation that an altered environment would result in higher intellectual functioning; due to a complex interaction of both environmental and hereditary factors.

custodial —under complete care.

cyanosis —a bluish skin color resulting from insufficient oxygenation of the blood.

dB —the symbol for decibel.

deaf, deafness —absence of functionally useful hearing.

deafened —unable to hear, often used to suggest that the individual was able to hear at birth or until language was acquired.

decibel (dB) —the unit of measurement in the assessment of hearing.

decoding —converting or transforming a symbolic message into ordinary language. The process of deriving meaning from vocal, graphic, and/or gestural activity.

deep structure —the linguistic event that is cognitive in nature and represents what an individual wishes to say. (Also called base structure or underlying structure.)

deglutition —the act of swallowing.

dementia —abnormal behavior or mental debility.

dental —pertaining to the teeth.

dependent retarded —the term used to describe the severely retarded. Often considered to include individuals who test between 0–35 on formal intellectual measures and need total care.

development —the process of maturation of an organism.

dextral —right-handed dominance.

diagnosis —the procedures by which the nature of a disease or condition is determined.

dialect —a regional variety of a spoken language.

diphthong —a vowel-like sound made while the articulators are in rapid movement from the position for one vowel to that of another.

disability —an incompetency in some area of function.

discrimination —as used in communication, the ability to make judgments between or among sounds.

disorder —a generic term for any abnormal condition.

distinctive feature —the unique characteristics of sounds that make it possible to distinguish one from another; for example, voicing, manner of production.

distortion —an articulation error in which the phoneme is produced incorrectly yet clearly not identifiable as another phoneme.

Down's Syndrome —see mongoloid.

dull normal —a term sometimes used to classify individuals who test between educable (mildly) retarded and average—75-90 on formal tests.

dys- —pertaining to inadequate function as opposed to "a-," which pertains to lack of function.

dysarthria —articulation disorders resulting from neurological dysfunctioning of the tongue.

dysfunction —abnormal behavior of an organ.

ear —the organ of hearing consisting of three major parts: outer, middle, and inner ear.

echoing —the communication behavior in which a child utters a sentence that is in part unintelligible, and a listener imitates but replaces the part not understood with a "wh" word.

echolalia —the parrot-like repetitions of verbal material.

educable mentally retarded —the term used to classify mild retardation; often considered to include individuals who test between 50 to 75 on formal intellectual measures.

efferent —nerve impulses coming from the brain or spinal cord to the muscle system.

embedded —in complex sentences, the process of combining sentences by inserting a second sentence as a relative clause.

encoding —transforming information into a code for transference.

endocrine —pertaining to glands such as the pituitary and thyroid that secrete directly into the blood stream.

endogenous —pertaining to mental retardation attributable to familial factors without demonstrable structural defect of the brain; present in the genes.

ENT —ear, nose, and throat; used to describe a medical specialist.

enuresis —inability to hold urine, particularly after three years of age.

epilepsy —a cerebral disorder manifested by transient disturbances in motor and/or sensory function.

etiology —the cause of a disease or condition.

eustachian —the tube or passageway connecting the middle ear to the posterior area of the nasal chamber or the throat.

evaluation —an appraisal of factors such as intelligence, personality, communication, and achievement.

exogenous   —pertaining to mental retardation attributable to external causes with demonstrable structural defect of the brain; not present in the genes.

expansion   —the communication behavior whereby a person imitates a child but adds something more complete and corre   the utterance.

experience   —a broad term referring to the totality of activities that have occurred during the existence of an individual.

expression, expressive language   —the outgoing aspect of the language system; the encoding and transmission of verbal symbols.

familial   —pertaining to a strong tendency to occur among more than one member of a family. Thought to derive from genetic or cultural influence.

feeblemindedness   —a term used synonymously with mental deficiencies, particularly a legal definition; in England it is used to signify mild retardation.

fetus   —the prenatal organism after the sixth week following conception.

fluency   —the freeflowing nature of ideation or speech; lack of interruption.

free form   —any part of speech that can stand alone.

free morph   —the parts of morphological units that can stand alone; the aspects that laymen consider "words."

frequency   —the number of cycles occurring per unit of time; in hearing, expressed as cycles per second. Contributes to the pitch of a sound and is expressed in Hertz (Hz).

fricative   —speech sound made by forcing the air stream through a narrow opening; *th, v, f.*

frustration tolerance   —the ability to endure frustration.

functional   —referring to the behavior of an organ in contrast to structure or physical condition.

gene   —the bearer of heredity that lies in a chromosome.

generative grammar   —a system of rules that assigns a structural description to sentences in explicit and well-defined ways.

-genic   —a suffix indicating "cause of," "source of," or "result of."

gerontology   —the study of, and interest in, the aged.

Gestalt   —pattern or configuration; integration of the whole.

gestures   —motor bodily activities used to provide or enhance expression.

gigantism   —unusually large stature as a result of glandular dysfunction.

glide   —speech sounds that consist primarily of movement of an articulator rather than it being held in a static position.

glottis   —the space between the vocal folds.

grammar   —study of the system underlying formal language features such as morphemes, words, and sentences; the knowledge of a language that is possessed by every native speaker.

grand mal   —major type of epileptic seizure.

graphemes   —written symbols or alphabet letters.

growth   —progressive development of an organism toward maturity.

guttural   —pertaining to the throat.

habilitation   —therapeutic improvement in a skill or level of adjustment.

habit   —a learned response in which the action is fairly well established and almost automatic.

handicapped   —a problem sufficient to reduce one's efficiency in carrying out the demands of the culture; reduction of social, emotional, educational, and/or economic functioning so that an individual cannot perform to inherent ability level.

haptic   —referring to both tactile and kinesthetic factors.

hearing loss   —the difference between an individual's hearing thresholds and hearing acuity considered "normal."

hereditary   —pertaining to the biological mechanisms by which characteristics are transmitted to offspring.

holophrase, holophrastic   —a single-word utterance that appears to express a phrase or sentence idea.

homo-   —denotes "like" or the same.

homophenes   —words that are visibly identical in production in that the articulator action appears the same.

homophones   —words of different meaning but similar sound, "blue" and "blew."

hydrocephalic   —water on the brain, increased secretion of serum into cranial spaces; diagnosis of an organic condition.

hygiene   —the study of the principles of prevention of disease or disorder.

hyper-   —a prefix denoting excessive amounts.

hyperactivity   —excessive and often meaningless movement displayed by children and often considered to be the result of C.N.S. or behavioral difficulties.

hypo-   —a prefix denoting reduced amounts.

Hz (hertz)   —unit of frequency of a sound referring to one cycle per second.

idea   —a broad term referring to a concept or mental image.

idioglossia, idiolalia   —a unique, original language code invented and used by a child or children. More likely to occur in twins or siblings of close age levels.

idiopathic   —of unknown origin or etiology.

idiot   —the term formerly used to describe severely retarded children; the lowest grade of mental defective.

idiot savant   —a term applied to mental defectives who display particular skill in one specific area of endeavor.

illiteracy   —the condition of being unable to read or write as a result of lack of opportunity or mental deficiency.

imbecile   —the term previously used to describe moderately or trainable retarded children.

imitation   —the reproduction, in language, of heard symbols.

impairment   —a defective function.

incidence   —the frequency of occurrence of any given trait or condition at the time of birth.

incidental learning   —that which is acquired as a by-product of intentional learning or as a result of profiting from experience.

incompetent   —in the legal sense, inability to manage one's own affairs.

individual differences   —the measurable unlikenesses of people, which tend to be distributed statistically in predictable ways as displayed in the curve of normal distribution.

infancy   —the first eighteen months of life.

inflection   —a shift in pitch during the utterance of a syllable; changing words by altering segments of the word, which may cause different grammatical and syntactic relations.

innate   —instinctive or inborn rather than learned or acquired.

innate linguistic competence   —the language universals, according to the nativists, that each individual possesses at birth.

innateness hypothesis   —holds that the structure of language is, to a considerable degree, specified biologically.

inner ear   —the vestibular apparatus, semicircular canals, and cochlea.

inner language   —the language used in the thought processes, which may or may not be transferred into verbal symbols.

IPA   —the International Phonetic Alphabet or system of symbols whereby each sound has only one symbol and each symbol one sound.

instinct   —a complex pattern of unconditioned reflexes or an unlearned inner drive to biologically purposeful action.

intelligibility   —a measure of an understanding of speech and language.

intelligence   —basic mental potential or native intellectual ability; in measurement, the assumed intellectual ability based on test results.

intelligence quotient (IQ)   —an estimate of the intellectual status of a child based on a ratio determined by dividing the mental age, obtained from formal testing, by the chronological age (both in months) and multiplying by 100. This describes a child's functioning rather than native ability and is, in part, culturally determined.

intelligence tests   —measurement instruments that purport to determine an individual's intellectual functioning level.

intonation   —a manner of producing or uttering tones, particularly with regard to pitch or loudness.

intransitive verbs   —verbs that do not take an object.

ITA   —Initial Teaching Alphabet, a system of symbols based on phonetics and consistent relationship of sound to symbol. Used principally in beginning reading.

jargon   —the production of inflectional patterns without intelligibility or apparent meaning.

labial   —pertaining to the lips.

lalial   —speech.

lallation   —defective articulation, particularly of the (l) phoneme.

lalling   —meaningless repetition of a sound.

lalopathy   —any disorder or speech function.

language deviation   —a condition characterized by an inability to adequately use the linguistic code of an individual's environment either through lack of development or loss of function.

language universals   —similarities attributable to the general form of language in languages everywhere.

lapsus linguae   —a slip of the tongue in which a true or unconscious meaning is revealed.

larynx   —the voice box.

lateral lisp   —defective sibilant production in which sound energy is directed over the side rather than over the front of the tongue; usually occurs with *s* and *z*.

learning   —a broad term referring to modification of behavior as a result of experience.

levels   —the functional complexity of an organism's communicative behavior usually classified as either "meaningful" or "nonmeaningful" (automatic).

lexical unit   —a single entry in a dictionary such as "go, goes, gone, going."

lingual, lingua-   —pertaining to the tongue.

linguistic   —those aspects of language that particularly relate to its grammatical, ideational, and intellectual components.

linguistic competence   —is the set of principles that a person must have in order to be a speaker of a language.

linguistic performance   —the translation of linguistic competence into linguistic action; involves competence, memory, distraction, and perception.

linguistic relativity   —holds that individuals experience the universe differently because of their varying linguistic communities.

linguistic theory   —the science of human language.

lip reading   —comprehending speech by watching the lips, face, and visible articulatory organs.

lisp   —generally considered as the defective production of the *s* or *z,* but sometimes used to describe the defective production of all sibilants.

loudness   —the psychological correlate of volume.

macroglossia   —abnormally large tongue, which may impede clear speech.

macrognathia   —unusually large jaw.

magic, magical thinking   —belief in the accomplishment of certain outcomes or effects that transcend the normal limits of human capability or the realistic likelihood of occurrence.

maladjustment   —any mild disturbance of the personality in which there is difficulty in securing a satisfactory adjustment to the environment, especially to other persons.

malformation   —any type of abnormal growth or development of the body or its parts.

malocclusion   —a failure of the lower and upper teeth to meet properly.

mandible   —the lower jaw.

manipulation   —in behavioral terms, the attempt to influence others in personally desired ways through purposeful behavior.

marker   —the bound morphemes that indicate number and tense when added to free morphemes.

maturation   —the development of various physical, emotional, social, and intellectual factors.

maxilla   —the upper jaw.

mean   —the sum of scores divided by the number of cases.

mean length of response (MLR)   —average number of morphemes in an utterance or response; mean length of utterance is more commonly used.

mean length of utterance (response), (MLU)   —average number of morphemes in a speech utterance.

median   —the point on the frequency distribution of scores that divides them in half; where half the scores are above and half below a determined score.

memory   —the power, function, or act of retaining information, images, feelings; recall; in a testing situation, the ability to exactly reproduce a given stimulus (rote memory). In the latter instance, meaning is disregarded.

mens   —mind, mental, pertaining to the mind.

Mental Age (M.A.) —mental development measured by comparison with performances of average persons at various levels of chronological development.

mental deficiency   —inadequacy of intelligence or learning capacity and social incompetence; a term reserved for adults by some authors.

mental hygiene   —measures that serve to alleviate conditions of persons with mental problems.

mental image   —mental pictures or impression of objects, sensations, or actions.

mentalism   —the emphasis on psychological events or states explored by introspection; as opposed to behaviorism.

microcephaly   —abnormally small head, usually with a cone-like appearance and marked recession of forehead and chin.

micrognathia   —unusual smallness of lower jaw (mandible).

minimal pairs   —pairs of words that differ in only one sound and differ in meaning, too.

mirror writing-strephographia —a form of writing in which the alphabet characters are reversed but appear correct when held to a mirror.

modal verbs   —auxiliary verbs such as "will," and "can," that signify the possibility of an action.

mode   —the most frequently appearing score in a series.

monaural   —pertaining to a single ear.

mongolism (Down's Syndrome)   —a type of mental retardation with distinctive physical characteristics that include a smaller head, sloping eyebrows, broad and short hands and feet, a large tongue with transverse fissures, and slightly slanting eyes.

moron   —the term previously used to classify the mildly or educable retarded child.

morpheme   —the minimal recurrent and meaningful unit of language in speech. In "walked," both "walk" and "-ed" are morphemes.

morphology   —the study of the structure of words; the means of constructing words from morphemes.

motive   —a goad to action; the cause or purpose of behavior.

motor   —pertaining to the activities of the organism in contrast to incoming or sensory experiences.

mutism   —inability or lack of desire to speak.

nasal   —(1) in phonetics, those sounds that are primarily resonated nasally, (2) pertaining to the nose.

native   —inborn or developed through maturation as opposed to learned.

nature-nurture controversy   —the argument regarding the relative importance of heredity and environment.

negation   —the opposite of affirmative sentences; contains a negative or "no" morpheme.

neologism   —a new or original word coined by an individual, which may have no meaning for other persons.

neonate   —the infant from birth until one month.

nervous system   —brain, spinal cord, nerves, and ganglia collectively.

neurosis   —functional disorders involving maladjustment.

noise   —in psycholinguistics, any activity that introduces error or interference into a system of communication.

non-fluency   —interruptions in the flow of speech which, under 7½ years of age, are often considered within normal limits.

norm   —a standard of reference in making judgments.

normal   —the average or that which is acceptable to a culture; statistically, within one standard deviation of the mean.

normal distribution   —the frequency of occurrence of various traits or behaviors based on mathematical probabilities.

nosology   —disease or symptom classification.

noun   —a word used to denote a name, a person, place, thing, quality, or act.

nystagmus   —spasmodic oscillations of the eyeballs, which may suggest certain types of organic pathology.

oligophrenia —the French term for mental deficiency; in America, used especially in medical contexts.

omission —an articulation error in which a phoneme is left out of an utterance.

ontogeny —the growth and development of the individual.

open class —words that are not in the pivot class, but can stand alone or be paired with them in a child's language development; the larger class of words that combine with pivots in "blanket on, toy on, on doll," "blanket, toy, doll" are open class words.

ophthalmologist —physician specializing in the examination, treatment, and study of the eye.

order —the sequence of morphemes in a sentence.

ortho- —a word unit signifying the correct or normal condition and sometimes indicating the correction or improvement of a typical condition.

organic —referring to the body or specific organs.

orthodontist —the dental specialist engaged in the practice of straightening or aligning dental structures.

orthography —the writing system of a language.

orthopedic —refers to the skeleton or locomotor apparatus.

otitis media —infection of the middle ear.

otologist —physician specializing in the examination, treatment, and study of the ear.

overlearning —denotes any learning over and beyond that required for one correct production of material.

overt —outward or external.

paradigm —model; standard.

paralanguage —associated aspects of language expression.

paraphrase —transforming or reproducing phrases or sentences using different morphemes while preserving meaning.

passive voice —denoting a verb form used to indicate that a subject is the object of an action.

perception —meaningful awareness and interpretation of incoming stimuli.

perceptual disorders —primarily visual or auditory difficulty in accurately receiving incoming stimuli; problems in organizing the whole of the stimulus and accurately identifying figure-ground relationships.

performance —an individual's language usage observable auditorily.

perinatal   —around or about the time of birth.

perseveration   —a continuation of an activity after cessation of the causative stimulus or after the activity has fulfilled its purpose; difficulty in changing sets.

petit mal   —the minimal type of epileptic seizure.

philology   —the study of the beginnings and growth of languages.

phon   —the unit of sound level.

phone   —any speech sound considered as a physical event whether or not it is part of the phonology of the dominant language.

phoneme   —the minimal unit of sounds with distinctive features that establishes exclusive groups of speech sounds; a class of sounds, in a language, considered equivalent.

phonemic transcription   —indicates the phoneme to which each sound uttered belongs and is represented by the major symbol. Sounds are enclosed in parentheses.

phonetics   —the alphabet of sounds in which fine distinctions are retained, even within sound classes.

phonetic transcription   —an accurate recording in phonetic symbols of the exact characteristics of an utterance. Sounds are enclosed in brackets.

phonics   —the system that assigns the possible oral sounds to alphabet letters.

phonological rules   —relate underlying representations to the phonetic representation of the morpheme.

phonology   —study of phonemic aspects of speech and language; the rules whereby the pronunciation of a sentence, including stress and intonation, is determined.

pica   —perverted appetite; craving for things not fit to eat (plaster, wood, human discharge).

pitch   —the psychological correlate of frequency.

pivot class   —words in a child's beginning speech that are used frequently with many different words from a larger group called "open class." Serve as "pivots" for these later words. For example, "on" can be used in: "blanket on," "toy on," "on dolly"; also referred to as modifier, operator.

plosive   —a consonant sound produced by stopping-up the voiced or unvoiced breath stream, building up pressure and then exploding it.

postnatal   —subsequent to birth.

prefix   —an affix that precedes a word, is attached to it, and changes or modifies its meaning.

premature —condition in which an infant is born before the full gestation period or weighs less than five pounds.

prenatal —before birth.

preposition —indicates the relation of a noun to a verb, an adjective, or another noun.

prevalence —the frequency of occurrence in the general population of any given trait or condition.

processes —learned habits required to obtain meaning from linguistic stimuli; decoding, thinking, or encoding.

prompting —a type of verbal exchange between parent and child during which a parent asks a question, and then asks another one, with the second ordered in a partial, possible, response form. For example, "What did you do?" "You did what?"

pronoun —one of a class of words that function as substitutes for nouns.

propositionality —the information content or meaningfulness of a message.

prosody, prosodic features —variations in length, loudness, pitch of phones, and other factors such as inflection and phrasing.

prosody —aspects of linguistic patterns created by modifications of pitch, quality, and strength, duration, and rhythm, perceived primarily as stress, phrasing, and intonational patterns.

prosthesis —any man-made device intended to compensate for a bodily abnormality.

psyche —the mind.

psychiatry —the branch of medicine that deals with the diagnosis and treatment of mental disorders.

psychodrama —Moreno's technique for achieving mental catharsis by having an individual act various roles.

psychogenic —a disorder of mental origin; causation due to psychological rather than organic factors.

psychology —the science of mental life; the study of human behavior in its mental, intellectual, social, and emotional dimensions through observation, testing, measurement, sampling and other forms of assessment; the provision of remedial measures for aberrant performance.

psychometrics —the administration of psychological tests.

psychoneurosis —see neurosis.

psychosis —a mental disorder characterized by lack of, or distorted, contact with reality.

quality   —vocal color or timbre that provides the characteristics by which one voice can be distinguished from another.

question   —requesting a response for information. (1) "yes-no" questions call for either a "yes" or "no" answer, (2) "wh—" questions begin with a "wh—" word such as "who," "what," "where," "when," "why."

raw score   —a score that has not been subjected to statistical treatment.

reasoning   —the act of thinking in conformity with the principles of logic; common sense judgment.

reception   —receiving incoming messages; a more active process than hearing since a message may be "heard" without being actively heard or received.

reception, receptive   —the incoming aspect of a language system; the decoding and accepting of verbal symbols.

redundancy   —the repetitious nature of language whereby more symbols are used to encode messages than are necessary in order to insure message transference.

referent   —an entity that a word stands for; the human, animal, tree, for which a word is substituted.

referential theory   —words or symbols that stand for something else. "The something" is a referent.

reflex   —an immediate, unlearned response to a specific stimulus.

rehabilitation   —the process of restoring an individual to functioning.

reinforcement   —the facilitative influence of one neural pattern upon another; rewarding behavior to increase the likelihood of recurrence.

resonance   —the effect of the cavities of the head and structures of the body upon the quality of sound.

restriction   —rules governing the possible combination of words to prevent the occurrence of ungrammatical sentences.

retarded   —individuals functioning at a lower level on some scale or measurement of behavior than those upon whom the norms were established; often used to mean "behind others of similar chronological age."

reward   —the incentive used to motivate animal and human subjects.

rhinolalia   —nasal resonance.

rhotacism   —defective articulation of the *r* sound.

screening test   —a method of appraisal in order to discover those individuals in need of study in greater depth.

selection restriction —limits on possible combinations of words. For example, "bachelor's wife" is not a possible linguistic unit.

semantic feature —markers that express a part of the meaning of a word.

Semantic —the behavioral discipline that uses semantics in habilitative measures.

semantics —the study of meaning in language including the relationships between a word and an object it represents and replaces; the rules whereby individual word meanings are combined to form the meaning of a sentence.

semology —perception of linguistic information.

sentence —an ordering string of morphemes that has structure to it.

sequela —after-effects of a condition or disorder.

sibling —brother or sister; a person of the same parentage.

sign language —a code of communication employing visible signs.

sinistrality —left handedness.

slow learner —see dull normal.

socio-linguistics —combining the expertise of the two disciplines suggested in the word.

somatic —pertaining to the body.

sonant —a speech sound that has a component of tone generated by vocal-fold activity.

speech reading —see lip reading.

stimulus —any form of energy or event eliciting a response.

stimulus deprivation hypothesis —contends that mental retardation is largely due to early cultural inadequacies, deficient social environments, and/or early maternal deprivation.

strabismus —crossed eyes.

stress —that accent or emphasis placed upon a sound or syllable spoken loudest in a given word or phrase.

stuttering —a disorganization in the rhythm of speech. (Also referred to as "stammering.")

subjective data —not directly accessible to other investigators and which cannot be readily quantified; based on an observer's interpretation or judgment.

substitutions —articulatory errors whereby one sound inappropriately replaces another.

suggestion —influencing the beliefs or actions of another person without resort to direct orders.

suprasegmental factors   —see prosody.

surd   —a speech sound that does not depend on action of the vocal folds.

surface structure   —the linguistic event that represents what an individual actually says in contrast to intent.

symbol   —any stimulus, such as an object, spoken word, or ideational element, which elicits a response originally attached to another stimulus.

symbolic function   —use of one action or object, concrete or mental, that stands for another.

sympathetic nervous system   —the portion of the autonomic nervous system that consists of paired chains of ganglia and efferent fibers innervating the visceral organs, duct and ductless glands, and muscle walls of blood vessels.

symptomatology   —the study of symptoms.

syndrome   —a pattern of symptoms indicating a given disorder.

synonymy   —words having similar meanings.

syntax   —study and science of sentence construction.

tactile   —pertaining to the sense of touch.

telegraphic speech   —speech that consists of nouns, verbs, and adjectives, with functor words omitted.

thinking   —problem-solving behavior.

token   —each particular occurrence of a speech word or unit.

trainable retarded   —a term used to describe moderate retardation; often considered to include individuals who test between I.Q. 35 to 50 on formal tests of intelligence.

transformational grammar   —according to the rationalists, sentences have two sets of rules or structures. Structure is the relationship between the morphemes of a sentence. Surface structure deals with word class arrangements and the phonological and syntactic rules used to form sentences. Deep structure gives the underlying meaning in a sentence and is not identical to surface structure. Deep and surface structure are related by applying transformations.

transformations   —syntactic rules that modify a basic phrase or sentence and result in a structure that is less abstract.

transitive verbs   —verbs that take an object.

tree diagram   —a means of diagramming words in a sentence.

type   —all similar tokens classed together as a group.

type-token ratio (TTR)   —the relationship between the total number of words used and the number of different words used in a speech sample.

underlying structure   —see deep structure.

unvoiced sounds   —sounds produced without vocal-fold action.

uvula   —the least-accessible portion of the soft palate that can be viewed in the oral cavity. When split (bifid uvula), it has no real effect except that this is often associated with a short velum.

velopharyngeal sphincter   —the muscle ring that controls the airway between the oral and nasal cavities.

velum   —the soft palate.

verbal   —pertaining to words.

verbal style   —differences in individuals' communication that exist in the presence of normalcy and despite a relatively common-language background.

verb phrase   —a verb followed by its modifiers; a verb and its modifiers.

visual channel   —the viewing channel through which information is obtained.

voiced sounds, voicing   —sounds that are produced with the vocal folds vibrating.

voiceless sounds   —see unvoiced sounds.

vowels   —voiced speech sounds produced by the vocal cords and resonated to a great degree, orally, by changing the cavity through alteration in tongue posture, position, and tension.

word order   —implicit in language to indicate the syntactic structure of sentences.

words   —arbitrary vocal or visual symbols that replace and represent people, places, things, actions, abstract concepts, and also the supporting symbolic structures necessary to connect the primary word-carrying symbols; any sequence of meaningful symbols set off visually by a blank space or auditorily by silence.

REFERENCES

1. Alson, L., and Swindler, A.: A Pilot program for language development in the educable adolescent. *LSHSS,* 7:2, 1976.
2. Anastasiow, N. and Stayrook, N.: Miscue language patterns of mildly retarded and nonretarded students. *Am. J. Ment. Def.,* 77:4, 1973.
3. Backus, O.: *Speech in Education.* Longmans, Green. New York, 1943.
4. Baer, D. and Guess, D.: Teaching productive noun suffixes to severely retarded children. *Am. J. Ment. Def.,* 77:5, 1972.
5. Baroff, G. S.: *Mental Retardation: Nature, Cause, and Management.* Halstead Press, Hemisphere Publishing, Washington, D.C., 1974.
6. Baskervill, R. D.: The speech pathologist as a resource consultant in assisting classroom teachers in enhancing standard English competency among inner-city children. Unpublished paper presented at ASHA convention, Washington, D.C., 1975.
7. Baum, D., Odom, M., and Boatman, R.: Environment-based language training with mentally retarded. *Ed. and Trng. of Ment. Ret.,* 10:2, 1975.
8. Bateman, B. and Whetherall, J.: Psycholinguistic aspects of mental retardation. *Ment. Ret.,* 3:3, 1965.
9. Bereiter, C. and Engelmann, S.: *Teaching Disadvantaged Children in the Primary Grades,* Prentice-Hall, Englewood Cliffs, 1966.
10. Berry, M.: *Language Disorders of Children: The Bases and Diagnoses.* Appleton-Century-Crofts, New York, 1969.
11. Bilowsky, D. and Share, J.: The ITPA and Down's Syndrome: an explorator study. *Am. J. Ment. Def.,* 70:1, 1965.
12. Binet, A. and Simon, T.: *Mentally Defective Children,* Longmans, New York, 1914.
13. Blessing, K.: An investigation of psycholinguistic deficit in educable mentally retarded children: detection, remediation and related variables. *Ment. Ret. Ab.,* 2:3, 1965.
14. Bliss, C. K.: *Semontography,* Semontography Publications, Sydney, Australia, 1949.
15. Bloom, L.: *Language Development, Form and Function in Emerging Grammar,* M.I.T. Press, Cambridge, 1970.
16. Bloomfield, L.: *Language.* Henry Holt and Company, New York, 1933.
17. Bonnell, J. A.: The oral language program of the Grand Rapids Public Schools. *Mich. For. Lang. News.,* 1:3, 1972.
18. Bricker, W. and Bricker, D.: Development of receptive vocabulary in severely retarded children. *Am. J. Ment. Def.,* 74:5, 1970.
19. Bricker, W.: A program of language training for the severe language handicapped child. *Except. Child.,* 37:10, 1970.

20. Bricker, W., and Bricker, D.: Assessment of verbal imitation with low-functioning retarded children. *JSHR,* 15:4, 1972.

21. Buium, N., Rynders, J., and Turnure, J.: Early maternal linguistic environment of normal and Down's Syndrome language-learning children. *Am. J. Ment. Def.,* 79:1, 1974.

22. Bush, W. J. and Giles, M. T.: *Aids to Psycholinguistic Teaching,* Charles E. Merrill, Columbus, Ohio, 1969.

23. Capobianco, R. and Dunn, L.: Mental Retardation: Chapter III. *Rev. Ed. Res.,* 29:3, 1968.

24. Carrow, M. A.: The development of auditory comprehension of language structure in children. *JSHD,* 33:2, 1968.

25. Chalfant, J., Kirk, G. and Jensen, J.: Systematic language instruction: an approach for teaching receptive language to young trainable children. *Teach. Except. Child.,* 1:1, 1968.

26. Chomsky, N.: *Syntactic Structures.,* Mouton and Company, The Hague, 1957.

27. Cornwell, A.: Development of language, abstraction, and numerical concept formation in Down's Syndrome children. *Am. J. Ment. Def.,* 79:2, 1974.

28. Dale, P. S.: *Language Development.* The Dryden Press, Hinsdale, Illinois, 1972.

29. Davies, P. (ed.): *The American Heritage Dictionary of the English Language,* Dell Publishing, New York, 1970.

30. DiCarlo, M.: The nonverbal child. *Child Ed.,* 44:2, 1968.

31. Dever, R. B.: Proposal to teach English as a foreign language to educable mentally retarded children. *Except. Child.,* 35:4, 1969.

32. Durel, M., *Speak English—a practical course for foreign students,* Barnes & Noble Books, New York, 1972.

33. Ervin, S. M.: Imitation and structural change in children's language, In *New Directions in the Study of Language,* E. H. Lenneberg, ed., M.I.T. Press, Cambridge, 1964.

34. Ezell, D.: The effects of verbal reinforcement on the language behavior of mentally retarded children. *ASHA* (abstract), 2:7, 1960.

35. Firsh, S. A.: Training generalized receptive prepositions in retarded children. *J. Appl. Beh. Anal.,* 7:4, 1974.

36. Fitzgerald, E., *Straight Language for the Deaf.* Volta Bureau, Washington, D.C., 1954.

37. Fraser, C., Bellugi, U., and Brown, R.: Control of grammar in imitation comprehension, and production. *J. Verb. Lrng. and Verb. Beh.,* 15:2, 1964.

38. Fraser, W., and Grieve, R.: Recent studies of communication problems in the mentally handicapped. *Health Bull.,* 33:11, 1975.

39. Freeman, G. G. and Lukens, J.: A speech and language program for educable mentally handicapped children, *JSHD,* 27:3, 1962.

40. French, N. R., Carter, C. W., and Koenig, W.: The words and sounds of telephone conversations. *Bell Sys. T. J.,* 9:6, 1930.
41. Friedlander, G.: A rationale for speech and language development for the young retarded child. *Trng. Sch. Bull.,* 59:1, 1961.
42. Frost, J. L.: in Guiding Children's Language, *Learning,* P. Laub, ed., Wm. D. Brown Co., Dubuque, Iowa, 1967.
43. Gardner, W. I.: *Behavior Modification in Mental Retardation,* Aldine-Atherton, Chicago, 1971.
44. Goertzen, S. M., Speech and the mentally retarded child, *Am. J. Ment. Def.,* 62:2, 1957.
45. Goodstein, H. A.: Performance of mentally handicapped and average-IQ children on two modified Cloze tasks for oral language. *Am. J. Ment. Def.,* 75:3, 1970.
46. Gordon, M. L., Ryan, D. H. and Shilo, T.: *Helping the Trainable Mentally Retarded Child Develop Speech and Language.* Charles C. Thomas, Springfield, Illinois, 1972.
47. Graham, J. T. and Graham, L. W.: Language behavior of the mentally retarded: syntactic characteristics. *Am. J. Ment. Def.,* 75:5, 1971.
48. Gray, B. and Ryan, B.: *A Language Program for the Nonlanguage Child.* Research Press, Champaign, Illinois, 1974.
49. Griffith, B. G. and Spitz, H. H.: Some relationships between abstraction and word meaning in retarded adolescents. *Am. J. Ment. Def.,* 63:2, 1958.
50. Grinnell, M., Detamore, K., and Lippke, B.: Sign it successful—manual English encourages expressive communication. *Teach. Except. Child.,* Spring, 1976.
51. Guess, D. and Baer, D.: An analysis of individual differences in generalization between receptive and productive language in retarded children, *J. Appl. Beh. Anal.,* 6:2, 1973.
52. Hammill, D. D. and Larsen, S. C.: The effectiveness of psycholinguistic training, *Except. Child.,* 41:1, 1974.
53. Hardy, W. G. and Pauls, M. D.: Atypical children with communicative disorders. *Child.,* 6:1, 1959.
54. Haring, N. G., Hayden, A. and Nolan, P. A.: Accelerating appropriate behaviors of children in a Head Start program. *Except. Child.,* 35:10, 1969.
55. Harrison, S.: A review of research in speech and language development of the mentally retarded child. *Am. J. Ment. Def.,* 63:2, 1958.
56. Haviland, R. T.: Stimulus to language development: the institutional environment. *Ment. Ret.,* 10:4, 1972.
57. Heber, R. and Garber, H.: An experiment in the prevention of cultural familial mental retardation. In *Entering the Era of Human Ecology.* Report of the President's Committee on Mental Retardation, MR. 71, 1971.

58. Henderson, L.: Increasing descriptive language skills in EMR students. *Ment. Ret.,* 9:3, 1971.

59. Hunt, J. M.: *Intelligence and Experience,* Ronald Press, New York, 1961.

60. Jacobovits, S. and Miron, M.: *Readings in the Psychology of Language.* Prentice-Hall, Englewood Cliffs, 1967.

61. Jakobson, R.: *Selected Writings of Ramon Jakobson.* Mouton, The Hague, 1962.

62. Jordan, T. E.: in *Language and Mental Retardation,* R. L. Schiefelbusch, R. H. Copeland, and J. O. Smith, eds., Holt, Rinehart and Winston, New York, 1967.

63. Keane, V. E.: The incidence of speech and language problems in the mentally retarded. *Ment. Ret.,* 10:4, 1972.

64. Keehner, U. A.: A comparative study of linguistic and mental abilities before and after a development-remedial language program with mentally retarded children. Unpublished Masters thesis, University of Wisconsin, Madison, Wisconsin, 1966.

65. Kent, L.: *Language Acquisition Program for the Severely Retarded,* Research Press, Champaign, Illinois, 1974.

66. Kirk, S. A. and McCarthy, J. J.: The Illinois Test of Psycholinguistic Abilities—an approach to differential diagnosis. *Am. J. Ment. Def.,* 66:3, 1961.

67. Lasser, L. R., and Low, G.: Symposium on assessing and developing communicative effectiveness in mentally retarded children, *Asha,* 2:7, 1960.

68. Laub, P.: *Guiding Children's Language Learning.* Wm. Brown Company, Dubuque, Iowa, 1967.

69. Leberfeld, D. T.: Speech therapy and retarded children. *Trng. Sch. Bull.,* 53:7, 1967.

70. Leberfeld, D. T. and Nertz, N.: A home-training program in language and speech for mentally retarded children, *Am. J. Ment. Def.,* 59:3, 1955.

71. Lee, L. L.: Developmental sentence types: a method for comparing normal and deviant syntactic development. *JSHR,* 31:3, 1966.

72. Lees, R. B.: The promise of transformational grammar. *Ling. in the Class,* National Council of Teachers of English, Champaign, Illinois, 1963.

73. Lees, R. B.: The basis of glottochronolog. *Lang.,* 29:2, 1953.

74. Lenneberg, E. *Biological Foundations of Language,* John Wiley, New York, 1967.

75. Lenneberg, E.: *New Directions in the Study of Language.,* M.I.T. Press, Cambridge, 1964.

76. Lindsley, O. R.: Direct measurement and prosthesis of retarded behavior. *J. of Ed.,* 147, 1964.

77. Lozar, B. and Wepman, J.: Syntactic indices of language use of mentally retarded and normal children. *Lang. and Sp.,* 16:1, 1973.

78. Luria, A. R.: *The Mentally Retarded Child,* Pergamon Press, New York, 1963.
79. McConnell, F., Love, R. J., and Clark, B. C.: Language remediation in children. In *Communication Disorders.* S. Dickson, ed., Scott, Foresman, Glenview, Illinois, 1974.
80. McLean, J.: Lecture, Communication Problems of the Retarded Workshop, State University College at Buffalo, New York, 1967.
81. McMullen, D.: Teaching protection words. *Teach. Except. Child.,* 7:3, 1975.
82. McNeil, D.: in *The Genesis of Language.* J. Smith and G. Miller, (eds.), M.I.T. Press, Cambridge, Massachusetts, 1966.
83. Menyuk, P.: A preliminary evaluation of grammatical capacity in children, *J. Verb. Learn. Verb. Beh.,* 15:2, 1963.
84. Menyuk, P.: Comparison of grammar of children with functionally deviant and normal speech. *J.S.H.R.,* 7:1, 1964.
85. Milgram, N. A. and Furth, H. G.: The influence of Language on concept attainment in educable retarded children. *Am. J. Ment. Def.,* 67:5, 1963.
86. Miller, J. and Yoder, D. E.: On developing the content for a language teaching program. *Ment. Ret.,* 10:2, 1972.
87. Miller, G. A.: *Language and Communication.* McGraw-Hill Book Company, New York, 1963.
88. Minskoff, E. H.: Research on psycholinguistic training: critique and guidelines. *Except. Child.,* 42:3, 1975.
89. Mueller, M. and Smith, J. O.: The stability of language age modification over time. *Am. J. Ment. Def.,* 68:4, 1964.
90. Murphy, A. F.: Speech pathology and mental subnormality: a person conception. *J. of Ed.,* 147:1, 1964.
91. Naor, E. M., and Balthazar, E. E.: Provision of a language index for severely and profoundly retarded individuals. *Am. J. Ment. Def.,* 79:6, 1975.
92. Naremore, R. C. and Dever, R. B.: Language performance of educable retarded and normal children at five age levels. *JSHR,* 18:1, 1975.
93. O'Connor, N., ed., *Language Cognitive Deficits and Retardation.* Butterworths, London, 1975.
94. Odom, M., Longhurst, T. M., and Boatman, R. R.: Improving oral language skills in a classroom for the educable mentally retarded. *Ed. and Trng. of the Ment. Ret.,* 8:12.
95. Olson, J., Hahn, H., and Herman, A.: Psycholinguistic curriculum. *Ment. Ret.,* 3:4, 1966.
96. Osgood, Charles, A Behavioristic Analysis, *Contemporary Approaches to Cognition,* Harvard University Press, Cambridge, Massachusetts, 1957A.
97. Osgood, Charles E., *Motivational Dynamics of Language Behavior,* University of Nebraska Press, Lincoln, Nebraska, 1957B.
98. Papinia, N. A.: A qualitative analysis of the vocabulary response of institutionalized mentally retarded children. *J. Clin. Psych.,* 10:6, 1954.
99. Peale, N. V.: *The Power of Positive Thinking,* Fawcett World, New York, 1975.

100. Poole, I.: Genetic development of articulation of consonantal sounds in English. *El. Eng. Rev.,* 11:6, 1934.

101. Premack, D.: *Intelligence in Ape and Man,* Lawrence Erlbaum Associates, Hillsdale, New Jersey, 1976.

102. Rankin, P. T.: Listening for learning in *Listening and Speaking: A Guide for Effective Oral Communication,* Edited by R. G. Nichols and T. T. Lewis, William C. Brown & Co., Dubuque, Iowa, 1954.

103. Rittmanic, P. A.: An oral language program for institutionalized educable mentally retarded children, *Am. J. Ment. Def.,* 63:3, 1958.

104. Ross, A. O.: *Psychological disorders of children: a behavioral approach to theory, research, and theory.* McGraw-Hill, New York, 1974.

105. Rossi, L. E.: Associative clustering in normal and retarded children. *Am. J. Ment. Def.,* 67:5, 1963.

106. Ryckman, D. B., and Wiegerink, R.: The factors of the Illinois Test of Psycholinguistic Abilities: a comparison of 18 factor analyses. *Except. Child.,* 36:2, 1969.

107. Sailor, W., Guess, D., and Baer, D. M.: Functional language for verbally deficient children: an experimental program. *Ment. Ret.,* 11:3, 1973.

108. Schiefelbusch, R. L., Copeland, R. H., and Smith, J. O.: *Language and Mental Retardation.* Holt, Rinehart and Winston, New York, 1967.

109. Schlanger, B. B.: Speech therapy with mentally retarded children. *JSHD.,* 23:3, 1956.

110. Seitz, S. and Marcus, S.: Mother-child interactions: a foundation for language development. *Except. Child.,* 43:5, 1976.

111. Semmel, M.: Lecture, Communication Problems of the Retarded Workshop, State University of New York College at Buffalo, 1968.

112. Siegel, G. M.: Adult verbal behavior in 'play therapy' sessions with retarded children. *JSHD Mon. Suppl.,* 10, 1963.

113. Siegel, G. M. and Harkens, J. P.: Verbal behavior of adults in two conditions with institutionalized children. *JSHD Mon. Suppl.,* 10, 1963.

114. Skinner, B. F.: *Verbal Behavior,* Appleton-Century-Crofts, New York, 1957.

115. Sloan, W.: Progress report of special committee on nomenclature. *Am. J. Ment. Def.,* 59 5, 1954.

116. Slobin, D. I. *The Ontogenesis of Grammar.* Academic Press, New York, 1971.

117. Smith, J. O. Group language development for educable mental retarded, *Except. Child.* 29:2, 1962.

118. Smith, J. and Miller, G.: *The Genesis of Language.* M.I.T. Press, Cambridge, 1966.

119. Snyder, L. K., Lovitt, T. C., and Smith, J. O.: Language training for the severely retarded: five years of behavior analysis research. *Except. Child.,* 42:1, 1975.

120. Sommers, R. K.: Factors in the effectiveness of articulation therapy with educable retarded children. Final report of project number 7-0432, U.S. Department of Health, Education and Welfare, 1969.

121. Stalin, J.: *Marxism and Linguistics,* International Publishers, New York, 1951.

122. Stedman, D. J.: Associative clustering of semantic categories in normal and retarded subjects. *Am. J. Ment. Def.,* 67:5, 1963.

123. Stremel, K.: Language training: a program for retarded children. *Ment. Ret.,* 10:2, 1972.

124. Templin, M. C.: Certain Language Skills in Children. University of Minnesota Press, Minnesota, 1957.

125. Thomas, O.: Grammatici cortant. *Eng. J.,* 6:10, 1963.

126. Thorndike, E.: *Human Learning.* M.I.T. Press, Cambridge, 1931.

127. Thornley, M.: *Every Child Can Learn Something.* Bernie Straub Publishing, Seattle, Washington, 1975.

128. Totter, J.: Evaluating the Van Hattum syntax building program, unpublished paper, State University College at Buffalo, 1975.

129. University of Pittsburgh Cleft Palate Center: *General Stimulation Guide,* 1975.

130. Vanderheiden, D. H., Brown, W. P., MacKenzie, P., Reinen, S., and Scheibel, C.: Symbol Communication for the mentally handicapped. *Ment. Ret.,* 13:2, 1975.

131. Van Hattum, R. J.: Services of the speech clinician in schools: progress and prospects. *Asha,* 18:2, 1976.

132. Van Riper, C.: *Speech Correction.* Prentice-Hall, Englewood Cliffs, N.J.

133. Vygotsky, L.: *Thought and Language.* M.I.T. Press, Cambridge, 1962

134. Walker, H. J., Roodin, P. A., and Lamb, M. J.: Relationship between linguistic performance and memory deficits in retarded children. *Am. J. Ment. Def.,* 79:7, 1975.

135. Wepman, J.: in *Readings in the Psychology of Language,* L. Jacobovits and M. Miron, eds., Prentice-Hall, Englewood Cliffs, N.J., 1967.

136. West, R., Kennedy, L., and Carr, A.: *The Rehabilitation of Speech.* Harper and Brothers, New York, 1947.

137. White, B. L.: *The First Three Years of Life,* Prentice-Hall, Englewood Cliffs, New Jersey, 1975.

138. Whorf, B. J.: *Language, Thought and Reality.* M.I.T. Press, Cambridge, 1956.

139. Wilson, F.: Efficacy of speech therapy with educable mentally retarded children. *J.S.H.R.,* 9:3, 1966.

140. Winschel, J. F. and Lawrence, E. A.: Short-term memory: curricular implications for the mentally retarded. *J. Spec. Ed.,* 9:4, 1975.

141. Wiseman, D.: A classroom procedure for identifying and remediating language problems. *Ment. Ret.,* 3:2, 1965.

142. Wolinsky, G. and Walker, S.: A home-safety inventory for parents of preschool handicapped 'ldren. *Teach. Except. Child.,* 7:3, 1975.

Subject Index

Author Index